While the Music Lasts

While the Music Lasts

My Life in Politics

William M. Bulger

Faber and Faber
BOSTON • LONDON

Published in 1997 by Faber and Faber, Inc.,
53 Shore Rd., Winchester, MA 01890.

Published by arrangement with Houghton Mifflin Company.
For information about permission to reproduce selections
from this book, write to Permissions, Houghton Mifflin Company,
215 Park Avenue South, New York, New York 10003.

ISBN 0-571-19927-5

Library of Congress Cataloging-in-Publication Data
Bulger, William M.
While the music lasts: my life in politics / William M. Bulger
p.   cm.
1. Bulger, William M. 2. Legislators — Massachusetts —
Biography 3. Massachusetts. General Court.
Senate — Biography. I. Title.
F71.22.B85A3   1996
328.744'092'2 — dc20   95-46803
[B]   CIP

Printed in the United States of America

Book design by Robert Overholtzer
Jacket design by Peter Blaiwas

10 9 8 7 6 5 4 3 2 1

To my wife, Mary,
and to Bill, Jim, Sarah, Patrick,
Mary, Dan, Kathleen, Chris
and Brendan — with all my love

THE STANDUP GUY

There were tangos and waltzes — the whole jamboree,
And beauties to cut in upon.
There was lure and romance in the songs that they sung me.
I cared not a fig for the flings they'd have flung me —
Which made some so mad that they'd like to have hung me!
But I always dance with the gal that brung me.
Yes, I'm hers while the music lasts.

— *Anonymous*

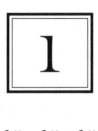

I**N THE DISTANCE** soared the pale towers of Yankee Babylon, their alien frigidity made bearable by what we perceived as the warmth and color of the hanging garden of South Boston, where we lived.

The center of the city was, at the same time, next door — and remote as the Pole. It depended on your definition of distance.

Our roots were local. They ran deep. They kept us from being merely a part of the whole. We valued our mélange of cultural traditions, and we had a shared sense of security. We were a *Neighborhood:* an enclave so discrete that we sang "Southie Is My Hometown" and referred to a trip into the central part of the city as "going to Boston."

We were aggressively urban, if less urbane than people from other areas. We had names and numbers for some thoroughfares, but most people lived on streets identified by letters of the alphabet. Our houses were largely two- or three-story wood or brick buildings facing on sidewalks, many of them perched on hills that tumbled steeply to the sea. The houses looked a bit worn, a far remove from the grandeur of Boston proper. Behind most of them, on sunny days, family wash danced in the relentless northeast breeze, like brazen flags of our ethnic community.

We washed our windows. We swept our sidewalks. We went to

school and we went to church. Families were stable: a divorce was a whispered horror. We had our share of bars and bookies and sin, but the area then, as now, had the city's lowest rate of serious crime. And on the rare occasions when someone crossed the line into heavy felony, he alone was condemned. The Neighborhood was wonderfully free of the star-chamber mentality that indicts and ostracizes entire families, even in many self-consciously liberal communities.

It was, as it still is, a largely blue-collar area. The men were mostly longshoremen and artisans — carpenters, plumbers, ironworkers. Most women were housewives, but some worked in shops or in a variety of part-time jobs, some of them unusual. The Gillette Safety Razor Company, in South Boston, paid women to perspire. It was part of a process for testing various deodorants. It was quite common to hear a woman say, "I'm working as a sweat at Gillette."

I was four years old when my parents moved, in 1938, from the abutting district of Dorchester to the Old Harbor housing project in South Boston. There were three children then: Jean, the oldest, then James. I was the youngest. Carol, Jack and Sheila came later, in that order. We lived in apartment 756, third floor left, in a building at 41 Logan Way. The rent was $29 a month.

Tenancy was temporary. We were told that was a firm rule. But inconvenient rules in the Neighborhood were not strictly enforced. We were still living there twenty-three years later, when I left after getting married.

Outsiders were unable to tell where Dorchester ended and South Boston began. But that meant nothing. Close didn't count. One was born in South Boston or, tragically, one was born elsewhere in the city.

Strangely, immigrants from Ireland, Poland, Lithuania, Italy, even Russia, seemed to enjoy a more ready acceptance. But those who first opened their eyes in another part of Boston were guilty of an original sin for which there was no facile absolution. It was just something you hoped everyone would forget. In my case, for some happy reason that I never fully understood, my alien origin was overlooked.

I was reminded of that years later, during my first political campaign, by one James Dahill, a local celebrity by virtue of being a first cousin to Richard Cardinal Cushing of South Boston.

"I hope," Dahill said, "that you give Fitzgerald a good trouncing."

"Why is that?" I asked. "He seems a good enough guy."

"No," said Dahill, "he comes from Roxbury. Only moved here in 1935. Now he's trying to take over."

I felt no duty to remind Dahill that Fitzgerald had three years seniority on me as a resident.

Being young was a happy adventure. We had Boston's most beautiful beach. We had a fabulous emerald — two miles wide — called Columbus Park, with a baseball diamond, tennis courts and lush acres where you could lie in the summer sun or build forts when the city was huddled under a February snow.

Most of us were poor, but if someone earned a dime running an errand, he rarely spent it entirely on himself. Kenny Mulhall owned a bike, but we all rode it. Our baseball equipment was sparse, but we shared it. We were quick with our fists, but fights were brief, soon forgotten, and never rooted in the diversity of our national origins. There was a distinct coolness, rooted in history, toward the English, under whose rule one third of the population of Ireland had perished. I never knew any conspicuously English residents in South Boston, however, so we fought over *important* things, like the relative merits of professional athletes.

Few of us went to college, but few of us were stupid.

I used to sing a lot — mostly Irish songs — with or without invitation. I still do. Hearing me sing "The Rising of the Moon" and other hymns to the rebellious Celts, my mother would often ask, "How'd you get so Irish?" My young friends were used to my breaking into song whenever the spirit was on me, and tolerated it without close analysis of its quality. At times, they'd join in. No one would have confused us with a choir of nightingales, but no one told us to be quiet.

We walked around a lot, dressed in dungarees or in knickers and black stockings, often wearing a scally cap. When in a hurry, we would take the trolley. It ran from Andrew Square up Dorchester Street, up Pill Hill — where the doctors had their offices — to Flood Square, then down East Broadway to City Point, where Admiral Farragut's statue stood. We never paid the fare, of course. Only adults paid. We hopped on the back of the cars and no one bothered us.

We stuck together. Contrary to Frost's aphorism, close neighbors *did* make close friends in South Boston, and many friendships were lifelong. We lived in a relaxed ambiance: when my dog, Skippy, followed me to school, it didn't upset anyone, even when he slept in the cloakroom.

Except for money, we had it all — or at least my chums and I believed we did, which was just as good.

April is not crueler anywhere than in Massachusetts. Frozen lumps in the infield would drive us to move our baseball games from the diamond in Columbus Park to the tennis courts. We were very unpopular there. The police would chase us out. Sometimes they would confiscate our baseball, which was devastating.

I recall an occasion when a massive police hunt was in progress to learn who had broken a streetlight on O'Callaghan Way. We were told that a recently impounded baseball would not be returned unless we identified the lamp breaker. We were disgusted with the miscreant, since essential equipment was being held hostage because of him. But we loathed informers. It wasn't a conspiratorial thing — our folklore bled with the names of informers who had sold out their brethren to hangmen and worse in the lands of our ancestors.

Even the police, who in those days mostly shared such sentiments, might have loved the treason — but they would have hated the traitor. Of course, they did not get the name they sought. And when they persisted, a light was broken at the nearby corner of Logan and Devine Ways.

There was more than a little rebellion in many of us. That distressed Mrs. Eudalia Cummerford, who was a well-intentioned social worker at the housing project. She was a quiet, intense woman with a long face, big teeth and the clenched jaw of the dogged do-gooder. She had great difficulty rounding up the children to march to the flagpole at Logan Way and Old Colony Avenue to salute the colors. Everyone would scurry at her approach. My friend Joe Quirk and I would hide in a hallway on McDonough Way. That was not because we were loath to affirm our respect for the flag — we did that in school every day. We just didn't like being lined up and marched about. Perhaps we sensed in Mrs. Cummerford the menacing shadow of things to come, of a troubled time when social engineers would try to march us about in step with their dehumanizing experimentation.

Much of our lives centered on our church.

I celebrated my first communion at St. Monica's, an old wooden structure in Andrew Square. It remained my church for almost a generation. I was one of four altar boys, and all of us would walk there carrying our cassocks and surplices, feeling splendid as a parade of cardinals. I quickly memorized the Latin, though I had no notion what it meant. To me it was simply a chant of sorts that colored the magnificence of the Mass with beautiful sound.

There was a curate at St. Monica's named Leo Dwyer, a gentle, ingenuous soul who looked more like an old boy than a young man: a superannuated altar boy called to holy orders. He was forever assuring us that we could expect miracles if only we were good and had faith. He would tell us the story of Hungary's Saint Elizabeth:

"She disobeyed her husband, who was a selfish man," Father Dwyer said, "and filled her apron with loaves of bread to give to the poor. Her husband stopped her and asked what she was carrying."

At that point he would pause for dramatic effect. Then he would go on: "She was terrified, the poor dear. She told a lie. She said she had gathered roses from the garden and had them in her apron. Her husband said, 'Show me.' So she opened her apron — and what came out?"

"Bread?" one of us would suggest.

"Roses," Father Dwyer would say, his face ecstatic. "Dozens of roses. Nothing but roses."

True or false, it was a lovely story, and I think of it often.

Father Dwyer had a mundane side. He told us in a diffident manner accentuated by reflective hesitations — and with the air of one sharing a dreadful secret — that some in the surrounding city considered us provincial. To dispel such an incredible delusion, he took groups of us to visit his old parishes in nearby Amesbury and Haverhill. He took us to Hampton Beach in New Hampshire. We would trek a score of miles on foot, back and forth from Mattapan Square to Houghton's Pond in the Blue Hills.

"We're doing these things," Father Dwyer explained solemnly, "so that you can see the world!"

Sometimes we really did get a glimpse of the world. I recall a pack of us returning from a boat ride to Nantasket Beach and seeing the illuminated sign on South Station flashing news of the devastation of the Japanese city of Hiroshima by what was described as a mystery bomb.

The pastor of St. Monica's, the Reverend Cornelius J. Donovan, was loud and arrogant, cantankerous as a thorn bush. He was a gruff man, vainly proud of his feats as a football player at Notre Dame. I respected the cloth, but not the man wearing it. He and the mild-mannered Father Dwyer shared an uneasy relationship, electric as a gathering storm. We waited in delicious anticipation, hoping for it to break.

One day as I carried the missal to Father Donovan on the altar, the book slipped from my hands. All the ribbon place markers fell out. When I picked everything up and delivered the wreckage, Father Donovan said, "Watch out I don't kick you in the groin, boy." Miss Collins, my fifth grade teacher, who was in the congregation, was shocked. "Why, that book was bigger than you," she said. Father Dwyer was horrified. He asked me, "What did you think when Father Donovan said that?"

We were scrappy and spirited in the project, and I didn't hesitate to tell him exactly what I thought: "Father, if he kicks me, I'll kick *him* where he won't like it."

Ham Slowe, a dedicated drinker who had strayed from the Church, was a particular object of Father Donovan's disapproval. When Ham was on a bender, which was most of the time, he and his mates would hole up in an abandoned building near Leed Street. On cold nights Father Dwyer would give them blankets so they wouldn't freeze. He threw the blankets down to them from a window to avoid being caught in the act by Father Donovan. Ham was so grateful that he finally promised Father Dwyer he would attend church.

The next Sunday, there was Ham in the congregation, target of a scornful glare from Father Donovan. The pastor's hortatory homilies, never diluted by brevity, abounded in gusty football imagery. I do not recall them literally, but they were along the line that we should block the devil and hit the line for God. The sight of Ham inspired him to thunderous heights.

After a quarter hour of the white noise emanating from the pulpit, during which most of us had taken refuge in a shared somnolence, Ham rose to his feet and clambered to the aisle.

"I'm walkin' out," roared Ham. "And anyone in this church with a brain in his head will walk out with me."

In the awful silence that followed, we all looked at Father Donovan, who stood glaring in apoplectic rage. Ham continued up the aisle, pausing at the door to shout over his shoulder, "I could give a better sermon than Donovan, and I wouldn't have to be sober to do it!"

Father Dwyer knew that somehow he would be blamed, because he had brought Ham back to the Church. He was so shaken that he repaired to the chancery the next day and pleaded for assignment to another parish, anywhere beyond the reach of Father Donovan. After a brief investigation, his wish was granted and he was sent to St. James parish in Haverhill.

For a long time I despised Father Donovan as a bully, but in later years I came almost to pity him. I realized that in a sense he had died on the playing field at South Bend some golden day in his youth when *he* had been the one to shake thunder from the sky for old Notre Dame. During that transient glory he had known the ineffable frisson of fame, however fleeting. He had never been given the grace or the intelligence to realize the relative triviality of that moment, so nothing that came later could approach the memory. All his ensuing years must have been merely retrospective, the penance of the has-been. I thought of Housman's pensive lines:

> . . . lads that wore their honors out,
> Runners whom renown outran
> And the name died before the man.

I would always feel scorn toward him, but my active anger ended, like a game clock running out at the end of the fourth quarter.

South Boston was, and arguably still is, the most politically active community in Massachusetts. It abounds both in widely known politicians and aspirants lusting to replace them in office.

I can remember no time in my life when we were not fascinated by the color and trappings, the cadence and cacophony of campaigns — past, current or contemplated. Politics was a cottage industry, a spectator sport and, I suppose, the nearest thing we had to a real-life drama, sitcom or game show. We actually *listened* to speeches. We actually *read* the handbills and advertisements. In the process, we became devotees, critics, even connoisseurs of political exposition.

And we have always dearly loved a grand parade!

Lampposts are still seasonably festooned with placards. Volunteers, from children to ancient partisans, carry banners and hand out flyers. Sound trucks deliver the promises and importunities of office seekers in a gamut of voices — young or mature, grim or happy, strident or mellifluous. In short, politics, in all its shades and subtlety, all its artistry and buffoonery, continues to pervade the air of our Neighborhood.

As a child, I would stop on my way to the beach or the playing fields of Columbus Park to listen to corner orators holding forth from Andrew Square to East 8th Street. I relished their clashes with hecklers in the crowd — a bare-knuckled repartee that often began when someone with dilated pupils and an attitude shouted something like, "McCarthy, you're a bum!"

As a youth, I would attend lively rallies at the VFW hall and the German Club or join a claque organized to cheer the efforts of a candidate speaking from the bed of a pickup truck. When I grew a little older, I sought out the Neighborhood's old lions, men retired from the political wars. They were pleased to dispense their wisdom to a respectful listener, and I was a most eager novice. I sat in many of their old-fashioned parlors, rooms full of the bric-a-brac and souvenirs of past campaigns. Often, much of my host's history was preserved on the surrounding walls in sepia photographs, like bits of his life trapped in amber. Today, so many decades later, I remember that guidance with advantage.

South Boston residents turn out and vote. Rain or snow, hot or cold, they can be relied on to do that. As a result, the area — only a few square miles — has produced, in extravagantly disproportionate numbers, men and women who were elected or appointed to office. There was John McCormack, Speaker of the U.S. House of Representatives; his nephew Eddie McCormack, who became Massachusetts attorney general; Louise Day Hicks, who went to Congress; Raymond Flynn, who became mayor of Boston; John Powers, who became president of the state Senate. There was Jim Kelley, who is now president of the Boston City Council. There was Joe Moakley, who served in state government and went on to the national House, where for so long he was chairman of the Rules Committee, the powerful panel that decides which bills will reach the floor of Congress for a vote. And there are many, many more who went from South Boston to prominence in municipal, state and national offices.

Joe Moakley is older than I am, but I had lived at 41 Logan Way when he lived at number 51, and we were close friends. Once, walking at Carson Beach, he told me he found politics more exciting than baseball. Even at that early age I realized what he was going to do with his life — and as I thought about it, I wondered whether he might have spoken for me as well. That notion became a certainty later, when I worked in his many campaigns.

As children, we were fascinated by the community's characters. There were many of them, some very colorful, some very weird. Their antics provided a sort of vaudeville show that enthralled us.

One of my earliest recollections is connected with the campaign of John J. "Ombo" McStow, who ran for state representative. A phalanx of children came marching through our project carrying a banner that stretched across Logan Way. It read: "Help Ombo to Help Us." A rumor spread that Ombo was bringing a famous horse named Black Thunder from a farm in the wilds of Dracut to the Old Colony project on Pilsudski Way to give rides to children.

We flocked to Pilsudski Way, our heads filled with anticipation of a proud beast with a coat like midnight, rolling its fiery eyes, flaring its nostrils, its hoofs striking sparks on the concrete walkway. But when we got there and saw Thunder, there was no hint of lightning in him.

He was a muddy-brown creature, more like a weary pony than the spirited beasts we saw in westerns at Saturday matinees. He was swaybacked, lumpy and immobile. He looked like the handiwork of a failed taxidermist.

Thunder's head, hanging toward the ground, suggested ennui. Nothing moved. His half-closed eyes seemed not to blink. Aroused to at least a semi-stupor by our cries of encouragement, he was prevailed upon to walk slowly, perhaps twenty feet and back to his starting place. There he would stand, a wretched still life, waiting for the next rider.

It was a letdown. And our nascent political acumen led to a communal judgment that Ombo had won not a vote with Thunder.

Indeed, the most arresting moment of the spectacle came when it was discovered that the horse trailer was gone. There were no stables at the Old Colony project, no shed, no barn, not even a patch of pasture to accommodate the animal until the trailer could be brought back.

The dilemma was solved when a resident took the animal into his apartment. We watched him lead Thunder — very nimble for a creature that seemed so moribund — up the stairs to the second floor. "I don't know what the super would think," the man called back, "so say nothing about this." His secret was safe. No one would learn from any of us that a horse was living in an apartment on Pilsudski Way. Snitching, as I have indicated, was not highly regarded in the Neighborhood.

I remember the postman, Mr. McCool — I never knew his first name. In common sense, he was deemed to be several pennies short of a nickel. But he was cheerful and his seraphic face looked red and healthy as a polished apple. He had a reedy voice, spoke with a whistling sibilance and was fond of saying, "God invented whiskey to keep the Irish from taking over the world." He was an acknowledged authority on that subject, since he tarried in most of the bars he passed in order to, as he put it, take on some fuel. Withal, to everyone's wonder, his delivery of the mail was flawlessly on schedule, however uncertain his gait.

There was Mrs. Mulligan, who lived in the project on Devine Way. She insisted she was descended from a famous Indian warrior. It might have been true: she had a face like an ax — stern, sharp features with high cheekbones and a jutting nose, like the noble visage of the feathered brave on the logo of the Shawmut Bank.

There was something — at the time I didn't understand exactly what — that made me wish her well. I know now what it was: she looked at you through eyes that had seen too many right things go wrong. I remember saying to Joe Quirk that I wished something nifty would happen for her.

In some ways, Mrs. Mulligan was without shame. She had a strained relationship with the project superintendent, who suspected her, among other things, of taking light bulbs from the corridors, which she certainly did. And she was in a virtual state of war with Martin Looney, the manager of the First National store, a man who exuded the warmth and geniality of a peregrine falcon. Looney accused her of an impermissible informality in acquiring his grocery products.

He would say, "She's got a short attention span. When she buys things she forgets to pay for them."

Looney became obsessed with Mrs. Mulligan. He installed two-way mirrors to keep her under observation when she strolled the store's aisles. He would rise before the sun and sit in his car to stake out the early-morning milk delivery. She was endlessly resourceful, however, and when she would call me in to run an errand, she'd often say blithely, "Have a cookie and a glass of milk, Bill. I got 'em both on the cheap from that idiot Looney."

She flagged me down one day and gave me two dollars and ten cents. She said I might keep the dime if I gave the two dollars to the bookmaker in the back room of the Car Stop Cafe on Broadway. She wrote her betting selection on the back of an envelope.

"This is a sure tip," she said, "at very big odds. It's going to change my luck, Bill, and I'll wave all my winnings in Looney's ugly face."

It was while I was returning from the errand for Mrs. Mulligan that I saw the postman, McCool, sober as a bishop, striding down O'Callaghan Way.

"What's with McCool?" I asked Mrs. Mulligan. "I just saw him. He doesn't look like himself."

"He's sober," she said, a little sadly it seemed. "The poor man is having delusions. He thought he saw a horse looking at him out of a window on Pilsudski Way. It took him very hard. He gave up the drink."

I knew the horse was not a delusion. But neither I nor anyone who knew the truth would break silence and tell the story of Black Thunder, and that caused some short-term problems, because the mail wasn't on time from the day McCool stopped drinking.

Later, after a trailer appeared and took the animal back to the farm, the facts came out. They apparently prompted McCool to decide his sojourn into sobriety had been premature. When next I saw him, he was being propelled by a full load of fuel down Dorchester Street — and the mail was back on time again.

We collected baseball cards. We called them baseball pictures. They were handed out free with certain grocery items, fancier products that were rarely on our simple shopping lists. John and Mary Karp, fugitives from the persecution of Jews in Russia, ran a little store on Devine Way where they began giving away the cards left behind by uninterested adults.

When I heard about that, I went to the store and approached Mary, who was sitting on a milk crate, and asked, "Have you got any pictures?" "No," she said in an accent that rolled like the mighty Volga, "but we have some very nice plums."

"Mary," her husband said with a superior air of strained patience, and an accent as full of borscht as hers, "the boy is not looking for *peaches*. Listen better if you want to talk American."

When I was a little older and looking for odd jobs instead of baseball cards, they hired me. I swept floors, tended the counter and delivered bundles for the Karps for several years. They were very good to me and were always asking me to sing "Linda" for them, because that was their granddaughter's name.

During that time the Karps hired a second employee, Ralph.

"I am a Communist," Ralph told me.

When John Karp heard that proclamation he roared his disapproval. Then, steadying himself, he added, "*I* am American. We have no use for Communist nonsense in this country." His manner suggested an unbroken lineage to the *Mayflower*.

"What's wrong with being a Communist?" Ralph asked. "I just want a world where everybody isn't crazy for money."

I recall his words clearly. They astounded me. I had never met a Communist before, at least no one who admitted being one. I knew from countless Sunday sermons that Communists were thoroughly bad guys, but I could discern no horns on Ralph. He seemed genial. He had an almost apologetic deference and a gentle voice.

I watched Ralph closely. I watched for him to do something sneaky or unpatriotic, or say something rotten about God. He never did. Finally I asked Father Dwyer how Ralph could seem so likable and still be a Red.

Father Dwyer told me that Communism was evil, but that didn't mean all Communists were evil. That confused me even more. The concept of parts being opposite in nature to their whole was beyond me. I decided to stop fretting about it until I was older and wiser — twenty-one or -two, perhaps — when I would probably be smart enough to understand almost anything.

Edward "Knocko" McCormack was easier to understand than socially acceptable Communists, or at least I thought so. I did not dream in those days that he would become an important personage in state and even national politics. I would have been astonished had I known that there would come a time when I would work for him.

He wore a tam-o'-shanter and rode a white horse named Jerry in our St. Patrick's Day parades. He was loud and fat and boasted of having been a bootlegger during Prohibition. He had sold what he represented as Molson's Ale from his garage. It was generally believed he brewed the contraband in his cellar.

To counter such talk, Knocko would often appear with sand on his arms, which he would brush off, ostentatiously saying, "Had to unload a big shipment on the beach last night."

But with all his bluster, and the tales, true or false, of his many misdemeanors and enormities, he was somehow likable. You had the feeling that Knocko just couldn't help it.

Mayors came and mayors went, but Knocko survived in his job in the city's Department of Weights and Measures. He was the brother of John W. McCormack. Brother John served in the state legislature for six years before going on to Congress, where he was majority leader three times. He served as Speaker of the House for nine years. While brother John was soft-spoken and faultlessly courteous, brother Knocko was self-effacing as a bass drum.

Knocko owned a bar at 6th and P Streets called the Wave Cottage. It was a busy place in the summer. Long before we were old enough to be allowed in, we would sit outside watching the show through the open door.

Knocko would tend bar wearing only severely abbreviated shorts. He always kept a big block of ice mounted in front of an electric fan, supposedly to cool the air. But there was a great deal to Knocko, and every pink-and-white inch of his body continued to drip sweat as he cruised back and forth filling glasses. Heat never seemed to bother him. He never looked tired, never slowed. No matter how steamy his exterior, Knocko appeared to be cool *inside* — which enabled him to bring to his bartending a certain sweaty savoir-faire.

The license required that food be served at the Wave Cottage, but the menu was limited. Knocko didn't believe in any nonalcoholic inventory. On the rare occasions when someone ordered a steak, a runner would be sent across the way to Coogan's market to buy one.

"Can't get fresher meat than that," Knocko would boast. Like much Knocko said, it made no sense.

Regulars in Knocko's bar would always watch for a stranger coming up from the beach to get a cold glass of beer. The newcomer, seeing that Knocko's chest and stomach were covered by nothing but moisture, would — sooner or later — strain forward as unobtrusively as he could to see what Knocko was wearing below the bar. Usually such limited reconnaissance revealed only the additional florid terrain of Knocko's billowing underbelly.

The scenario would then unfold along predictable lines while we rolled about in the doorway stifling our laughs. The newcomer, plainly puzzled, would look at the poker faces of the other patrons, obviously wondering whether he was the only one who considered a naked bartender an oddity. Finally, unable to contain himself, he would stretch across the bar until he discovered Knocko's modest concession to convention.

That produced an expression of almost palpable relief and, almost inevitably, an order for another beer. Knocko, shrewd as they come, was well aware of the redundant episodes. He believed they resulted in beer sales that might otherwise not have been made. He was probably right.

Over the bar at the Wave Cottage, along with the beer, Knocko dispensed guidance to the forlorn and work — or at least the promise of work — to the jobless. He had a special relationship with the Public Works Department and would pass out what he called "snow buttons," entitling each recipient to a stint shoveling for the city in the winter.

Some would approach Knocko seeking permanent employment with a city department, and Knocko never said no. He would tear a blank page from a book he kept behind the bar and on it write "Okay." He would sign it "Knocko."

Never did I know of a single instance in which one of Knocko's "okay" notes resulted in a job. Yet to my astonishment, no one blamed him. They would say, "Knocko went through for me, but . . ." and then the failure would be attributed to a departmental mix-up, treachery on the part of a city official or, among the truly naive, the explanation "Well, nothing yet, but thanks to Knocko I'm first in line when something opens up."

The ways of politics, I thought watching him, are very strange. Here was Knocko viewed as a power broker for failing to accomplish *anything*.

His awed constituency saw him as a person of parts who cut a figure in politics, counseling, public relations, employment services, commerce and a miscellany of other activities — a sort of rough-cut renaissance man. All this, when really all he did well was pour beer. I have observed a similar phenomenon with respect to other public figures over the past three decades — and I suspect some of them couldn't even pour beer.

There came a wonderful day a few years later when James Condon, a South Boston politician, distributed passes for the SS *Steel Pier*, and much of our Neighborhood went to sea.

The oddly named *Steel Pier* was an excursion boat that plied between Boston and the picturesque community on the tip of Cape Cod called Provincetown. I had my pass and seventy cents in my pocket and looked forward to a grand time. I wasn't disappointed.

Most of the teenagers clustered at the dance floor. The girls danced with each other. The boys — few knew how to dance — loitered about watching them. The prettiest girl on the floor was a slim, lissome creature whose smile gladdened her whole face. I was bold enough to cut in. The fact that my knowledge of dancing was at best rudimentary was no restraint.

She was cheerful and very much at ease, a graceful girl with merry hazel eyes and high cheekbones that brought tiny lilac shadows to her face when she moved her head in a certain way. I had never noticed that in anybody else. Her name was Mary Foley, and I learned that she lived on Pacific Street, a small street on the slope below Dorchester Heights. We enjoyed talking with one another and spent the entire day seeing the sights of Provincetown.

The fishermen were friendly. Mary and I savored the rich aroma of spicy Portuguese cooking that emanated from their waterfront homes. We were bemused by the mostly failed painters, poets and writers who seemed almost absurdly happy in their indigence. When we walked the endless beach, we saw flimsy shacks where many of them lived among the dunes. We looked in the shop windows and were surprised so many stores were closed. That meant, a policeman explained, that the proprietors had been overcome by a yen to go fishing or do nothing, which, we were told, happened often.

I was delighted with Mary Foley. She had a quick sense of humor, the kind that provoked a cheeriness in others. I showed off shamelessly. I sang "Paper Doll" and "Don't Sit Under the Apple Tree" and other popular songs for her, as well as "I'm a Typical Irishman" and "Shall My Soul Pass Through Old Ireland." She seemed to enjoy it all. I bought her some fried clams — in fact, I spent my whole seventy cents on her, and would have spent more if I'd had it.

When the trip was over, we said goodbye in South Boston. After I had gone a few steps, I remember stopping and looking back at her as she walked away. My head was filled with political aspirations by then, and she had told me during our walk in Provincetown that she planned a future in public health. Her agenda and mine were demanding and divergent, which made it unlikely we would share another day together. The thought didn't crush me, but for a while it was a little uncomfortable, like having a pebble in my shoe.

Mary became a happy memory. People like the Karps remained warm friends. Characters — Ombo, McCool, Mrs. Mulligan and all the rest — continued to be fun and in some ways instructive. But the principal influences of my early years — three of them — came from other sources.

I found one unexpectedly, downstairs in St. Monica's Church, while waiting for Sunday school to begin, when I heard Wally Clifford and Joe Quirk talking about the ninth grade at Boston College High and Boston Latin School, schools known for their high academic standards. I had just completed the ninth grade in public school, but they were talking with animation about things of which I knew nothing. It disturbed me intensely.

I walked through the Neighborhood thinking about those schools, especially BC High. People I knew waved or spoke to me. Some stranger in me responded with automatic banalities. But I was in another room of my mind, lost in dilemma, wondering how to get into a school my family could not afford and for which I was not qualified. The real me was so deeply involved in the problem, so sequestered in inner silence, that later I could not recall whom I had met or what had been said.

Finally I knew what I had to do. BC High was then on St. James Street in Boston's South End, near City Hospital and the Immaculate Conception Church. I put on my Sunday suit and walked into the school without an appointment. I felt quite confident — a lifelong failing.

Charles Doherty, the school registrar, happened to be at the lobby desk. I introduced myself and explained that I wanted to go to BC High, but that my family couldn't afford it and I wasn't qualified. However, I said, hurrying to get it all out before he could say anything, I would repeat the ninth grade and earn the money myself for the tuition. "So, you see," I concluded, "I can handle the whole thing."

He looked at me through steepled fingers for perhaps five seconds — it seemed like five hours — and then he nodded and said in the most casual of voices, "I think you can do it."

It was one of the most important events of my life.

A second seminal influence was the fact that I came into great wealth at an early age: I discovered books. Almost from the beginning of that windfall, that unguided adventure, when I had to read with a dictionary open beside me to look up the words, I was deeply moved. I realized I had found something of the greatest value. What began as an infatuation rapidly escalated to an almost febrile addiction. The more I read, the more I wanted to read — trivia, trash and classics, the lot; it was all one to me at the start, some of it utterly useless, much of it beyond my ken.

I would take long walks and try to make sense of what I had not understood. I often failed. But at times, at soaring moments of sudden revelation, I would discern, like a dazzling epiphany, a meaning that had been eluding me. I have rarely relied upon spirits to raise my spirit, but I know what drunkenness is, because I became drunk on books, an intoxication from which I never sobered, nor ever wanted to.

Books took me to worlds never hinted at by Father Dwyer. They often disturbed me and made me long for something I could not identify or perhaps someone I had yet to meet. They produced a contrapuntal sense of exhilaration and optimism.

Sometimes I found that books filled my head with vast and stunning thoughts. They seemed so novel that I wondered whether anyone else had ever thought such thoughts before. They came like storms whirling through my mind, leaving me uncomfortably embarrassed when normality returned. I remember thinking once that the only permanence was space and silence. All the racket we make, I thought, all the noises of man and nature, were merely interstitial trivia between the alpha and omega of the nothingness in which the world began and with which it will end under a burned-out star. The conception struck me as momentous, but a short while later I shook myself mentally and wondered what was the matter with me.

What was the matter with me, of course, was that I was seventeen.

The third great influence was an extraordinary human being. He was slight, sinewy, standing perhaps five and a half feet tall in his stout work shoes, but surprisingly strong, a small sledgehammer of a man.

He was a product of the North End. When he was young, that blue-collar section of Boston was, in the words of the historian Doris Kearns Goodwin, more crowded than Calcutta. He began life lost in that crowd, without patrimony or prospects, but with bone-deep faith in hard work. He was a Catholic — indeed, his sister was a Dominican nun; but he was not ardent in his practice.

He belonged to what some then termed the newer races, immigrants and their progeny. His fair skin and ruddy complexion — and those eyes, fathoms deep and blue as the Irish Sea — reflected his ancestry. He was part of that symbiosis between the Yankee bosses and those they thought of as huddled masses yearning for a day's pay at hard labor in the yards and factories. The city's burgeoning industry was then a mill that ground its crudest fodder exceeding fine, as it did him.

He never learned an artisan's skill. He had little formal education. In his youth, laboring in a railroad yard, he was pinned between two freight trains. A doctor explained that his left arm was of no further use and cut it off. A straw boss explained that a one-armed laborer was of no further use and fired him. The railroad calculated the wages due him — up to the time he had fallen, mangled, to the cinder bed — paid him and forgot him.

He acquired a prosthetic arm, crude by today's standards, which he fruitlessly tried to conceal by keeping the wooden hand in a pocket. He married a wise and wonderful woman, twenty years his junior, with whom he raised a large family. To support them, he pursued with an invulnerable ebullience a succession of odd jobs, always managing to find them, always convinced that what he was doing was important.

He never owned a home. He never owned a bond or a share of stock. He never had a bank account. He was born poor, lived poor, died poor, yet he had a quiet puissant pride and rejected even a suggestion of concession to the physical infirmity he never acknowledged.

His name was James Joseph Bulger, and he was my father. To a great extent, it was the things he taught me — directly and indirectly, purposely and inadvertently — that made me, for better or worse, what I am.

He was an instinctively gentle man. Women and elderly people liked him for his courtesy, an innate sense of manners that might seem anachronous to some now. Young men learned swiftly that when he was threatened or otherwise crowded, his gentility faded like the snap of a light switch, and he was tough as the streets he came from.

Roy Green, a former boxer from Charlestown, told me of a street fight — if it can be called that — in which another boxer, named Danny Johnson, was pounding an adversary into bloody insensibility.

"Your old man came along," Green recalled, "and he said, 'Danny, don't you think he's had enough?' But Danny was boiling. He said, 'You're next, Bulger.' After a few seconds your dad said, 'Hey, Danny,' and Danny looked toward him and was hit dead on the chops by a punch that must have started at your old man's ankles. It sounded like a ball going off a bat at Fenway Park. Down goes Danny, out cold."

Green added, "I had a lot of fights, you know. I could always handle things. But I'll tell you, your father is one guy I never wanted to get it on with."

I asked my father about the incident. All he said was "Bill, stay out of fights." Then, after thinking about it for a few moments, he said, "But if you can't avoid it, don't stand on ceremony."

That wisdom is not restricted to physical threats. Politics can be the key to useful public service; it can be fun; but it can also become a blood sport when some feral types, driven by ambition, think they perceive a lowering of your guard. Many times during the past thirty years I have remembered with advantage not to stand on ceremony.

My father was given to occasional periods of silent brooding, but the secret demons that tormented him at such times never altered his conduct. He loved and respected my mother. He fought the world with one arm to support us. He gave us everything he had to give. I have never wished there had been more.

My mother, Jane Veronica McCarthy, lived on Corey Street in Charlestown when she met my father. He was two decades older than she was, but that apparently did not deter their courtship or marriage.

She was a strong-minded woman. As a girl, she had made up her mind that she didn't like her name. She thought Veronica was much too fancy and Jane much too plain, so she had decided she would be called Jean. When she put her mind to something, she usually got it. Accordingly, everybody called her Jean, including my father.

She looked to my father, as did all of us, for leadership. He was the decision maker. But on the rare occasions when she felt strongly about something, he would inevitably defer to her. She was amused by the passionate interest he brought to current events, his addiction to the radio newscasts and his involvement in the broadcasts of baseball games. I remember coming home one day and my mother saying to me, "Your father's in the front room, managing the Red Sox."

She was an attractive woman, ever youthful; a fair-skinned brunette, blue-eyed and optimistic. When tragedy came, as sometimes it did, she endured it stolidly. She was not the sort to faint. She was sparing of the feelings of others. When she lay dying, she would say, "Now, you must not let it bother you." Or: "This happens to everyone. It's nothing to be sad about." Always "it" or "this," never "death." She would not darken the room for others by saying the word.

The older we get, it seems, the more wondrous becomes the theater of our memory. It is often suffused with a merciful magic that smoothes the rough edges of the past, so that we see our childhood through the eyes of the child we once were. It is that phenomenon, I suppose, that makes those days, somewhere on the edge of remembrance, seem to have been free of the wickedness and pain that now beset the human condition. If that illusion, or blessing, exists in my case — and I suppose it does — then, like being born in Dorchester, I can do nothing about it. I can only describe what I remember the way I remember it.

I remember my father for his wisdom and courage. I remember my mother for her strength and compassion. And I remember the South Boston of my childhood as a place where it seemed inconceivable that youth and summer would ever end.

All of that, of course, was a long time ago. Since then, South Boston's reputation has been trashed nationally by the media.

It could hardly be otherwise. The community's standards, traditions and aspirations have been ravaged and ridiculed by social activists. Some of them have had the best of intentions. Some of them have been motivated by hateful or contemptible goals. Some of them appear to have had nothing better to do with their time. Most of them have been articulate and sophisticated.

The defense by residents, couched in terms of blue-collar bluntness, reduced to fragmentary quotes and catchy sound bites, often elliptical, has been inadequate and easily misconstrued.

It has been a debate between completely mismatched advocates.

The result is that a cruelly false portrait of South Boston has been headlined and broadcast to the nation. It has been said that the rootless have always had contempt for the rooted, which may explain why social engineers chose our community for their disruptive experimentation. In the process, they displayed a wonderful disregard for the suffering of those affected, and damned as ignorant — or worse — any who tried to call that suffering to their attention. The media, for their part, heard words, seized on words, dealt only with the surface of words, and ignored the meanings beneath the words. The media were enthralled by the fiery prophets of social salvation, who in turn were blinded by the incandescence of their panacea of the moment.

Both groups, in their arrogant certitude, could no more see the true character of the Neighborhood — its ethos, if you will — than they could see the stars at noon.

But all of that comes later.

2

TELEVISION takes Americans to South Boston's L Street baths annually to see the Brownies, a male swimming group. I always associate them with the beginning of my political career.

It is when winter has turned the ocean to liquid ice that the Brownies perform, frolicking about in brain-numbing waves like a pale pod of happy seals.

They tended in years past, as they do now, to be men past the physical splendor of youth. Many wear bathing caps on bald heads. Everyone seems out of breath. The figures are less than Greek. But there is a certain bravura to their antics. They wear shorts for the cameras; otherwise they swim naked as squid.

I was hanging (as we used to say) at the baths one February day in 1960 when the Brownies were splashing in all their glacial glory. I had strolled over to see the show. A former boxer named Roley Rennihan, who was then working on the garbage trucks, came in. We talked for a while. That wasn't easy. He spoke very slowly. He never said much, and when he did, he still didn't. He had a masterly command of clichés and, after prolonged reflection, would say things like "He's a prince," and "She's a queen," and "You got to put your shoulder to the wheel." After a while it made your teeth ache.

In time — inevitably in South Boston — the subject became politics. Roley said, "There's a rumor you're going for the brass ring, Bill." I said I wanted to run, but wondered whether I'd be considered too young. Roley, as I have suggested, was not quick, which may have accounted for his retirement from the ring. He spent several minutes reflecting on what I had said. It would have required time-lapse photography to capture the process. At last he had it worked out. "I'll keep my ear to the ground," he promised with that virtuosity he had for metaphor.

I knew Roley lacked the sang-froid of the master information gatherer, but I thought, Why not? He might be able to sense the general attitude. It would, in a way, be my first poll, however unscientific. I began to feel excited about it. At least it was a start — which shows how much I knew about such things at the time.

I waited anxiously for several weeks to hear from Roley and finally went looking for him. He was in Connolly's Tavern in Andrew Square. I joined him at the bar and said, "I thought you might have something to say to me, Roley."

"Well," he said, "I do."

There was the usual long pause, and then he asked, "During the summer you work on the girls' side at L Street, don't you, Bill?"

I couldn't see what that had to do with his research, but acknowledged it was true. He lowered his voice to a whisper, and the battered face came close to mine. "Bill, don't ever say I asked you this, they'll all be laughing at me . . . but do they wear bathing suits on the women's side?"

So much for my opinion poll. I realized he'd forgotten all about it. It was the first of many personal disappointments in politics, but the good part is that they become less shattering as they mount up, because you expect less. I stayed calm and assured him that the women did indeed wear bathing suits.

"Yeah," he said a little sadly, "I thought so. But," he added, brightening perceptibly, "the day will come when they don't, Bill. You'll see, it'll come."

Roley may have been a disaster in opinion research, but it is likely he was ahead of his time sociologically. Examples of relaxed beach attire abound, from the Riviera to the Caribbean. Even as I write this, the harassed New York City Transit Police are confronted by a "Free Mammary Glands!" campaign. A woman advancing that cause recently stripped to the waist in a crowded subway car, where she stood waving a little flag. The press report did not describe the flag — under the circumstances, it probably was not closely studied. But it is a long way culturally from New York's subway to the L Street baths, which remain a citadel of feminine decorum.

I was disappointed in Roley, but I still had the feeling that I had made a beginning, so I was not discouraged. I also like to think I had the toughness of spirit that was the endowment of my origins.

There was much in my background that would help me in a campaign of my own. I had begun political work — the unglamorous dog work of politics — years before when I was in high school. I ran errands, stuffed envelopes, carried signs, canvassed and joined confederates at designated spots to hail our candidate as he passed by. It was on-the-job training to which, in the beginning, I brought little more than a tireless enthusiasm and an iron constitution. I remember a lieutenant of Joe Moakley's saying, "Well, one thing you've got to give young Bill — he may not know what he's doing, but he sure works at it like hell."

He was right. I knew little. But I was learning, and enjoying it.

Besides Moakley, I had worked for John McCormack and Johnny Powers and many others. Bill Carr, who said he found World War II relaxing after playing football at Boston College, was the most casual campaigner in my experience. I recall his wife saying, "You're a do-nothing candidate, Carr — get out of here and do *something*." He was a charming fellow and he'd always answer, "Everything will work out." Somehow, it always did.

The dumbest I ever worked for was a man named James Sullivan, who ran for sheriff against the incumbent, Frederick Sullivan. Jim had been a hanger-on in the campaigns of James Michael Curley, and I assumed he'd get Curley's endorsement. He never did. One day Tommy "Jabber" Joyce and I went out with Jim to distribute flyers and a trolley passed by with a sign on it bearing

Jim's picture and the question "Will *You* Vote for James Sulli-van?"

Sullivan began shouting to pedestrians, "There I am on the back of that streetcar! My God, look at me, look at me!"

Nobody looked at the trolley. Everybody looked at Sullivan the way people stare at someone having a fit. Jabber was so embarrassed, he stuck all the Sullivan flyers under his shirt. I asked, "Why are we wasting our time with this guy?" Jabber, the brother of Francis X. Joyce, who now heads the Massachusetts Convention Center Authority, said he was wondering that too.

Later it dawned on me that Jim Sullivan was not meant to win. He had been put in the race by Curley to split Fred Sullivan's vote.

I had been able to put so much time into political work because my sister Jean, first-born of the children, helped me with my high school tuition from time to time. Of course, I also kept busy at odd jobs: I worked at Karp's. In bad weather I went to the city yards where the straw boss, John McGlone, a neighbor on Logan Way, would pick me out to shovel snow. On other days I'd go to the docks where Joe Comfrey, another neighbor on Logan Way, picked teenagers from the shape-up to act as helpers at what we considered the astronomical wage of $3.50 an hour. We were called scalawags. I scalawagged a lot. In good weather, I had my job as a lifeguard at the L Street baths.

There were no student loans in those days, and even with Jean and my jobs I would not have been able to afford the tuition when I entered Boston College — a staggering $400 per year. But the Jesuit fathers agreed to pay for my first year, so that worry was gone.

By the time I was ready to graduate from high school, I had made a firm decision to run for office eventually. It was simply a matter of when. Meanwhile, I had more immediate problems, like finding a date for my prom. I had never been a major force on the dating front because I was always broke. But now I had a few dollars in my pocket, and I remembered Mary Foley, the girl on the SS *Steel Pier:* slim, vivacious, good-natured, gentle, and when I really thought about it, beautiful. I recalled that I had made a smashing impression on her when I sang "Shall My Soul Pass Through Old Ireland." I convinced myself she'd be delighted by the invitation. I had, obviously, no serious problem with self-esteem.

When she answered the phone, I announced the good news as though she had just won a lottery. "This is Bill Bulger," I said in my usual suave way. "Do you want to go to my school prom?" I didn't add, "You lucky girl," but it was there in my voice.

After a brief silence, she asked, "Bill who?"

That wasn't exactly what I'd expected. My mind flitted back to cruel Megan O'Malley, who had broken my heart in the third grade when she told me she hated all boys, including me. But I kept talking, and Mary finally said she recalled dancing with me. She laughed, not unkindly, a soft contralto laugh, and said, "I thought you were measuring the floor." Then she said, "I'd like to go to your prom, Bill."

I brought her yellow flowers. I don't know what kind they were, but they looked bright and cheerful. They made me think of her. Her mother, who had been born in County Galway, tried to give me money to "help get through the date," but I already had five dollars in my pocket, surely enough.

Things went so well with us that the following year, when Mary graduated from Gate of Heaven School, where she had gone for twelve years, she invited me to *her* senior prom, where I measured the floor for hours.

Jean — who at the time of her graduation had been voted the prettiest girl in South Boston High School — made our family happy by marrying Joe Toomey, a young man from South Boston. Joe was a West Point graduate and, at almost six feet six inches, had been the tallest cadet during his years at the academy.

In a matter of weeks, Joe was ordered to Korea, where he was decorated for his conduct in action. But second lieutenants of infantry are prime targets, and we were informed that he had been wounded and captured when China committed its troops to help the battered North Korean forces. Young men are the tools of war, and South Boston always seemed to supply more than its share.

There followed a period of silence, which in some ways was particularly distressing. Joe's capture was the first really bad thing that had happened to us, and I felt a foreboding. I was reading *Macbeth* at the time, and I recall being strangely upset by Malcolm's poignant words: "I would the friends we miss were safe arrived."

At last word came that Joe had been starved to death by his captors. Survivors, less cruelly treated, told of seeing that huge, powerful body waste away from malnutrition, until Joe simply lay down, closed his eyes, and died.

All the shock, grief and anger that ravaged my family was muted by our empathy for Joe's widow. I can never forget Jean's stricken face. In the desolation in her eyes I could see her taking sad inventory of her lost future with Joe, all the unlived years. They had been together so briefly, and seventeen years would pass before Jean was ready to marry again — a long threnody indeed.

I would see Mary Foley occasionally during this period. She worked at the F. W. Woolworth store at the corner of Broadway and F Street. It was poorly lit and cavernous, filled with counters. There was no air conditioning, and in the summer it had the ambiance of a dank cave.

I had a summer job at the City Laundry on Dover Street, near where the *Boston Herald* building now stands. When my shift ended at noon, I would stroll up Broadway to Woolworth's for a few words with Mary. Then I'd be off to my lifeguard job at L Street, my swimming trunks hanging from the back pocket of my shorts. Mary knew I was headed for the beach while she faced a long afternoon in the Woolworth cave. It never occurred to me that I was being thoughtless.

After my first year at Boston College I volunteered to be drafted. The call came quickly. I was sent to Fort Dix in New Jersey and then to the Army base at Fort Bliss, Texas, where I spent eighteen months. In all, I was in service two years, from September 1953 to August 1955.

I came home to the greatest shock of my life, a tragedy that the family had kept from me while I was away: my older brother, James, was in jail awaiting trial on a charge of bank robbery.

For almost forty years, newspaper and television reporters have urged me to talk about Jim. I never have, except to say that he is my brother and I love him. But I cannot write an honest memoir and ignore the subject.

Jim, next-born after Jean, was my senior by five years. I had seen him change from a blithe spirit to a rebel whose cause I could never discern. He was in a constant state of revolt against . . . I'm not sure what. He was restless as a claustrophobic in a dark closet.

"Where's Jim?" my mother was always asking. "I turn my back for a second and he's out the door. He's always out the door. Where does he go?"

I couldn't answer. I didn't know. I don't think Jim knew where he was going most of the time — just *out*.

He was a physical culturist and kept himself in prime condition. He neither smoked nor drank. He was so concerned with impurities that he would plead with our mother not to spray Flit or other insecticides in our house. He abhorred addictive drugs. He had an abundance of good humor and a wildly creative talent for impish mischief — like the time he came home with an ocelot he had acquired as a pet. He named the animal Lancelot.

My mother refused to go into the room where Jim and I slept so long as Lancelot the ocelot prowled there. She would remind Jim that pets were forbidden in the project.

"Gee, Mom, everybody's got dogs," he'd say, "and it's dogs and cats that are forbidden. Read the rules. Where does it say anything about ocelots?"

The beast grew at an alarming pace, and our father eventually, to our mother's evident relief, had Jim take Lancelot to the zoo.

Jim's scrapes were small in those growing-up years, but in time there were enough of them to make him known to the police. That created a dangerous situation. Some policemen used their billy clubs more than their brains. And Jim was defiant and wouldn't give an inch. His speech was bold. He was often beaten, sometimes savagely. For a while I thought *all* police were vicious.

Jim, I have always believed, had a quicker mind than mine and the intelligence to excel academically — had he wanted to. But he found school boring. His teachers, like my mother, often discovered that Jim was suddenly missing. Once he was in the wind for several months: the Ringling Brothers and Barnum & Bailey Circus came to town; when it left, Jim left with it. He was what the circus called a roustabout, a sort of gofer. He loved it.

Jim and I did not share the same friends. His were older, of course, and they listed, like Jim, to the wild side. They looked on him as a leader, which was the only role he would tolerate. He was the sort who rarely had to raise his voice when he wanted something done.

His cronies were in awe when Jim began dating a performer from the Old Howard, a burlesque theater in Boston's Scollay Square, in those days a rallying point for sailors on shore leave. Her work sometimes took her to Chicago, and she sent him postcards signed "Tiger Lil."

Our mother was horrified. Jim would get hysterical watching her reaction. He was still a teenager.

The city's school system finally required him to attend Brandeis High, a trade school near the Bradford Hotel in midtown Boston. He finished there and immediately joined the Air Force. He did that so suddenly I had to pick up his diploma for him after he had left.

He wrote to me often. It was clear he was enjoying himself. The Air Force apparently had more rules than planes, and he delighted in breaking or circumventing a great number of them. It appeared from his letters that he contrived a new system each week for being absent without leave, and did so with impunity. His conduct was not from any lack of patriotism. He was just being Jim. I believed then, and I believe now, that he would have performed well in combat.

Jim was honorably discharged from the Air Force, but then fell in with some much older men who were experienced in bank holdups. He accompanied them on robberies in Indiana. He was also wanted in Massachusetts. I am not suggesting that bad companions were entirely to blame for his crimes. Certainly they contributed, but Jim made his own decisions and never blamed anyone else for them.

For jurisdictional reasons, his trial took place in federal district court in Boston, before Judge George Sweeney, a strict but fair man. I went to court the day Jim was sentenced. He was found guilty of participating in three bank robberies, sentenced to twenty years, and sent to the federal penitentiary in Atlanta, Georgia. He accepted the verdict and the sentence stoically.

I was twenty-one at the time. He was twenty-six.

I borrowed the money to take my parents to Atlanta to visit Jim. My mother said, "Take your father, my place is with the children." I knew it was pointless to argue with her. I did what she said.

Later, when Jim was transferred to a prison at Lewisburg, Pennsylvania, I bought a stripped-down Chevrolet and drove my father there. Some guards, knowing Jim lifted weights, had thrown the weights out in the ice and snow to punish him. Jim's hands were swollen and the palms were covered with open red sores where they had frozen to the iron. I was angered, but Jim thought it a huge joke that the guards could think he'd be stopped by a little pain. "You have to score very high in the stupidity test to be a guard in this place," he said.

When I asked him whether any of the prisoners had given him trouble, he smiled and said, "Nothing I couldn't handle."

We did not know it was customary for visitors to deposit money in the commissary, and never left a cent for Jim. Being Jim, he never asked us to.

At that time, a prisoner became eligible for parole after serving one third of his sentence, so we expected Jim to be free in seven years. But he was no more docile in prison than out. He was caught with contraband of some sort that prison authorities said was to have been used in helping another prisoner to escape. Jim was sent to the maximum-security prison called Alcatraz, a scientifically harsh house of dungeons on a bare wet rock in San Francisco Bay.

In all, eleven years passed from the time Jim left Boston until he was paroled and came home.

Since that time, there has been much speculation in the press, many lurid allegations. From everything I could see, he appeared to have taken enormous steps to separate himself from the environment that led to his early misbehavior. It's left to me, as it has been to others, to speculate about what, if anything, is valid in the dark rumors published about him. I am confident much of it has been circulated as an oblique political attack on me. I *know* some of the allegations and much of the innuendo to be absolutely false. Other matters I cannot be sure about, one way or the other. I have no way of knowing and can only hope. But he is my brother and I love him, and pray that he will not damage himself again.

Joe Toomey's terrible death and the thought of my brother locked in a prison cage — both coming in the space of a very few years — I found almost insupportable. My moral landscape, the contours of good and evil, reward and punishment, substance and chimera, seemed suddenly evanescent. And the Kafkaesque nightmare was not solely due to my shock at the suffering of others. It was in part self-centered. To put it baldly, I wondered why such things had happened to *me*.

Priests and philosophers taught that the key to happiness was avoidance of sin, and while I was peccable as the next one, I had tried. No matter what anyone else might think, I had *tried*. Why, then, was I so unhappy? I am ashamed of my preoccupation with my own hurt, but there it is: that was how I felt.

Truly — except for the mad, who in some respects may be the happiest among us — we all know life cannot be serene. Like forces of nature, external influences — coincidences, the behavior of others, acts of God, call them what you will — impact our lives as surely as oaks are riven by lightning bolts. Why, then, are we startled by sudden griefs? Why do the storms and floods of our personal lives bring a vague sense of injustice? Why do we not expect such things? Perhaps that is the way it is meant to be. Perhaps, as Isak Dinesen speculated, God made the world round so that we could not see too far down the road.

It is painful when illusions die, when innocence is lost. But self-pity is the loneliest of agonies; no one really can share it with us; few want to. In time we seek for countervailing influences to provide a sense of recovery. My mind turned almost at once to Mary. It seems to me wonderfully coincidental that, in seeking a fresh beginning, a new day as it were, I should have thought first of Mary — namesake of her whose emblem is the morning star.

Mary and I had corresponded a few times while I was in the Army. Now we began to date on a regular basis. Her infectious good humor was a tonic, but she also had the rare gift of being able to share silence happily when that was the most supportive thing to do.

Soon she had me singing again, songs like "Boys from the County Mayo" and other hot numbers of similar ilk, and I enjoyed it because it amused her so. I began to miss her greatly when we were apart.

We'd go to a parish dance or to a motion picture occasionally, but most of the time we walked around South Boston, talking or singing or just being with one another. We strolled the strand way down the beach, past the L Street bathhouse, then out onto Castle Island to Kelly's Landing, where we'd share a box of fried clams and a box of French-fried potatoes. She usually had more money than I did, so she'd pay for the expensive clams and I bought the fries. We'd go to Dorgan's, a restaurant on the corner of the G Street hill, and order something at the take-out window. We had a lot of routes and we varied them.

I don't think I spent $100, all told, during that time.

Mary's mother, Sarah Foley, lifted my spirits. She was a strikingly beautiful woman. Sarah had left the village of Carna and come to South Boston as thousands from that area had done before her.

Sarah was deeply superstitious, totally persuaded of the efficacy of a host of charms and taboos. When she went to the church hall to play bingo, she would place a rabbit's foot beside her board.

I noted a particularly disturbed expression on her face once when I made light mention of leprechauns, the little people who are said to run about the Irish countryside doing magic. I teased her by asking with a straight face whether she believed in such creatures.

"I'll not get into that particular matter," she said primly.

I suggested that leprechauns existed only in fairy tales.

"Well," she said, "you can think whatever you think, I'm sure. And that's an end to that."

I asked her if she had ever *seen* a leprechaun.

She was a master of indirection. "Well, I personally knew a woman in Carna had the evil eye," she said. "If I hadn't known her myself, I suppose you'd be telling me the evil eye is a fairy tale."

"Some say it *is* a fairy tale," I said.

"That's what the priest said," Sarah recalled triumphantly. "So when he came riding into the village, that woman cast the eye at him and his horse fell right out from under him."

I asked whether the priest was ever able to ride a horse again.

"Oh, only ignorant people think the curse lasts forever," she said airily. "That's just superstition. If you take a scrap of the witch's clothing, boil it and drink the water, the curse is gone."

Thanks in considerable part to Mary's healing presence, my thoughts were turning increasingly to the future — and my plans for a career of public service were becoming less amorphous. This renascent preoccupation was fueled by the fact that 1959 had been a watershed year politically in Massachusetts. James Michael Curley had died in November of 1958, and with his passing had gone the last vestiges of the flamboyance, the bossism and the heavy-handed hurrahs of the era he created. The thought was not entirely free of poignancy as I remembered the old warrior's personal charm and wit.

I had an aimless affection for Curley. His personality and

shrewdness had sustained him in successful campaigns for mayor of Boston, governor, and Congress. His politics were not mine, but even when I was in high school he seemed bigger than life to me. My father would caution me: "Curley's done good, but he has faults."

He did indeed. He had unlawfully taken a civil service examination for a friend and had been imprisoned for mail fraud. President Truman had issued a full pardon to Curley in 1950, but he was never pardoned by his enemies and critics. It was said he accepted graft, but that was never proved; he lived modestly and left little for his heirs when he died. With all his faults, whatever they may have been, I found the sheer *Irishness* of his personality beguiling. I always loved listening to him. I heard him speak often.

After I returned to Boston from the Army, Curley had tried a comeback, running for mayor against John B. Hynes. Joe Moakley asked me to vote for Hynes.

"You'll be wasting a vote on Curley," he said. "He's gone."

"I know, Joe," I said, "but I can't help your man. Once in my life I want to cast a vote for Curley, and this looks like it might be the last chance."

Moakley looked at me as though I had lost my wits, which I probably had.

Curley ran a distant second in the preliminary election. That meant — in Democratic Boston — Hynes would win in November.

I went to the Brunswick Hotel the night of that loss to hear Curley speak. I wondered what he could say to his disconsolate supporters, politically wise men and women who knew the end had arrived.

The place was crowded. Everyone was wearing the face of a victim. I worked my way through the solemn army of people in the lobby and eventually reached the door of the ballroom where Curley was to speak. It was not possible to go another inch.

There was a sudden commotion behind me and here came Curley, imposing as a royal personage, big as a tank. He advanced grandly through a silent crowd that opened for him like the Red

Sea parting for the Israelites. When he passed me, I fell in behind him and followed on his heels to the front of the ballroom. I stopped when he climbed the three steps to the speaker's platform, realizing I had the best spot in the place, directly in front of the raised dais.

Curley began speaking. That deep, mellifluous voice rolled like gentle waves over the glum audience. The soft cadence had a healing quality, gradually washing away their anxieties. Then, having calmed them, the voice grew stronger, the words sharper and quicker. I was fascinated by the performance, the man's power. You could feel a swelling current moving the crowd, a roiling sea before an approaching storm.

"Remember John Paul Jones," he thundered. "Remember him on the splintered deck of the *Bon Homme Richard,* sails torn, rigging shredded, blood running in the scuppers, even his brave and faithful officers urging him to surrender.

"Yes," he said, the voice leveling before beginning its final crescendo, "I want you to remember the great victory of John Paul Jones . . . for tonight I say to you what he said then: *I have not yet begun to fight!*"

The crowd went wild. Reason was shelved. Rational disbelief was suspended. The venerable walls of the Brunswick shook with cheers, whistles and stamping feet. Curley had converted a wake to a rally. He was Lazarus rising from his winding sheet. The flushed faces raised to him glowed with courage and confidence and faith.

In a short while, of course, they would all come to their senses and realize the fight was over, the battle lost. They would know that he had somehow hypnotized them merely by reciting clichés they had long ago seen chalked on blackboards in their elementary schools. Then they would find themselves puzzled, perhaps vaguely disturbed, wondering what had happened to them in that crowded ballroom.

I walked home that night knowing he would lose, knowing I would vote for him anyway, but knowing I had witnessed a political magic show.

Today, when young men and women read of Curley, many find little depth or importance in anything he said. They acknowledge he had wit, but they attribute his power to sway an audience to what they perceive as the unsophisticated times in which he lived. His actual words — like his dramatization of John Paul Jones — they find suggestive of the turgidity of a high school valedictorian. The result is they then dismiss him as a colorful relic of a gullible era, the tribal totem of a simplistic ethnic culture of the past.

They are partly right — and totally wrong.

Curley undoubtedly had innate speaking talent, but he had studied under Dr. Delbert Moyer Staley, the great rhetorician who later trained Jack Kennedy and other luminaries. Curley was his mentor's star pupil. He could and did hold thousands enthralled, spellbound not by the banality of what he said, but by the way he said it, the musical sounds in his voice. It was the range, the timbre, the soaring flights, the poignant glissandi, the lingering echoes of that resonating, reverberating voice.

One will never understand the man's magic by reading his words. It is discernible only by the ear, not the eye. The power of Curley's song was not in the lyrics, it was the instrumental.

I had no delusion that I had Curley's vocal gift. Nevertheless, I felt I could succeed in politics. I aspired to model my public service, to the best of my ability, on my political idols: Roosevelt's social conscience, Truman's grit, Jack Kennedy's ability to inspire hope, Moakley's capacity for service. Large ambitions indeed.

I bought Mary an engagement ring at a little shop on Beacon Hill. We went to my home to show it to my family. My mother was startled because she knew I had no money.

My father asked, "How are you going to get married when you can't support her?"

Mary said she had some savings from her job at the Public Health Department. I reminded him that I'd soon graduate from law school and expected to build a thriving practice very quickly.

My father said, "For God's sake, don't tell anybody about this!"

In 1960, when I was going into my last year at law school, Mary and I were married in Dorchester, at St. Margaret's Church.

On our honeymoon we went to Cape Cod, where we had found a place with the tacky name of Settle Downs, in the town of Brewster. I was so excited that when we emerged on our first morning, I greeted a man and woman at poolside with the words "Hi, this is Mary Foley and I'm Bill Bulger."

In those days, people sharing the same motel room were expected to share the same surname — and the reaction to my words was glacial. We finally got it all sorted out, and I tried to get things back on track by saying, "I'm planning to run for political office." The man turned and walked away.

After a brief pause, his wife said, "Don't mind him. He hates politicians."

"Tell him to look on the bright side," Mary suggested. "Bill might lose."

We rented an apartment at 1596 Columbia Road, at the corner of K Street in South Boston. Our parish was Gate of Heaven Church. In 1966 we bought a house at 828 East 3rd Street, where we live today. Our parish became, and still is, St. Brigid's. Our first son, Bill, was born in 1961, James in 1962, Sarah in 1963, Patrick in 1964, Mary in 1965, Daniel in 1966, Kathleen in 1968, Christopher in 1969, and Brendan in 1974.

Mary continued her job in the Public Health Department at the statehouse when we arrived back from our honeymoon in July of 1960. I got down to the business of politics.

My old friend Joe Moakley had vacated his seat in the Massachusetts House of Representatives to run for the state Senate against the incumbent, a wily veteran named John Powers. I was still in law school, but decided to run for Joe's seat.

So did fifteen others!

I had no organization, no money, and certainly no experience as a candidate. But none of those things is as important in politics as timing — and the vacancy left by Moakley determined the timing.

I could not work for Joe in his campaign, because I was a

candidate. I decided to watch his fight carefully for whatever guidance it might offer.

Powers had a high, thin voice, a petulant manner of delivery, and once started he would go on interminably. He had been infuriated by Moakley's slogan, "It's Time for *That* Change," and couldn't stop talking about it. But he had a large and efficient organization that served voters well — and got them to the polls. Moakley lacked the manpower and money to match that.

Apparently it *wasn't* time for a change. Powers prevailed in a fierce struggle. The campaign was instructive: I learned from watching them that a superior candidate can be defeated by a superior organization. But I also suspected that no organization could sustain indefinitely a flawed campaigner.

Powers was a capable, self-educated man with many virtues: he drove himself hard; he got things done. He served many years in the Senate and was elected to the presidency. But to Powers, politics was a world of limitless paranoia: he discerned in the most fitful and capricious occurrences evidence of malevolent conspiracy. He was a close accountant of the slightest criticisms, and it was said he never held grudges longer than three or four decades. Worse, he lacked control. He not only picked fights with a cruel, hyperbolic tongue, he picked *unnecessary* fights. He became increasingly the product of his past misjudgments, and I suspected the ineluctable arithmetic of that process eventually would drive him from office, as indeed it did.

My hopes for assistance from Moakley's organization vanished, because those who were not occupied with his campaign were among the group running against me. They felt they and others with long service in political wars had earned the succession. They viewed me as an upstart with pretensions beyond my proper station.

Technically, there was a second House seat open. But it was certain to be won by James Condon, the incumbent. Condon, an experienced politician — the man who had distributed the tickets for the *Steel Pier* excursion, where Mary and I met — was another source of anticipated support. He had encouraged me to run and

had said he would help me. I knew his experience and organization could be powerful weapons in my campaign.

When he did nothing, I reminded him of his promise and he
said, "I'll be there for you when the time is right."

That is the political equivalent of telling you the check is in the
mail.

Obviously, Condon had not expected the army of aspirants
that declared for Moakley's seat, and he saw no political sense in
making one friend and fifteen enemies. It was clear I could count
on nothing from Condon.

I was alone, but even that didn't discourage me. Jack Kennedy
was running for president; the air was electric with visions of a
New Frontier. The notion of public service, the value of it for its
own sake, filled my head with lofty aspirations. I believed we were
on the verge of a quantum leap in social progress, a time when
good things would happen, when all the old promises would be
kept. I was determined to be part of it.

One of the problems of building an organization from scratch
is dealing with enthusiasts who are more likely to hurt you than
help you, and dealing with them in a manner that won't offend
them. You still want their votes.

Some bring baggage too heavy to carry. For example, there was
a local radical, a salesman of social indiscipline and other unthinkable causes. There was his opposite, our Neighborhood law-
and-order advocate of draconian remedies for all the ills of society. Both men appealed to small groups of confused people, and
were considered crackpots by all the rest.

I didn't want either of them slowing down my political wagon
by their affiliation, but I didn't want to alienate any votes — even
theirs. I assured both that their positions were highly original,
which was certainly true. I asked each to write detailed position
papers for me so that I could make thoughtful decisions on their
proposals. I hoped that would keep them occupied until after the
primary election — without alienating them. Both later told me
they had voted for me. Perhaps they did. You never really know.

More difficult by far is the problem of maintaining the active support of those campaign workers whose political naiveté makes them vulnerable to fears and doubts that can sap their enthusiasm. Such people tend to believe the most idle of rumors and to spread them, innocently, but harmfully. I recall going through Andrew Square one Sunday and encountering a group consisting of Ham Slowe, Joe Wetwash and a character known, for some reason, as The Good Robb. They weren't regular campaign workers, but they were available at times, when sober, to carry signs or pass out literature. They regularly loitered in the square on the Sabbath, because the VFW post was open after Mass and the drinks were cheap and plentiful.

Ham was sober only on special occasions, and this wasn't one of them. The Good Robb was of a similar persuasion. Joe Wetwash — so called because he drove a delivery truck for the Peninsula Laundry, which was considered a major career move for him — was a less dedicated drinker, but very simple.

"They're selling out over in Connolly's," Wetwash told me. "There's a Republican over there and he's setting up drinks for everybody. They're all signing cards to vote for him."

"We've got a big problem here," Slowe told me grimly. The Good Robb shook his head sadly over such betrayal.

"Those guys will be ashamed when they wake up in the morning and remember that they have to vote Republican," Wetwash said.

Of course, there was no chance of that. What the Republican was getting for the drinks was signatures, not votes. Many of those at the bar probably wouldn't vote anyway, and those who did would no more vote Republican than they would embrace apostasy from their church. To avoid argument, though, I assured them that the drinkers in Connolly's were all supporters of Jerry O'Leary, an opponent.

"O'Leary's losing the votes," I told them, "not I."

That made them happy.

I felt I had as good a chance as anybody else: I had grown up breathing politics. I had worked in the vineyard, doing the menial jobs that I would have to teach to others if I were to build an organization. I knew the Neighborhood well. Most important of all, I had the faithful and tireless Mary Foley at my side, typing for me, organizing my schedule, encouraging me.

I believed there were five men I had to defeat in order to win:

There was O'Leary, who had been a football hero at Holy Cross College. He was widely known, experienced and a hard campaigner. Personally, I found him more interesting when he *stopped* talking, but many considered him the favorite.

There was Jack Walsh, son of Stretch Walsh, a popular South Boston figure. Jack later became a bodyguard for the Kennedy family. He appeared in many news photographs when he accompanied Jackie, John and Caroline to the isles of Greece. Some said Jack Walsh would be helped by the Kennedys, but I doubted it.

There was John Fitzgerald, a perennial candidate who believed his turn had come. He had a substantial organization, but I believed that in his many losses he had lost his heart for politics. When your heart stops in politics, as in life itself, you're dead. Still, he could not be ignored.

There was Thomas Belmonte from I Street. He was a bit of a mystery to me, but he was the only candidate of Italian ancestry in the race and had to be taken seriously. Before the campaign was over, he would prove a bigger mystery than he had been at the start. The astonishing thing about Tom was he never left his home area on I and 8th Streets. He'd always be there when we went by with our signs. Even years later, in other campaigns, when we'd pass by, Tom was still in the same place. He was a nice fellow, but strange.

There was Jim Collins, who later became treasurer of Norfolk County. He was a tragic, peccant figure who abused his office and went to prison. His family split apart, and he died of a heart attack while on a work-release program. But he had a pleasant personality, spoke well, and when I was running against him, he was well funded by his father, James M. Collins Sr., an ex-bookmaker who bought a new Cadillac every year. Collins senior spread word in the Irish areas that I was really Polish or Lithuanian.

A candidates' night was held at the South Boston Social Club. I took a sizable contingent to the affair with me. The other candidates spoke episodically of their achievements, but with becoming modesty. They were very polite to one another.

O'Leary got carried away with the gentlemanly atmosphere and informed the audience that *all* the candidates were well qualified. As a group, I knew my opponents disliked and resented me, but they treated me with a distant civility.

I spoke last. At least I got up to speak. I had prepared my remarks carefully, but suddenly I couldn't recall a word. The thought flashed through my mind of Maimonides — the learned Rabbi Moses ben Maimon — who had written of the flutist who rose to perform and realized he had forgotten how to play his instrument. I suppose it was the excitement of making my first formal speech that made my memory go blank. But I had to say *something.*

"Forget everything you've been told tonight," I said.

I heard my voice as though I were listening to someone else speak.

"O'Leary says all the candidates are equally qualified," I went on. "That's not so. I'm more qualified than any of them."

All of that just spilled out of me. I don't know where it came from, and I certainly didn't know where I was going next. But it didn't matter: the crew I'd brought with me began to cheer and howl, and soon most of the audience was carried along and joined in.

After that, everything I said brought resounding applause.

When the speaking was over, I noticed some of the candidates talking with a dark, saturnine man known as Bob Dineen the Crazy Marine. Elizabethan writers had a word — "grinigog" — to describe someone who is always smiling, even when there is nothing to smile about, and that was the word for Dineen; he was a smiler, a grinigog. Finally the conversation broke up and he came across the floor. He leaned toward me with a studied insolence in his eyes that gave the lie to the painted grin on his face.

"You belong in prison with your brother," he said. The word "prison" had a sneering sibilant stress. It was a hiss.

I knew he'd been sent to say that. I knew they expected me to lose control, and lose the crowd in the process. It was hard not to. But I spoke very softly to him. "Bob, a dog that will fetch a bone will carry one. So go back and tell them it didn't work."

I knew, though, that sometime, somewhere, Dineen and I would have to come to understand one another better.

Our campaign battleground was South Boston's Ward 7, stretching from the L Street bathhouse into Dorchester. Three of the precincts were in Dorchester, seven in South Boston.

I had absolutely no money. Bill Carr, the former representative in whose campaigns I had worked, told me, "Bill, you've got to *ask* people for money. That's the way it's done. You go ask Joe Barry, he's a generous guy."

It was a very hard thing for me to do. I would rather have gone to the dentist with a root canal problem than to Joe Barry's liquor store in Perkins Square that day. But I had gone to school with his son-in-law, Scott, and I hoped that might break the ice. I went to the store, told Joe I was running and said, "If there's anything you can do to help out, it would be great."

He reached in his pocket and drew out $65, which he handed to me. I was overwhelmed. At the time it looked like ten times as much.

It was a touch-and-go campaign with so little money, but I had great support from friends. Will McDonough, who became an outstanding sportswriter for the *Boston Globe* — and who now also does commentary on TV for National Football League games — became my campaign manager. I would tell Will that with his intelligence he could get a good job somewhere instead of frittering his time away writing about sports. Now I budget to pay college tuitions while Will negotiates million-dollar contracts, which says something about my talent as a career counselor.

In those long-ago days, his major concerns were such things as finding residents who would allow my signs to be erected on their property. I recall one night when Coley Walsh — brother of Father Michael Walsh, who was then president of Boston College — breezed in after a sojourn at the Cornerstone Pub.

"I own that three-decker across the street," Coley said. "Go nail a sign up on it."

Will, accompanied by Bill Sweeney and Ed Phillips, put a ladder against the building and began nailing a sign in place. A window opened and a man's head emerged.

"What the hell do you think you're doing?" he demanded. "You've already knocked a picture off the wall."

"Coley Walsh owns this place and said we could put up a sign," McDonough explained.

"All Coley owns is the clothes he's wearing," the man snarled. "I own this house, and you get away from it and take your damn sign with you."

McDonough doesn't lie, but he has reflexes like those of the great receiver Jerry Rice. Knowing the angry man could not see the name on the sign, he said, "We're leaving, but I still hope you'll vote for O'Leary."

"Not after you're hammering my pictures off the wall," he was told. "Tell him I'm voting for Bulger."

McDonough shook his head sadly and left.

Mary tried to help with the financial nightmare. She bought a budget envelope with compartments for rent, food, medical expenses, and the like.

"We're going to systemize everything," she told me. "No more panic."

A few nights later I met her at Andrew Station and said, "Mary, I raided the envelope to buy some bumper stickers."

She asked me how we were going to pay the rent.

"Now, Mary," I advised her, "don't worry about things like that."

She smiled and said, "Come on, I'll buy you some fried clams."

That's the way Mary is. I never heard more about a budget envelope.

Our campaign headquarters cost us nothing. Old friends — Stogy, Munu and Fredyu Krupa — had a shack made of corrugated metal on Preble Street, near the Old Harbor project. The Krupas were a Polish family, and they distributed newspapers, using the shack as an assembly point. Fredyu, whom I knew best, made it available to us.

We stored signs there. We met there in the early morning to plan the day, and then we'd meet again at night to review what we had done. When things went well, someone would buy a case of beer, and we would celebrate. When that happened, Skunky Dolan, an old man who lived nearby in an abandoned car, would hammer on the door and tell us to quiet down.

Skunky reeked of alcohol. It was an act of reckless courage to strike a match in his close presence. His personal hygiene, or lack of it, exposed him to constant criticism, but that never bothered him.

"I'm too old to apologize for anything," he'd say.

On the nights when he pounded on the door of our headquarters, we'd give him a can of beer, and he'd go back to his abandoned car and leave us alone.

During the campaign I sought advice from several political veterans. Some helped, some did not.

I met with Joe Kane, a first cousin to Joseph P. Kennedy. He was a vigorous old-timer who would walk in from Jamaica Plain and sit downstairs in the Waldorf Cafeteria on Beacon Street.

He had enormous influence with Jack Kennedy — and with good reason. Jack began his first campaign for Congress without bothering to register properly in advance as a Democrat. When he realized his oversight, it was too late to correct it, which made him ineligible for election. He went to the Waldorf and found Kane.

"Uncle Joe," he said, "I have a problem."

Joe and a friend at city hall, a woman who had worked for Maurice Tobin, a former mayor of Boston, went into the city's vault. They searched through the jungle of records until they found Jack's registration. When they left, he was a registered Democrat, a proper candidate. One wonders what effect it might have had on Kennedy's career if his first campaign had been aborted by a technicality of registration.

Kane wanted to talk to me about Kennedy. He had nothing else on his mind.

"He's so tight, it's embarrassing," Joe said. "I went to Litchfield's with him and some of his friends. When the check came Jack announces, like he always does, that he has come without a cent." Kane said that he had paid for lunch. "That's the end, though. I told him I wasn't going to lunch or anywhere else with him unless I saw his money first."

As Joe talked, my mind wandered to the many stories I had heard of Kennedy's caution in spending money. There was the time Willie Sutton, a campaign employee, was asked to take Jack's mother, Rose, from the Ritz-Carlton to Logan Airport. Willie, being on the payroll, called a cab. Rose decided to ask the driver how things looked for this young congressional candidate here in Massachusetts.

"It looks very good," the driver said. "He seems like a nice man, young Kennedy — a war hero and all. A nice kid."

"That's just wonderful to hear," Rose said.

By now the cab was in the North End of Boston and Rose told the driver, "I'm Rose Kennedy, Jack's mother, and I come from this area we're driving through."

With that, the driver slammed on the brake. "I'm glad to run into you," he said. "Jack owes me two dollars and eighty-five cents from the last time he was in my cab."

When Rose got out of the cab at the airport she said to Willie Sutton, "I think from now on it will be less expensive if we don't identify ourselves."

The young congressman's parsimonious habits annoyed more than Joe Kane. I knew of one group of businessmen Jack had stiffed at lunches who invited him to Boston's most expensive restaurant. They ordered generously from the extensive menu, drank the congressman's health in vintage Montrachet, and then, one at a time, departed on one pretext or another and left him alone. When the waiter presented the bill, Jack had to telephone his office to send his driver, Peter Cloherty, down with cash.

Cash and Peter Cloherty were a dubious combination. One day, Kane told me, Jack burst in on him at the Waldorf and said, "Uncle Joe, I'm going to the district attorney's office to get a complaint against Peter Cloherty."

"Well, why?"

"Because he's got his hands on my credit cards and he's eating meals all over town. He bought a suite at the Ritz. He's been doing all these various things and I can't catch up with him, so I'm going to get a complaint."

Joe told the congressman to sit down. "Jack, listen to me carefully. You are now a congressman. That means you get people *out* of trouble, not *into* trouble."

Jack went back to his office, but he never forgave Cloherty and soon found another driver.

Peter Cloherty later became a state representative from Brighton. He was a friendly, ebullient sort, a great hand-shaker. When Jack Kennedy, then president-elect, came to the statehouse to deliver a speech, Peter blocked the aisle and grabbed Jack's hand in welcome. I had the impression Kennedy was almost desperate to get away.

Peter went to the 1960 Democratic national convention. To attract attention, he started a fire on the floor in the midst of his fellow delegates. It was featured on network television — as were Peter's courageous efforts to extinguish it. Thus Peter started a fire to frighten people and then put it out to become their hero.

Some politicians do that sort of thing all the time.

My visit with Joe Kane was enjoyable, but not productive. The only thing I got from him was the suggestion that I faced an uphill fight in a crowded field. I *knew* that. It was a secret shared by the entire population of South Boston.

Jim Twohig was different. He had served in state government and understood local politics. He was a jolly old fellow with a brick-red Irish face, and he wore suspenders over a starched white shirt. His law office in Perkins Square, with Jim sitting behind an ancient desk, looked like a Norman Rockwell painting.

"Well, I'm going to tell you," he said, gesturing with a liver-spotted hand, "you can win. If you go around and meet enough people, you can win."

I said, "I'll do that."

"I'm just telling you," he repeated, "that's what can elect you — meet a lot of people."

No candidate ever lacks advice. It's everywhere. If all those who offer advice would distribute literature or stuff envelopes or make phone calls, running for office would be easy. It is *good* advice that is hard to come by. I knew the advice from old Jim was good.

By the time of the primary, I had a large crowd of people working with me, mostly friends from the project. We were buoyed by a conviction that we were the have-nots fighting what we called the FIF, the First Irish Families.

We'd be at Andrew Station, at Columbia Station, along Broadway and at all the bus stops on East 8th Street. I remember an angry Jerry O'Leary saying, "Who do you guys think you are? You can't have all the bus stops."

We weren't cowed by football heroes. Roger Gill told him, "Get up earlier in the morning, O'Leary. Otherwise we've got them all."

I worked very hard myself. Following Jim Twohig's advice, I walked everywhere to meet people. I was out at six in the morning. I was at it during the evening. I remember one man laughing and saying, "Hey, this must be the tenth time you've asked me to consider you. I'm considering! I'm considering! I swear it!" But his manner was friendly, so I felt encouraged.

Some encounters were not so stimulating. I ran into old Mrs. Phyllis Ryan, a neighbor on Monsignor O'Callaghan Way whom I had known most of my life and counted on as a supporter. I told her I had heard great things about her nephew's progress in school.

She shrugged. "Well, I don't know," she said. "You were always reading Greek books, and look what that did to you."

It did not seem prudent to pursue that line of thought.

When things were slack, I would hurry to the Dorchester wards and walk the streets, greeting people and asking *them* to consider my candidacy. Then I'd head back to my lifeguard job at the L Street bathhouse. It didn't pay much, but at hectic moments I'm inclined to think that in some ways it might have been the best job I ever had.

We would put an ad in the *South Boston Tribune*. It cost from $60 to $120. Then I would have it reprinted, which produced hundreds of copies and made it all affordable. We would hand out the reprints up and down the streets.

I wrote the ads myself. They would have horrified a professional copywriter, but they compensated in raw nerve for what they lacked in technique. I would write a bold headline, QUALIFIED!, and then follow it with a list of my elementary schools, high school, college and law school. I would write QUALIFIED! again and list my memberships in the L Street Swim Club, the Knights of Columbus and whatever else I could think of.

Relevancy and materiality were obviously not requisites; my purpose was to fill every available inch. Niceties, such as the importance of white space in ads, were totally beyond my ken.

To scorn any knowledge or talent one does not have is surely a human failing, and I want to avoid that. But I wonder if those of us in politics do not at times overemphasize the importance of cleverness with words and expertise in their display. Some candidates go so far as to change their names to make them more euphonic. That is an absurdity. After all, there is a singer named Humperdink and an actor named Schwarzenegger, both enormously successful. Humperdink and Schwarzenegger! How do men with names like that become famous if the name's the thing whereby we catch the fancy of the public?

I never disparaged an opponent. I was proud of that, because as the campaign grew more intense, some of them began calling me Johnnie Upstart. Others, noting that I always wore the same blue suit when campaigning — it was the only one I had — referred to me as Same Suit Bulger.

Election night was stormy. There had been hurricane warnings. I rented a sound truck and drove through the Neighborhood urging everyone to stay off the streets. Residents were pleased that someone who wanted their votes would be advising them to stay home and be safe.

Other candidates were impressed: soon a half-dozen sound trucks roved the area repeating the same message. It must have been the most concentrated weather alert in the community's history.

Returns from the first precincts looked promising. After a few hours, it was evident I had won. I thanked everyone who had worked with me, and then I began making the prescribed rounds.

I went to the headquarters of the other candidates. I told those who had called me Same Suit Bulger, "I owe it all to my lucky suit." When I saw Jim Collins Sr. — who had told the Irish areas that I was Polish or Lithuanian — I said, "Jim, it was the Polish and Lithuanian vote that got me by." But I said it all lightly, and they knew there was no bitterness, so everyone joined in the laughter.

I went to the Ward 7 Democratic Club and stood on a table with Johnny Powers, our hands held above our heads in a victory gesture. Then I went to the VFW hall behind Andrew Station and the celebration continued. When I left that hot room and went out into the cold charity of the predawn air, it was four A.M., the lonely hour of the wolf; but I needed no company. I felt like a marching band. I felt like a one-man crowd. The lingering clouds of the passing storm held back daylight, but for me there was splendor in the streets that night.

My father had advised me to stay out of politics. He was apprehensive that my brother's problems might hurt me. But he was pleased that I had dared to run. He valued that.

The morning after the election, we walked together on Columbia Road along the South Boston waterfront in the slanting autumn sun. It was a rather brisk day, cool for September, with a sea wind from the northeast. We stopped at Carson Beach and stood looking out at the ocean and the screeching gulls lying on the wind.

Finally he said, "Well, you got what you wanted."

"I think so."

There was a long silence, and I thought the conversation was over. Then he said, "The old-timers have an expression, 'Dance with the gal that brung you.' I hope you'll do that. I hope you'll always stick with the things you told everybody you believed in when you asked them to vote for you."

I said I would.

"Just do what you think is right, Bill," he said, "and then, dammit, live with it. Always stand up."

Doing what you think is right is easy. Living with the reaction can be hard. In 1960 I had not neatly defined in words what I thought was right. Instead, my motivation had episodic and anecdotal origins:

I thought of the railroad's casual disposal of my father. I thought of Mrs. Mulligan, reduced in her last years to stealing milk. I thought of Father Donovan bullying a self-destructive soul like Ham Slowe. I thought of a boyhood chum who had been cruelly beaten by a drunken parent. It was my hope, admittedly unstructured and vague, that I could somehow make such things less likely to happen.

I thought of Genevieve Casey . . .

I remembered Mrs. Casey from my childhood as a mysterious and reclusive character, frail as a shadow, spooky as Halloween. She had long white hair, stringy and unkempt, and fierce brown eyes. She was crippled with rheumatism and hobbled about on a stout black cane that she would shake menacingly at us if we got in her way on the sidewalk. We thought her an alarming old woman.

One day, when I had the uncomfortable duty of delivering a small order to her from Karp's, she seemed quite different. I found her sitting alone in the dark, looking confused and miserable. Her electricity had been cut off summarily. She had to go to a window to read the bill I gave her.

"If they'd given me one more week," she told me, "I could have had the money from my nephew."

I stood there in the shadows, not knowing what to say, while she stared out the window and chewed in that way some older people do when their teeth are gone. Then she said, never looking at me, "Now I have to pay extra to get it started again — and where do I get that?"

Until then, she had always communicated with a glare, a shake of her cane and, in rare moments of loquacity, a growling noise of disapproval. It was the first time I had heard her actually speak. Her voice was whispery, like the rustle of dried leaves on the deserted ball field at Columbus Park in the fall. It was not at all what I expected from one so apparently ferocious.

I had no answer to her question that long-ago day — but now, elected to the House, I intended to make a law requiring utility companies to give reasonable notice before cutting off service. I resolved to make laws dealing with the wrongs in *all* those hazy vignettes that troubled me. It was not a sense of power I felt, but a joyful exhilaration at being able to make things better.

One learns in time that standing up for such values — dancing with the gal that brung you — can trigger savage attacks. Sometimes the attacks make you long for a more serene job: testing parachutes, taming lions, disarming bombs. But you don't think about that for long, nor very seriously.

Not while you still hunger to make a difference.

Not while you still think it's all possible.

Not while you can still hear the music.

3

I N 1961 when I entered the statehouse, seventy-year-old John W. McCormack was majority leader of the U.S. House. Thomas P. "Tip" O'Neill, who would succeed McCormack in that position, was a congressman from Cambridge. John Volpe came in as governor that year. Kevin Hagan White became secretary of state — he would later become mayor of Boston for sixteen years and a significant political presence in the city. Eddie McCormack of South Boston became attorney general. As a freshman legislator, I had of course no reason to know how significantly all of them would figure in my future.

Each generation seems to suffer from the delusion that it has discovered injustice and burns with a passion to end it immediately. I was no different. The agenda I brought to my first legislative term would, I had no doubt, benefit mankind enormously. I intended to propose laws of such patent merit that they would be enacted speedily by enthusiastic compatriots and received with acclaim by a grateful public. I insisted to myself that my motivation was not arrogance, but innocence.

To my astonishment, however, Mrs. Casey's bill — requiring notice before cutting off utilities — was stillborn in the House.

At first I did not understand what was happening. So I plunged ahead with a slew of what I deemed other eminently worthwhile initiatives . . . and got nowhere. I felt like a singer who had finally made it to the Metropolitan Opera, only to discover, when the curtain rose, that there was no audience.

I began to realize that the life of a new legislator is rarely a happy lot. The specific agonies vary from person to person, but there is a sameness in the quantum of frustration suffered by most newcomers impatient to write their ideals into law.

They are confronted by the fact that the same democratic system that makes possible so much good also requires procedures that delay, frustrate and at times abort the best of intentions. They soon realize that they can do little or nothing until they have learned how to deal with that system. Doing so was for me tedious and sometimes infuriating, but my background had produced a combative nature that perversely enjoyed the challenge. Some of the other newly elected men and women actually suffered. They were more sensitive, and to them the learning curve seemed to be made of barbed wire. It wounded them. In a few instances, it left permanent scars.

I was too feisty for that. I thought of the physician Asclepius, whose reputed cures in the fourth century were fabled to have been so great that the underworld of the dead was becoming depopulated. Zeus, who thought Asclepius was overdoing it, became annoyed and slew him with a thunderbolt. Many politicians have met similar fates for trying too hard. At least, I thought, I had no cause to worry on that score — no one was interested in the cures I offered.

All I needed, I told myself, was patience.

My immediate concern was the pressure of time. I was finishing my senior year at school, working on the *Law Review,* preparing for final tests and the bar exam.

The logistical problems were great. Prior to that final year at law school, my old friend Tom Finnerty had given me generous help. Tom, who was a year ahead of me, had then worked nights at the Boston Gas Company, and could always afford a car. He would give me a ride back and forth to classes. But now Tom had graduated and I was on my own, busier than ever and just as impecunious.

And that was the easiest part. The clamorous demands of my constituents — their variety and urgency and sheer volume — were brain-numbing. And I, who could not cope with a household budget, had little notion how to organize my schedule.

It appeared to me, as it does to most young men and women when they enter public life, that each person who telephoned or wrote seemed to believe he or she was the only one seeking help. Each professed to have a unique and compelling exigency. Many sought jobs. Many desperately required housing. There was a long line of victims — men and women outraged by bureaucratic abuse, harassed by brutal creditors, threatened with wrongful eviction. Some sought legal advice and scoffed at my explanation that I was forbidden to offer any until I passed the bar.

I gave endless assistance in filling out forms. I even helped find lost dogs and cats — gifted, irreplaceable animals upon whose recovery inevitably depended, I was told, the happiness of a forlorn child or the peace of mind of a dying grandmother.

I would pick up my mail and phone messages and take them by the trolley car that clattered down Commonwealth Avenue to the *Law Review* office at the school. There I could return calls because the phones had unlimited local service.

From law school I would hurry to the statehouse, hoping to do *something* to advance my ambitious legislative program. But the needs of constituents often required my rushing to administrative offices to deal with the petty malice of minor bureaucrats, or even to a police station, a venue not noted for eager cooperation or unfailing courtesy.

With all of that behind me, I would go home to do my studies. It was a full plate.

Meanwhile, slowly, I began to understand my problems in the House. Some were my fault. Some were not.

The first was the fact that in American legislatures, state and federal, a freshman is generally treated with condescension and, at times, even contempt. This behavior is not conspiratorial. It is simply a hoary tradition — a bad one, to be sure: unfair, unreasonable, unproductive and certainly uncivil — but a tradition nevertheless. Probably it is grounded in some of the less worthy instincts of humankind, the class-conscious snobbery of an establishment toward the perceived gate-crasher; the contempt of veterans for rookies; the distrust, even fear, with which some older men and women regard youth. Political veterans tend to be excessively territorial.

That attitude still exists, but it is not nearly so bad now as it was in 1961 when I became a member of the Massachusetts House. Then it was not far removed from the hazing of new cadets in our military schools: it served to preserve tenured castes by the humiliation and debasement of newcomers. I resolved that if I ever achieved veteran status I would extend myself to help newcomers. I have tried to do so.

Even outsiders had small regard for those of us who were new to office. I recall returning from lunch one day and being stopped in a corridor by a uniformed state police officer. He was a brusque, ruddy-faced man roughly the size of Mount Rushmore.

"Hey, Bill," he said. "You're Bill, right?"

"Right."

"Our pay bill's coming up today," he said. "You're for it."

"Probably," I said. "I've already voted for one pay raise for you people."

"So now you're voting for another one," he said. "We'll be watching you."

"You do that," I said. "You watch me."

There were only two votes against the pay increase that day, and mine was one of them.

I was distressed to see the extent to which some of my fellow freshmen were crushed by their treatment, so I would get them to join me in harassing the establishment. They seemed to enjoy the switch in roles, however brief. I rounded them up one day and announced, within the hearing of Representative Julius Ansel, one of the veterans, that the governor wanted the new representatives to come to his office.

"What for?" Ansel asked. "Why's he want to see you people?"

"Well, Julius," I said, "we've been asked not to discuss it."

"He's calling in the freshmen because he knows he can take you guys for a bunch of chumps," Ansel said. "You tell ol' Julius what it's about. I'll see we all get something out of any deal — jobs for our districts, whatever."

"Can't do it, Julius. When the governor asked us to keep this confidential, he mentioned you specifically."

Ansel thought about that and then broke into a grin. "You got a lot of chutzpah for a greenhorn," he said. "You're trying to put me on."

Ansel was a good man with an enormous sense of humor, even when he was the brunt of the joke. He had been born in Russia in 1908 and used to say, "The only thing good about Russia is leaving it." He came to the House from Dorchester, and his slogan was "My Heart Belongs to Ward 14." In time, we became good friends.

He tried to help me. He was constantly giving me advice based on his considerable experience. His tutorial methods were unique, his prolixity stupefying. I recall having dinner with him one night when he began lecturing me on strategy. "You have to have your backers set up to cover the divisions of the chamber floor," he said. He moved a salt shaker to a spot on the table and said, "There — you cover the first division." Then he arrayed my tea-cup and a butter plate beside the salt shaker. "See, now you have someone in the second and third divisions. You're covering the floor. You're ready to go." A waiter arrived with the entrée, but Julius let him stand there while he went on with his lecture.

Each election, I would go with him to his district where, on Blue Hill Avenue, stood the G & G Delicatessen — noted for attracting one of the most politically knowledgeable crowds in the state. At first, I enjoyed listening to the give-and-take. Later, I was often asked to speak. I liked the atmosphere and the friendly people. The G & G is gone now, and I miss it — it was unique.

Ansel's ability to imitate Curley's voice was incredible. While on the city council, before coming to the House, he would put on his Curley voice and call the Deer Island House of Correction, which had a turkey farm. Julius would identify himself as the mayor and order that turkeys be sent to every member of the city council and all department heads. Curley would try vainly to find out who was responsible. His chief suspect always was Julius.

Ansel had one conspicuous failing: he'd do almost anything to get into a news photo. Julius would wink at you and say, "Look, I know my limitations." I remember one day when he went out to Logan Airport to welcome a constituent who was being flown in on a stretcher from Florida. As she was being lowered from the plane, the media crowded about to get her photograph. Julius pushed in to make certain he was included. It became a shoving match. The unfortunate woman was pushed off her stretcher and slipped to the tarmac. Julius, who had caused it all, was a swift thinker: he lunged forward and knelt beside her, offering encouragement but staring into the cameras all the while.

"Don't just stand there," he shouted to the photographers, "help me with this poor woman."

He was not much on debate, but when a bill came up that had no opposition — an apple pie issue, as it was called in the House — Julius would rise and deliver an impassioned speech. His hands would saw the air as he pleaded with us to have the courage of our convictions and to pass this *vital* piece of legislation. The vote would approach 238 to 0, and then Julius would rise and thank us for following his leadership.

Ansel provided friendship and distraction, but my first-year problems continued. In fact, I found a new impediment. To one as young and eager as I was, it was an incredible discovery. I learned there were legislators who had simply become bored with the public office to which they clung.

That became evident when I approached Francis Marr and Joe O'Loughlin. I was determined to curb child abuse, I knew it would be a fight, and I needed the active support of veterans. Both men were decent and intelligent. Both had been effective members of the House. Both were sympathetic, and neither dismissed me as a callow beginner. Indeed, they promised to vote for my bill. But that was not enough: I needed some established people who would fight for the measure in committee and on the floor, and neither man would have any part of that. Neither was ready for the commitment of time and energy to do battle.

The drive that originally had motivated them was gone. They had lost interest. They were not unique. Later I found many others whose ennui was impenetrable. They were men and women who didn't want to stay in office, but didn't want to leave it. That was true then. It is true now. I suppose it always will be. It is a human phenomenon.

We are accustomed to seeing athletes, rich and famous beyond their wildest hopes, linger on in pain after their game has lost all enjoyment for them. Similarly, some men and women in public life, weary of being underpaid, overworked and casually vilified, do the same, even when enormous rewards are offered to them in the private sector. With some politicians, the reason is inertia or just plain cussedness. But most, I think, share with the aging athlete a strange reluctance to break with the past, with the memory of thrills and the distant echoes of a cheering crowd. There is a German word for it, *türschlusspanik*, the fear of closing doors. It is very sad.

To add to my woes, the Speaker of the House, John Thompson, a Democrat from Ludlow, was drunk. Not now and then, but all the time.

A big, muscular ape of a man known as the Iron Duke, Thompson had been badly wounded in World War II. He carried shrapnel in his body, particularly in his legs. I was told that when he came to the House he began for the first time in his life to drink, searching for a way to deaden his pain. Apparently he required constantly increasing dosage. His slips from sobriety became more numerous. By the time I met him, he was in free fall.

He thought I disapproved of his behavior. He would stop by me on the floor of the House and begin to talk defensively, as though he wanted to justify himself to someone who misunderstood him.

At such times he would inevitably lapse into anecdote of the most personal nature. That led me to break away as quickly as decently possible. I instinctively knew the folly of listening to any scabrous confidence, offered in drunkenness and regretted in the morning.

He wasn't a bully. In fact, he was kind when he thought about it. But he rarely thought about much beyond his next drink. He was at best a spectator, in charge of nothing — least of all himself. He would be at it all day, and when night fell he would leave for more serious carousing with his majority leader, Connie Kiernan, and with Bill Finnegan, a representative regarded by many members as a wit.

Thompson particularly liked the many restaurants and cafés in Boston's North End. While cruising those establishments, he would promise jobs to waiters and busboys and bartenders. On the gray mornings after his nocturnal bouts, Thompson would show up with scratches on his face. He insisted that he had a recurrent complexion problem, but I had seen the results of too many brawls to be entirely convinced. He would then settle down to drinking his hangover away.

Any restaurant or bar help he had hired the night before would begin arriving to claim their new jobs as court officers. He would never turn them away because, as he explained, he always kept his word.

Eventually, Thompson would collapse on a couch in his office. I believe that when he slept it would have taken a jolt registering eight on the Richter scale to rouse him.

Obviously, the business of a legislature is to legislate, and that was not happening. Routine matters moved along in due course. Bills for which there was overwhelming support got passed. But matters that were controversial were often doomed — or else got passed only by corridor deals among the lawmakers, a dubious process. The House was lost because its leader was lost. He had little idea of where he was, and none at all of where he was going. He was like the fabled navigator in a storm, with no guiding sun by day nor any star by night.

To me, he was a major reason why *I* was getting nowhere.

John Volpe, the Republican governor, was more attractive to me than the Democratic leadership. As a politician, he worked hard and, in many respects, effectively. He showed no disdain toward new legislators. He was bright, courteous, hardworking and able. He had established a reputation for integrity in the fiercely competitive construction business.

I never knew him to be cruel, and I believe he aspired to a strict code of ethics. It would surprise me to learn he was guilty of any offense against society more vicious than an overdue library book. His personal life, as far as I knew or ever heard, was circumspect. He professed to be a devoutly religious man, and I doubt he ever met a Catholic cleric he did not like.

He was also sober.

Like most of us, he was not perfect. He had the weakness that afflicts some self-made men — a self-adulation that exceeded the regard of those who appreciated him most. In Volpe there was a poignancy to this shortcoming: I believe he wanted desperately to be liked and admired. But the artificiality of his efforts to appear refined was irksome.

When he returned from his frequent visits to Rome, he would tell you how Bellini's columns inspired *him,* how *he* felt looking at the Trevi fountain, the thoughts that soared through *his* mind as he regarded St. Peter's. He would interrupt a conversation to say, "I must get to my office. I'm expecting a call from the Vatican."

One day when I met with him to discuss a bill, he told me, "We may be interrupted. I'm expecting to hear from the president of the United States." The call did not come while I was there.

It was unfortunate Volpe gave the impression of excessive self-esteem. It was too bad he tried so hard to impress people. He didn't have to. He was an accomplished man, and others knew it without his telling them. But he could not stop it.

In later years he worked hard to win votes for Richard Nixon in

Massachusetts, and Nixon made him a member of the Cabinet as secretary of transportation. But Volpe managed to talk away his welcome with Nixon: when the president came to Boston to deliver a speech over the facilities of a local TV station, the advance party asked the station manager to provide a room for Nixon as far away as possible from the room provided for Volpe.

Able and courteous as he might be, Volpe was of no help to me. It is said truly that a governor proposes, a legislature disposes. It was the Democratic leadership that controlled the legislature — and it was disposing my proposals into a wastebasket.

Into this sea of frustration waded Bob Dineen the Crazy Marine — he who had told me during my campaign that I belonged in prison with my brother. He arrived at my office and asked to see me.

Bob was constantly broke, except for one brief period after he had been paid damages for injuries allegedly sustained in a bus accident on East 8th Street.

He was called "Marine" because he claimed to have served in the Marine Corps. He was called "Crazy" because it was said he had climbed in a broken rear window of the crashed bus to qualify for his money damages. I do not know whether that story is true or a myth, but if it is the latter, then like most myths it is a lie that tells the truth: Dineen was a greedy man without scruple.

He asked me if I would help him pay his mother's rent. "I got it all but seven dollars," he said. "Bill, I'll pay you back — you can count on it — but I *got* to get seven dollars. She's awful old, Bill."

I was surprised that even one as thick-skinned as Dineen would seek help from a man he had attacked so savagely. I knew I'd never be repaid, but he seemed so desperate that I thought he just might be telling the truth about his mother. I bit back the things I wanted to say, went to the clothes rack to get my wallet, returned and gave him the money.

He said, "You're all right, Bill," and left with haste.

Soon after, I noticed that a new Cross pen was missing from my desk. That, coming as it did in the mood I was in, was too much.

On a hunch, I went directly to the Golden Dome Pub, across from the statehouse on Bowdoin Street. There was Bob, leaning against the bar, spending his mother's rent money.

I said, "I want my pen."

"What pen?"

I could feel a black and wholly disproportionate fury rising in me. I said, "Bob, in ten seconds I'm going to get my pen back. Either you're going to hand it to me or I'm going to wipe up this place with you and take it."

Without hesitation he reached into his coat pocket and produced the pen.

"Well," he said, "I'm sorry."

So we finally understood each other, Bob Dineen and I.

It felt good, I can't deny that, but it was probably the dumbest thing I ever did in politics, a field where even a grain of hurtful truth can in time develop into a bountiful crop of alleged character flaws.

Time cures youth; experience dispels political naiveté; but had I gone after Dineen with my fists, I might never have recovered from it. I probably would have been stereotyped as a barroom brawler. In the endless retellings, the additional adjective "drunken" would have been irresistible. The injury to my political aspirations could have been severe. For want of a pen — a five-dollar pen!

I shuddered at the fragility of reputation and at my own capacity for error. The bullet had missed . . . but not by much.

The bar exam was in July, and I was fortunate enough to pass it on the first try, enabling me to accept an invitation from Tom Finnerty to join him in the general practice of law. Our office was at 41 Tremont Street, Boston. Tom had worked a year in the law office of Joseph Graham, a Brighton representative, so we brazenly assured our clients we were experienced!

The law practice further complicated my legislative efforts by cutting into the time available to me. However, the need to support Mary and our first son, Bill, was immediate. It could only be accomplished by trying cases in the district courts. That was where I had to begin, carrying my new briefcase, dressed up in my lawyer suit. The fees were low, the clients almost always guilty. But to an observer of the human condition, as I fancied myself to be, it was instructive and rarely dull. I found some cases so entertaining I kept memoranda of them.

At that time, Thomas "Bobby" Linehan was the chief judge at South Boston District Court. He had an insatiable appetite for honorary degrees. He collected them. Linehan had honorary degrees from Northeastern University, Suffolk University and from wherever else he could get them. They covered his office wall like so many moose heads or other hunting trophies. They were dusted daily. He was fiercely proud of them.

At the opposite pole of authority, Daniel "Moon" Mellet was the broom at the South Boston court. (Janitors in public buildings are usually titled custodians, but in South Boston they are known as brooms.) Besides being the broom, Moon was a bookie. Now and then he would emerge from the closet he called his office to move the dust around briefly in the corridors, but that was a sideline, a mere showing of the flag.

Judge Linehan hated bookies.

"I don't care for that kind of activity," he would say. He said it with feeling, because he knew of his broom's true vocation, as did everyone else who worked or practiced in the court. Linehan schemed to catch Moon Mellet in the act of accepting or paying off a bet. Moon, resentful of any attempt to restrict his commerce, struck back. He had no degrees, honorary or otherwise, but he did have a Sunday school certificate signed by Monsignor Coppinger of St. Augustine's. He framed it and hung it on the wall of his tiny office in mocking imitation of Linehan's display. "There's *my* degree," he used to say.

"I know he's making fun of me," Linehan said. "One of these days I'm going to catch him doing what he shouldn't — and that's one broom that will get swept out."

One day I saw Moon accepting what looked like a betting slip from someone in a court corridor just seconds before Judge

Linehan walked around a corner into view. The judge apparently thought Moon looked guilty.

"Did you see anything going on here, Bill?" he asked, glaring at Moon as he spoke.

"Well," I said, "nothing out of the ordinary."

That was the truth. What could be more ordinary than Moon booking a bet?

Linehan shook his head in frustration and went on to his courtroom.

From that moment on, I had a broom in my corner. Whenever Moon heard something that might be helpful to me in a case — and he heard a lot — he would pass it on to me.

There was the matter of *Commonwealth v. O'Gara*. That involved old Johnny Foley, who owned the South Boston Social Club. Police called him one night and said the club's alarm had gone off and they had caught one Eddie O'Gara, my client, hiding behind a piano.

John told the police to throw the burglar in jail. They insisted he sign a complaint. He did so. Now he sat in the witness chair, peering through his wire-rimmed glasses at O'Gara.

Moon Mellet had stopped me in the corridor and explained in a stage whisper that Foley had been a bootlegger. "That might affect the poor man's license," Moon had said sadly, "if too much is made of it in court . . ."

"Now, John," I asked the complainant, "is it fair to say you know a lot about the rum business?"

"Well, I do. That's why I pay a lot of taxes."

"You've been in it a long time?"

"Ever since they brought it back," he said righteously.

"How about *before* they brought it back?"

The rules were very relaxed and John was allowed to answer. He seemed to be searching for the right words.

I said, "Well, we can get back to that, John. First tell us what happened that night the alarm went off."

"I went down to the club. The cops said O'Gara, there, he'd been hiding behind the piano. There was a broken window."

"Was O'Gara in the club *before* you closed?"

He hesitated. "Maybe," he conceded.

"When you locked up, did you look behind the piano?"

"Jeez, no."

"Could O'Gara have been sleeping behind the piano when you locked up?"

"I guess so."

"And John," I went on, "if a man awakens to find he's been locked in a bar — falsely imprisoned, mind you, *a serious crime* — is it not reasonable that he might break a window in an effort to escape?"

That, of course, brought a flood of objections, and the judge contributed by banging his gavel. But nothing could silence John Foley at that point.

"Hey," he said, "I don't want to stick anybody, but don't stick me. I don't even know this guy." He turned to the judge, whom he had known for years, and said, "Can I just ask you? Can you give the guy a break and let me get out of here?"

"You've all turned this court into a circus," the judge said, "and I won't stand for that. I'm going to find O'Gara guilty and sentence him to thirty days. But I'll suspend it and give him three months' probation. Now, all of you — get out of here."

Not the sort of case I'd thought about in law school, but it helped Mary keep us going, Mary who never complained and who encouraged me in my hopes to abate some of the woes of humanity.

In the legislature, I *was* becoming more professional. I had learned that rhetoric, however sincere, however grounded in merit, was ineffective. Facts and statistics were essential, and that meant doing research. There was no doubt in my mind that serious child abuse existed. I had known children who had been cruelly beaten by parents or guardians. I was driven by the memory of their hurt and frightened faces. The facts *had* to be there, if only I could dig them out, to prove a need for legislative action.

I met with social workers. I visited children's hospital wards. I talked with doctors and nurses who had treated fractures and similar traumatic conditions in children — conditions they were certain did not result from falls or the other explanations given. I learned that x-rays of children often revealed evidence of prior injuries, injuries never reported, never treated medically: nicked bones; bones that had been broken and allowed to knit themselves.

I remember visiting a hospital and seeing a child lying in a ward, obviously battered and bruised and still in pain, who insisted that he did not know how he had suffered his injuries.

I asked the nurse why he was shielding the person who had done such damage.

"Most of them are like that," she said. "They come in beaten to a pulp, sometimes with broken bones — but they won't tell."

"Why?" I asked her.

She shrugged wearily and said, "Some of them may be afraid. But I think most of them just love their parents. They care about them. They don't want to get them in trouble."

That made me all the more determined to make progress with my bill. I pressed it in Democratic caucuses, where members meet to plan legislative strategy. I accomplished nothing. The meetings were so poorly organized and so disputatious that little of anything was done.

The Speaker's chair might as well have been empty.

I had much to learn from the failings of that used and tormented man known as the Iron Duke. By observing the total lack of leadership, I began to understand what leadership meant and what it required.

To begin, it is first necessary that a leader truly lead. With time, I learned that legislative leadership cannot function through guile or coercion. Those are spurious techniques. Consider the Massachusetts Senate, made up of forty men and women who have earned their places by fighting for them tirelessly and doggedly, often in very spirited campaigns. They have the confidence of winners. They have strong convictions. They have promises to keep to their constituents. As a group, notwithstanding the chic cynicism often directed toward them, they are idealistic and intelligent.

It must be obvious that no one is going to *trick* senators into abandoning their legislative goals and jeopardizing their political careers. Sadly, some — though a minority — are coerced by the activist media to take positions in conflict with their preferences. But any presiding officer who tried such tactics would be ignored and swiftly replaced.

An effective presiding officer is one who works to bring about the consensus necessary to accomplish legislation seasonably — which is the reason for having a House and Senate.

I view leadership as a catalytic function. One discusses issues with members. One asks questions in an effort, not merely to know, but to understand diverse positions. To an extent, it is not unlike the role of a mediator.

The job requires a great deal of sympathetic listening — listening for points of agreement that can be developed into a base upon which to build, listening for areas of compromise, urging their exploration. A leader must welcome initiatives and encourage creativity to bridge any final gaps dividing members.

Certainly a presiding officer must offer suggestions and try to keep the process moving toward a timely resolution. But the end product — whether to support or oppose a bill, or whether to agree on a viable compromise — is not something that can be *inflicted* by leadership; it is a consensus resulting from the communal wisdom and goodwill of the membership.

In later years, when for a while I was entrusted with the Senate leadership, the media continually solicited my views on issues, an invitation to which I rarely responded. That has never been because I do not form opinions. It has always been because a legislative leader should not exacerbate divisions and risk polarization by choosing sides prematurely.

I have never found the media especially sensitive to that fact. And I frequently have been told in abusive editorials and commentary that I had an obligation to provide headlines and topical sound bites.

That duty has never been within my perception of the job description of a presiding officer. He or she is there to accomplish legislation, not to sell papers or enhance broadcast ratings.

There are, of course, occasions when the methodology of compromise is not available. Obviously no responsible person can abandon moral principle. In such cases one must join the debate vigorously and publicly, irrespective of title and without regard for personal consequences.

Issues of principle arise more often in rhetoric than in reality, however. In most instances a leader is morally free to be less than an activist, yet more than a mere moderator. The leader is not a captain with power to command, but he or she must be at the wheel, as it were, to navigate the vessel to a destination desired by — or at least acceptable to — the majority.

And it is reckless in the extreme to have a drunk at the helm, which was our tragic plight while Thompson led the House.

Despite the caste system, the bored members, the rudderless caucus and the dysfunctional leadership, I kept after my child abuse bill, lobbying it with anyone who would listen. I wouldn't let go.

My proposal required doctors and nurses to report suspected instances of child abuse to the district attorney. After all, such abuse, if proved, involved a violation of the criminal law. Tort lawyers lobbied against the bill, because it would immunize doctors and nurses from suit. That would mean lost legal fees. I had anticipated that opposition and dismissed it as contemptible. There were others who argued that the district attorney's office would be a disruptive force in dealing with a family that might otherwise be salvageable. I found *that* persuasive.

Clearly it would be better to have suspected abuse reported to a social agency — Welfare or the like — where the abuse might be dealt with and stopped, but the family still held together if it was otherwise a wholesome entity. I amended the bill accordingly.

While I was struggling with all this, Connie Kiernan, the majority leader and Thompson's drinking crony, was holding the House together — if his activity could be so described. But many of us were increasingly uncomfortable. Legislative leadership must be finely attuned to the membership — sensing discontent and accurately diagnosing it as mutinous, malcontented or merely muttering. We were in the muttering stage.

It reached the point where old Cornelius Desmond from Lowell reproved Thompson from the floor. He warned Thompson of what was happening to him. He urged him to read a book called *The Lost Leader.* It was a wasted effort. When Thompson was not listening to whispered remarks from a member of his leadership team, he was drowsing. He did not seem to hear the criticism.

Desmond was a respected legislator, but he was not the sort who could influence Thompson. I wondered who could, other than his cronies.

I began to think about those cronies.

There was Henry Sontag, a lawyer, and Tom Dougherty, a former representative from Medford. They seemed to be with Thompson every night. There was Finnegan, too immature for his inside position, whose wit was said to grow with each drink. There were others of lesser stature. All of them appeared blithely unconcerned with Thompson's incapacity. Certainly none of them made any discernible effort to sober him.

The stunning thought occurred to me that his condition might be precisely what some of those men wanted.

There was no evidence of conspicuous duplicity, but there seemed a constant agenda — issues that prompted them even to rouse Thompson to action. Those matters almost always involved, or so it appeared to me, things of interest to William Callahan, chairman of the Massachusetts Turnpike Authority. There was nothing necessarily evil in that; Callahan's work was of benefit to the state. But some of his tactics were disturbing.

Bill Callahan got things done. He built roads — and he built them well. He built Route 128, the north-south circumferential highway that runs around Boston from coast to coast. He built the east-west Massachusetts Turnpike across the commonwealth, from Boston through the Berkshires to the state of New York. They were the best highways in Massachusetts and among the best in the nation. What Robert Moses was to New York, Callahan was to Massachusetts.

His projects were targets of sustained and savage opposition from a host of adversaries. He seized the land he wanted by power of eminent domain, simply taking what he wanted, and no one seemed satisfied with the amount he paid for what he took. Communities feared a loss of business if traffic were to bypass their local stores. Some of the more snobbish towns did not want the influx of visitors or new residents they thought might result from easy commutation. Many individuals lusted after service and supply contracts that went to rivals. These adversaries had one thing in common. They all wanted Callahan's scalp.

Callahan battled them with evident delight. He was tough and resourceful. He schemed, he maneuvered, he charmed and he bullied. He would not change what he deemed to be the best route. He would not compromise on the quality of materials. He demanded first-rate construction and insisted that it be done on time. His bitterest enemies could not fault his results.

To hold his adversaries at bay, Callahan had to have solid legislative support. He always got it. His projects usually deserved support on merit — but I had the uneasy feeling that merit was not the sole explanation of his success.

Like Napoleon, he divided to conquer: he kept his plans secret so that communities were aroused only one or two at a time. He knew the legislators from affected municipalities would have to oppose him, which he pragmatically accepted because he had a large number of votes from unaffected districts to sustain him. To maintain that support, he dispensed jobs for constituents, awarded food franchises along the turnpike and, it was said, gave other things of value. He was ingenious, ruthless and at times, according to his critics, even criminal in getting his roads built.

He amassed no personal wealth. He had a cocky nature and a considerable mean streak, and he exulted mercilessly each time he crushed his opposition, which was most of the time. But his real satisfaction, I believe, consisted in the knowledge that he had built the greatest highways the state had ever known. Any wrongful means he employed cannot, of course, be justified by the spectacularly good ends he accomplished; neither can the latter fairly be ignored in evaluating that driven man.

The more I observed the situation — the more I watched the machinery at work — the more persuaded I became that Thompson's helplessness was being exploited. I became convinced that men he trusted, most of them able and bright men, were using him for their personal advantage.

I never proved it. But I thought it then. I think it now.

A few of us had grown so impatient with what was happening that we raised the leadership issue in caucus. Thompson, roused by his leadership team, walked among us, asking, "Are you on the reservation? If anybody is *off* the reservation, let us know. Would you just let us know?"

He sounded almost programmed. Only a handful of us spoke up. We were ignored. The message was that we had a duty to be quiet.

Representative John Toomey of Cambridge, seeing I was disgusted, drew me aside. "Don't let things like this get you, Bill," he said. "It's part of the game. Just think how great it is to have been elected."

"This is a do-nothing legislature," I said. "We don't have any leadership. We're expected to be robots. We're treated like dogs."

"Maybe," he said, "but isn't it great just to be here?"

I left, feeling almost hopeless.

Michael Paul Feeney of Hyde Park came to my office an hour or two later. He said, "Bill, I'm going to run against Thompson for Speaker. Will you help me?"

I told him he had my vote.

"Only a few of us complained in the caucus," he said, "so it won't be easy to pull it off."

"Well, let's try," I said.

Feeney was nearly right: it wasn't just difficult, it was impossible. After twelve-hour days of effort, we finally increased our group from five to twenty-six. That meant those willing to vote for a change amounted to little more than ten percent of the

Democratic membership. But our opponents fought as though they were in an uphill battle. They were veterans and knew the drill.

Representative Mike Catino of Quincy approached me. "Bill," he said, "you don't have the votes to put Feeney in."

"We need more than we have," I agreed.

"Why go down in flames? What's the point?"

I said I was troubled by a lot of unanswered questions.

"Let me tell you something," Catino said. "In politics, you should never mind the questions. Hell, there aren't any answers anyway."

I didn't know exactly what *that* meant, so I just told him my vote was pledged.

A few days before the vote, I was standing inside the statehouse door waiting for a shower to let up. Representative Leo Tauro of Worcester came in, his head covered with a newspaper to shield him from the rain. He stood there grinning, dry as a duck, holding a Styrofoam cup of steaming coffee. He was an amiable sort, but he had a disconcerting habit of beginning almost every sentence with the word "so." He would say, "So, what time is it?" or "So, how are you feeling?" or "So, let's have lunch."

On this occasion, he asked, "So, you still off the reservation?"

I told him I hadn't been on the reservation for a long time.

"So you'll lose," he said without rancor, "and you'll just have to live with it."

That seemed fair.

Representative David O'Connor from Mission Hill said, "You have the wrong idea about the Duke. You think he can't lead the House."

I said I didn't know whether he could lead the House; I had never seen him try.

"Bill," O'Connor said, "believe me — he's great when he's sober."

"How would I know?" I asked him. "I've never seen him sober."

The night of the vote, I received a call from the state attorney general, Eddie McCormack, whose candidacy for the U.S. Senate I supported. He asked me if I would meet with him in his office. I was told it was extremely important.

When I got there, Eddie said, "I have a phone call for you."

It was Speaker McCormack, calling from Washington. "Now, Bill, I'm calling you as a constituent. I want to be sure you understand that. I'm just calling as old John McCormack, your constituent from South Boston."

I said I was always glad to hear from him. He said he had been told I was not supporting Thompson for Speaker. I said that was true.

"Well, you've made your point, Bill," he said. "You've let the leadership know you're concerned. Now that you've *made* that point, I hope you'll see your way to support John and give him a chance to correct things. He has assured me that things will change. Give him a chance to change, Bill."

I admired John McCormack. He had accomplished many good things in Congress. And I owed much to him personally: he had tried to keep abreast of my brother's situation in prison, and he had been our only source of information about Jim through difficult years of worry. I remembered his saying to my father, "James made a mistake and is paying for it, but he can change if they give him a chance."

I remembered that while I stood there holding the phone, with neither of us saying anything, I knew it was going to be hard to refuse him.

"I know you won't break your pledge to Feeney," he said, ending the silence, "and I would never ask you to. Feeney's a reasonable man. He knows he's licked. He'll release you."

I said I did not feel I could *ask* to be released.

"You won't have to," he assured me.

He was right. When Feeney saw how few votes he had, and when he saw some of those turning against him, he released everybody.

"It looks like we'll have to give him a chance to change," Feeney said.

The words sounded remarkably familiar. I wondered if they were his own or whether he, too, had received a call from Washington.

We went along with the majority — in my case, not happily.

So Thompson had his chance, and of course nothing changed. One of the continuing problems was that he did not appoint the best men and women available to chair the various committees. That is something a legislative leader must do if the body is to function productively. Furthermore, the members know if someone has been appointed out of friendship or for some reason other than merit. They *know* — and they will not support a person they don't respect. There is often a price to pay for trying to choose the best; I have paid it many times.

As Senate president, for example, I was faulted for making Chester Atkins of Concord chairman of the Ways and Means Committee. Atkins was a wealthy, left-leaning Yankee, very unpopular with the rank and file of the Democratic membership. He was the best qualified, however, and I appointed him. As recently as 1994 I was challenged by Senator William Keating of Sharon, who was infuriated because I would not appoint him to head that powerful committee. He was not up to it, in my opinion. This disagreement led to a statewide battle; but that comes later.

I worked on the floor for my revised child abuse bill. There was some spirited opposition, but for the first time it appeared I was making some progress in the House. The situation in the Senate, where Senator Francis X. McCann of Cambridge busied himself rounding up votes against the measure, looked grim.

McCann was an older man, quite conservative. He was a zealot without the fury of the self-righteous. His weapon was not fire but ice, yet his support of the death penalty, however controlled in exposition, reached evangelical intensity. Someone said, "McCann wants four electric chairs — no waiting," and he felt complimented.

Surely he smiled sometime, someplace, at something or someone — but never when I saw him; certainly never at me.

Whenever I sought his support for anything, he inevitably refused. He would say something like, "We seem to have gotten along all right so far with things as they are." That struck me like someone arguing that the world got along all right before it had the wheel, which it obviously must have. But I restrained my natural inclination to say that. I realized that those who are impatient to act, as surely I was, are obliged by their disappointments to learn patience. I tried, I really did. But in McCann's case I got nowhere.

Even if I proposed something that accorded with views he had earlier expressed, it made no difference. He was uncompromising, and he let me know it in a soft voice that purred from a mouth that barely opened. He seemed harder to move than a graveyard. He would listen to what I had to say, mull it over, then look at me with his flat, wintry eyes and say very slowly, "No . . . no, I don't think so."

Whenever I left his presence I felt as though I were leaving a cold room.

I knew something was wrong with the man, but I did not know what it was. He often talked of his childhood in Scotland where he suffered cruel abuse. He and other Catholic boys were given menial jobs in a shipyard where bigotry often took the form of bolts and nuts showered on their heads by shipfitters working on the hulls. I wondered if that had helped shape Frank's bleak personality.

I knew *I* had done him no mischief.

When I spoke to him about the child abuse bill, he said he wouldn't support it because it was poorly drafted, but acknowledged that I was right that the legislature had to do something to protect children. His limited endorsement had the fervor of a cold cousinly kiss.

"I appreciate your saying I am right," I said. "I just wish you could keep the note of surprise out of your voice."

I went walking that day, as I often did when I wanted to think about something that puzzled me. It proved to be both an amusing and a disturbing outing, because I ran into Patsy Mulkern and Billy Reardon.

Both Patsy and Reardon belonged to a mysterious breed in our political culture, men of uncertain vocations who live on the fringe of events. Often well dressed, apparently solvent, such characters share a certain aplomb and seem to know everybody. They are founts of rumor, usually ranging from the improbable to the absurd. But not always. They will answer almost any question unhesitatingly and with an air of assurance, any question save one: *you must never ask one of them where he works.* To do so will not only end the conversation, it will probably end the relationship.

I encountered Patsy first. Patsy was said by many to be friendly with Joseph Kennedy. Perhaps he was. I always found him to be as light as one of those French soufflés Joseph Kennedy liked so much. Patsy wore a hat over his thinning gray hair. His squinted blue eyes seemed to be fixed on something beyond your right shoulder. His manner was insinuating, and you had to make an effort to hear his voice.

On this day he said to me, "You know the city councilor from South Boston, Bill Foley, the district attorney's son — well, I'll tell you something about him."

"Oh, what's that?"

"*He ain't Bill Foley,*" Patsy said.

I said that was extraordinary.

"Well, it's true," he said. "Nobody knows his *real* name because he was left as an infant on the D.A.'s doorstep. He's not even Irish. He's Polish."

I asked him how he knew Foley was Polish.

"Look at his head," Patsy said. "You can tell every time by looking at the head."

I was glad I had run into Patsy and his latest nonsense. He had been, as usual, good for a laugh, which I sorely needed. I thought I would share Patsy's crazy cranial theory with Bill Foley, but quickly decided I would not, because Foley, whatever his other qualities, had absolutely no sense of humor. Next I thought I would tell it to my friend Joe Alecks, an activist in protecting what he perceived as the interests of people of Polish ancestry. He was the sort who would demand that we name a fire hydrant after Chopin. But I remembered that Joe was currently unhappy with something Foley had said.

I decided to laugh alone.

It wasn't the same with Billy Reardon. He gave me nothing to laugh about.

Reardon loitered in the drugstore outside the statehouse day after day. Why, no one knew, and of course no one asked. When he wasn't there he was at Carson Beach sunning himself, keeping in shape, as he liked to say.

"Bill," he told me that day, "watch Johnny Powers. He's telling all his pals to cut you down. He's got McCann leading the pack."

"Why would he do that?" I asked, remembering election night when Powers and I stood side by side on a table, holding our clasped hands aloft like triumphant athletes.

"Powers never went to college, you did."

"But I've always admired the way he's educated himself," I said. "He knows that."

"He quit school."

"He never quit his education," I said. "He got his high school diploma while he was working at the Welfare Department. That wasn't easy."

"I'm just telling you," Reardon said. "Powers wanted to go to college, he didn't, and you did. He wanted to be a lawyer, he isn't, you are. Powers thinks he owns South Boston, but he don't own *you*. It's simple."

I told Reardon it didn't make sense to me.

"It will," he said, "it will."

Paranoia is an occupational disease of politics. I knew that before I knew the word. It is a dangerous and destructive malady. I refused to imagine the existence of a cabal on the basis of a rumor from a source as unreliable as Reardon. It was obvious to me that a number of persons could oppose you or even dislike you for the same or different reasons without being secretly joined in plotting against you. But as time went on, I found it more difficult to regard as benign the activities of McCann and other senators close to Powers, as well as his supporters in the House. I could not ignore the unfailing predictability of their opposition to me, nor its intensity.

It was not merely the fact that none of them ever supported my initiatives, it was that none of them was even *neutral* with respect to my most innocuous suggestion. What I proposed, they opposed. It was inevitable. I was compelled to wonder whether Reardon might have been right. I recalled Dr. Freud's observation that there are times when a cigar is merely a cigar — and applied that thought inversely to this entirely different context: There are times, I told myself, when what looks and smells like a clandestine plot is, in fact, just that.

I knew it was important to find out, one way or the other. Survival in public life requires that the real be distinguished from the fanciful in such matters.

While trying to decide what I was up against, I had a frantic call from Tommy McDonough, a typical client of those days, who said he desperately needed help. The timing of the call could not have been worse, coming as it did when I had to resolve swiftly the existence or nonexistence of a serious problem with Powers. But my duty to a client was clear. I had no choice but to shelve my concerns while I turned to Tommy's.

As usual, his were bizarre.

Finnerty and I had settled a workers' compensation case for McDonough. Tommy had received $28,000 — and it was spring. Tommy and a vivacious woman named Lulu Ketyirtis climbed in Lulu's car, a red convertible with imitation leopard-skin upholstery, and left South Boston. They rented an apartment at Nantasket Beach, ten or twelve miles away. Tommy, Lulu and the $28,000: a sort of Bermuda Triangle of romance — with a high probability of disaster.

Lulu was good-natured. A honey blonde of uncertain age, she had gone through a parade of boyfriends over the years. "Gone through" is a most appropriate phrase, because her liaisons were conterminous with exhaustion of the respective bankrolls.

Strangely, no one seemed to feel any bitterness toward her. Rather, she seemed the cynosure of a happy nostalgia. Lulu wasn't beautiful, wasn't witty or clever. But by repute she was warm and forgiving, and she flatly refused to take money from her companions. She just wanted to be around them while they were spending it — sharing the activities, the jokes and the laughs . . . while the money lasted.

But when the money went, Lulu went.

Tommy had been warned to expect a similar denouement, yet he never thought beyond the next twenty minutes. So when the money and Lulu ran out, he was amazed, saddened and then bored.

To liven things up, he telephoned the Nantasket police at midnight. "Look," Tommy said to the desk sergeant, "I'm blowing up the station in about three hours. You better get out of there."

The policeman said, "This is you, isn't it, McDonough?"

Tommy, not the sharpest tool in the shed, asked, "How'd you know that?"

All of which brought us to Norfolk County Superior Court, facing a bomb-threat charge before Judge Henry Leen.

It was an easy case. I pointed to the fact that Tommy's record, while it abounded in arrests for varying degrees of insobriety, showed no crimes against persons or property. Further, he had identified himself to the police, and no one had been placed in reasonable apprehension of harm. Judge Leen was a good judge, intelligent, experienced and fair, and I knew from his demeanor we were not facing a serious problem.

There was a recess, so we relaxed outside the courtroom, enjoying a coffee break while Tommy told me, "I had a great time in Nantasket. Lulu and I played the numbers and went to the track and all. The only thing was that all summer guys kept telling me, you know — when the money goes, Lulu goes."

I said I had heard something along those lines about her.

"Well, jeez, I told Lulu the dough was gone. So I wake up the next morning and there's this note from Lulu saying her mother needs her and she's gone back to South Boston. I mean, I felt terrible. And I haven't heard from her — why are you laughing, for God's sake?"

For a few moments McDonough's bewildered expression drove Powers and his cohorts from my mind.

I told him, "There's an old saying, Tommy, that those who won't learn from history are doomed to repeat it."

I don't think Tommy even heard me. He sat there looking at the floor, thinking of Lulu I suppose, and then he smiled and said very quietly, "There's nothing mean in her, you know. She ain't got a mean bone. I guess it's just her way. She's a great girl. I really like her. I had more fun with Lulu than I ever had in my whole life."

"I guess the twenty-eight thousand helped, too," I said.

"Well, yeah," he agreed. "There *was* that."

Clients like Tommy McDonough helped lighten my mood in my acclimatizing years in the legislature — and they were essential to Mary, who was bravely trying to balance our budget. But I ached to get back to the arena on Beacon Hill.

Evidence was mounting there that Reardon's warning had been sound. His "people," as Powers habitually described his supporters, most of them crusty old-liners like McCann, were now belittling me personally. And Powers himself had become involved.

Senator John "Rosary" Beades of Dorchester told me, "Johnny doesn't say much about you, but if he hears your name, he gets this expression on his face like he's just bitten into a bad clam." Senator Jim McIntyre of Quincy said, "Powers thinks everything's come too easy to you — and you should be made to earn your bones."

I heard similar comments from others.

The whole thing had an air of tragedy to me. I saw in Powers a combination of talent, resourcefulness and energy, all spoiled by a proclivity for pettiness and spite. Certainly he had done well in politics. He had served in the House seven years, from 1939 — when I was five years old — until 1946 when he moved on to the Senate. He served as president of the Senate from 1959 to 1964. He was an effective legislator, but seemed to find no peace in his successes. He was a troubled man, preoccupied with what he thought helped or hurt him, an ambit much too cramped for greatness. He worked as diligently to inflict a malicious hurt as to accomplish something worthwhile. He did not do so to advance himself; he did it to attenuate the difficulties of those he disliked or perceived as rivals. He appeared to dislike or fear a great number, often for inscrutable reasons.

Undeniably, and to me inexplicably, I was one of them.

Now that the fight was in the open, I plunged into it, clashing head-on in debate with my opponents for passage of a child abuse law. I fought the Powers people for their mysterious obduracy. I chided the tort lawyer lobby for being more concerned with fees than with the beaten and broken bodies of children. I reminded legislators who wanted to avoid involvement in a fight of the admonition that the hottest place in hell is reserved for those who remain neutral in times of moral crisis. I appealed to everyone that we had a duty to speak for those who could not or would not speak for themselves.

My bill passed in the House. I lobbied furiously in the Senate, and it was soon evident I was picking up substantial support there — Powers, McCann and their allies notwithstanding.

When McCann saw there was little hope of stopping the bill, he played his last desperate card. He announced he would vote for it if my name was removed as sponsor. Many of my compatriots bridled at that demand, and of course McCann thought my resistance would provide time to turn votes around.

I asked to have my name removed from the legislation. That not only silenced McCann and his cohorts, it won more votes for the measure from some fence sitters who were disgusted by McCann's pettiness.

The bill passed the Senate. It was promptly signed by Governor Endicott "Chub" Peabody, who had defeated the incumbent, Volpe, in 1962 and whose term had begun in 1963. The child abuse law has been revisited and improved often, just as one adds onto and improves a house. But the original structure was the bill hammered through in the early 1960s.

It was an intoxicating moment. It had taken me more than two years to bring about major legislation, but in the process I had become a professional. And I felt good. I told myself I had not been cowed by an oppressive system; I had learned much about the art of legislating; I had defeated powerful enemies. Most satisfying of all, and surely most important, I thought of those battered children I had seen in hospital beds and I could hope I had made Massachusetts a better and safer place for them to live.

Mary was so happy that she ravaged our budget to serve steak for dinner, and we dined by candlelight.

I don't know how many thousands of pieces of legislation I have brought to enactment since that day. I can't recall all the times we have celebrated such events in various states or on tropical islands or even in Europe. But nothing ever compares with the first time. It can only be compared with the time you kissed your bride, knowing it marked the beginning of a future filled with new and wonderful things.

Peabody, the governor who signed that child abuse bill, was far on the liberal left, but he had a candor I have not come in my career to associate with many of that persuasion. He was a better man than he was a politician — honest, decent, kindly and bright, but given to thoughtless pronouncements.

As Peabody reached the end of his term, there was an effort, which he supported, to repeal the death penalty. Had he been a politically sagacious man, Chub would have said that he was opposed to the penalty, wanted to see it eliminated and would do all in his power to do so. Even though a majority of the public wanted the death penalty, voters would not have faulted him for expressing an unpopular view on a single issue. The public, in general, is more tolerant than the press.

But that was not Peabody. Peabody said he was not only opposed to capital punishment, but that as governor he would commute all death sentences. He said he would never allow *anyone* to be executed while he was in office. In effect, he was saying that, on the basis of his personal views, he would set aside the verdict of juries and the judgment of courts and frustrate the law of the commonwealth. That plainly went beyond his right to disagree and amounted to abrogation of his oath to enforce the state's laws.

Shortly thereafter a gunman, fleeing a jewelry store he had just robbed on Washington Street in Boston, collided with a police officer in the doorway. Evidence indicated the officer was unaware of the robbery and was going into the store to make a purchase. Without hesitation, whether from panic or viciousness, the gunman shot the officer in the face and killed him.

Boston was shocked — and the city's anger turned on Peabody because of his provocative statement.

Peabody's teammate, Lieutenant Governor Francis X. Bellotti, knew Chub had been seriously weakened by the incident. He joined a plot to deny the primary nomination to his governor. His allies were Eddie McCormack and Mayor Kevin White. They succeeded in winning the nomination for Bellotti.

Bellotti was a staunch supporter of the death penalty, but his coup was a pyrrhic victory. Voters were disenchanted with Peabody — but they weren't too keen about disloyalty, either. They responded to Volpe, who was trying to make a comeback, and whose campaign was built around a single question: "Peabody trusted Bellotti — can you?"

The effect was devastating. Bellotti lost. Volpe returned to office.

For students of politics, it was a remarkable exhibition of how candidates can destroy themselves. Here were two capable and resourceful men, Bellotti and Peabody, Democrats running in a state in which their party was much more numerous than the Republican Party. Each made a fatal error that alienated voters. Peabody overreached his power; Bellotti was perceived as an opportunist. They were like protagonists in a Greek tragedy, and as Greek tragedies do, theirs played out to a fated and unhappy end.

It is interesting that Bellotti constantly imagined that *he* was the target of conspiracies and of underhanded tactics. He told me Volpe had defeated him with dirty tricks. He insisted Volpe sent people to restaurants on the Massachusetts Turnpike to hold loud conversations suggesting that the Mafia was helping Bellotti.

I asked him — with the straightest face I could manage — whether Volpe, a leading member of the Sons of Italy organization, might be anti-Italian.

He shrugged!

I felt certain that Bellotti had no involvement with the Mafia, and was aware that allegation was a canard too often and too casually used to discredit candidates of Italian ancestry. I also did not believe Volpe would have been behind a sleazy effort to discredit Bellotti. It just wasn't Volpe's style.

With the child abuse bill enacted into law, Tom Finnerty wanted me to devote more time to the law practice. "You can double or even triple your income in the first year," he said.

That was attractive, of course, but it wasn't what I wanted. I told him so. "I'm not going to keep score of my life in money," I said.

"Come on," Tom said, "your life isn't just some story you make up about yourself."

"That's exactly what it is," I told him, "and I don't want mine to be like everybody else's. I don't want it to be about merely gathering things."

"A lot of legislating is just plain scutwork," Tom protested. "You guys spend hours passing resolutions that Joe Jerk is a fine citizen or naming bridges and buildings in each other's districts. What's so great about that?"

I told him I thought all those grim-faced moneymaking lawyers walking around with their briefcases had to handle their share of trivia.

Tom said my conception of the importance of being a legislator sounded arrogant. I assured him that wasn't the case.

"Then what is it?" he asked.

That wasn't easy to answer.

"I went walking on Carson Beach one night," I told him. "I looked back and saw I had left no footprints. There was a stiff wind and it had blown them all away. The beach behind me was smooth as paint."

"So?"

"No footprints," I said. "I hadn't left any footprints. It gave me an eerie feeling, Tom. I don't want to look back one day and see I haven't left a footprint in the legislature."

I was thinking of the advice of Father Carl Thayer, under whom I studied Greek. He had told me, "Ultimately, what will count is what you view as important, and whether you pursue it." I could imagine nothing more dreadful than to be sitting in a nursing home someday saying, "I should have . . . I could have . . . why didn't I?"

Tom, for his part, seemed finally to understand me. It was agreed I would handle a light caseload so I might be able to budget my time better. That arrangement continued until I was elected to the Senate. After that, I was completely absorbed by legislative work and could no longer function as an associate. I became a consultant, working with Tom on cases in his office. Even that relationship diminished after I became president of the Senate — which made me a more conspicuous political figure, an identity that might possibly result in conflict detrimental to a client.

But for a while I had to plug away at occasional cases in the district courts. It was amazing how often defendants would undo themselves in such proceedings.

One of them, Chester Suchecki, was a mailman. In his off hours he worked as a doorman at the Polish Club on Boston Street. His principal duty was to alert a local bookie to any strangers who might be interested in terminating his community service. The burden of two jobs was heavy, and Chester at times fell asleep at the gate. When that happened he would often be arrested for aiding and abetting.

The court tended to be lenient with Chester, but was annoyed by the fact that he would always appear wearing his postman's uniform. Chester did that so his lawyer might more convincingly stress the dire consequences to Chester in his livelihood were a conviction to appear on his record.

The court, which did not perceive Chester as a serious criminal or a danger to life or property in the area, would continue the case without a finding. That meant that after a period of time — usually six months — the charge would be dismissed if there was no further offense. In the interim, someone else would have to work the door at the Polish Club.

The court's patience eventually wore thin. Judge Feeney called me to the bench for a conference and said, "I'm tired of this transparent effort to influence me."

I looked back at Chester, standing there in his summer uniform of stovepipe pants, wearing a forlorn expression on his face.

"You tell him," Feeney said, "that the next time he appears in my court with his uniform on, the mail is going to be late for a while."

But nothing could get the uniform off Chester. And every time he would enter court wearing it, he would be obliged to pay a fine before leaving. He was his own undoing.

It was even worse in the case of another client, Harry "Porky" Sullivan, a round man with a square face and a blaze of red hair. He was haled before the local court on a hollow charge of disturbing the peace. The evidence was thin. I told Porky not to worry.

He began to act very strangely when we went before the bench. No one heard what I had to say because all attention was on Porky, who was performing a series of contortions. He seemed to be trying to draw the judge's attention to a pin on his lapel.

The judge finally fixed Porky with a baleful stare. "Do you have an affliction? Some kind of twitch?" he asked.

In response, Porky gripped his lapel and held it forward, exhibiting the button. The judge, with an air of great weariness, looked into the distance as though he were thinking of the other careers he might have followed, other things he might have done with his life. Then he sighed and pronounced Porky guilty.

While Porky was paying his fine to the court officer, I asked him why he had made such a botch of things with his antics and the lapel pin.

He said, "That's Knocko's pin from the Yankee Division. He

lent it to me. Knocko said when the judge saw the button he'd go easy."

"Knocko's been trying to stick us with that pin for years," the court officer told him. "The judge don't care if you're Audie Murphy."

Knocko was, of course, Edward "Knocko" McCormack, and the name was like a bell tolling me back to my childhood. I had seen little of Knocko in the intervening years, but his son and namesake, Eddie McCormack, was now a candidate for the U.S. Senate. Since Eddie was a neighbor, I was dutifully pledged to his support. His opponent would be Edward Kennedy. It was going to be a rough fight.

Knocko had two sons. One was named John, after his famous uncle, but was always known as Jocko. The other, Edward junior, had been called Bubba in his youth.

Jocko was a wild spirit, another consort of the fabled Lulu Ketyirtis. He never saw a long shot he didn't like — until after the race was over. Jocko was once interrupted climbing with his luggage from a window in a Florida hotel after an unrewarding day at the track. He explained patiently that he had had every intention of going to the desk to check out, but it was Jocko's burden that few ever took him seriously. They didn't that time, either. His baggage was held until his uncle sent funds to redeem it.

Bubba, on the other hand, was graduated from the U.S. Naval Academy and Boston University Law School. It was at that juncture he discouraged further use of his nickname and announced that he was to be known henceforth as Eddie. That was more to distinguish him from his father than because of any penchant for informality. Unlike his brother, Jocko, who was a pie in the face of society, Eddie was smart and debonair, a study in silk: very smooth, very smooth.

He had been a city councilor. He was now attorney general, and it had been in his office that I had received the call from Speaker McCormack during the short-lived revolt against John Thompson. No one in South Boston was surprised by Eddie's candidacy for the U.S. Senate — we believed politics ran in families, like red hair or a predisposition toward bronchitis.

As such things so frequently happen, it was only a few days after the case involving the Yankee Division pin that I saw Knocko. I knew him to be a character of Homeric proportions, but his persona had undergone a dramatic change: he looked — *important!* I know no other way to say it. I soon learned why. He had been named manager of Eddie's campaign.

The choice, when I learned of it, astounded me. Since I was committed to the campaign, Knocko would be devising tactics and planning strategy, and I would be expected to execute his decisions. I wished I were not involved, but it was too late for that.

Knocko might have done well as an actor. He was always in the process of inventing himself. He had a chameleon-like capacity to adapt his superficial personality to the part he played — bartender, political fixer, a clown on horseback in a parade, whatever. Knocko could play any role. It was then not surprising that he now began to look like someone Central Casting might choose to play the role of a campaign manager.

He affected a frown of deep thought. His eyes were the eyes of the experienced inside player: knowing, crafty, alert. There was an aura of power and purpose to Knocko the Campaign Manager. To one who did not know it was all an act, he came across as a man of great consequence, walking down *his* street, through *his* neighborhood, to *his* sea front, looking out over *his* ocean.

It was, of course, a masquerade. A huge fraud. He was a disaster. He would phone at times to reveal his latest inspirations. Some of the calls came before dawn, since he'd be out during normal hours involved in whatever he did.

He called to tell me he was going to reveal the fact that Ted Kennedy, while in Harvard, had hired someone to take a Spanish examination for him. I suggested that using this information could make Eddie look desperate. But the story *did* come out and had a short-lived fling in the media. I don't know whether Knocko was the source, but I do know it didn't help Eddie.

In another call, Knocko asked me to talk to members of the

legislature and try to find out Ted's plan. I told him I already knew Ted's plan.

"Well, what is it?" Knocko asked.

"Getting elected to the Senate," I said.

Knocko, who had never run for a streetcar much less an office, was not amused. He told me I had a lot to learn about campaigning.

Once he called to share with me his decision that it would be a brilliant idea to hold a parade down Broadway for Eddie. I reminded him there were 351 cities and towns in Massachusetts, and that if Eddie was worried about votes in his native South Boston, he might as well forget the whole thing.

"Don't be so damned negative," he said.

I told him I felt positive about one thing, that Eddie could win South Boston without a parade. Knocko said I sounded as though I were in a lousy mood, which I was. Before he hung up he said, "Think about that parade. That could be a winner."

In each predawn call, Knocko would ask, "Hey, Bill, am I waking you up?" Each time I would assure him he wasn't. Why I did that, I don't know. I think most of us find it difficult to admit that a telephone call disturbed us. We will deny it in a sleep-drenched voice, while groping through the dark for a lamp switch. Perhaps we want to spare the caller any feeling of guilt. More likely, I suspect, is some puritanical legacy that makes sleep seem a slightly scandalous indulgence.

Because John McCormack was a power in Congress and Eddie was the state attorney general, winning in politics seemed a McCormack tradition. But it plainly was not Knocko's. That wasn't because he was stupid; he wasn't. He simply lacked political judgment, in consequence of which he was open to the feckless suggestions of brainless sycophants — the parade idea, for example. One can't live without a brain, we are told. But, I remember thinking, it *must* be possible. If one could not live without a brain, whence came people to advise Knocko or people to write editorials or people to run for the office of mayor of Boston — where one's career begins to die the day one is elected?

Ted's campaign was based on two premises: one, that he could get federal funds for our state because his brother was president; two, that he could be trusted because he was rich and needed nothing. The former hardly smacked of a New Frontier in political morality; the latter implied that candidates without wealth — Abraham Lincoln's name comes to mind — are inherently larcenists.

A conspicuous advantage was his father, Ambassador Joseph P. Kennedy, who had authored the sly slogan "He Can Do More for Massachusetts." The ambassador was a fiercely pragmatic man possessed of a resourceful intellect, and some $400 million to back it up.

Stephen Smith, Ted's brother-in-law, likable and intelligent, was listed as campaign manager. His responsibilities required no heavy lifting. That was done expertly by others, experienced professionals, and Smith was smart enough to stand aside and let them do it. But Ted's greatest edge, rarely mentioned for some reason, was the almost incredible fact that Eddie McCormack's campaign was managed — *actually* managed — by Knocko.

The first of Ted's supporters to approach me was Judge Frank Morrissey. Frank had been admitted to the Massachusetts bar through an unconventional procedure, and Jack Kennedy had persuaded Governor Foster Furcolo to appoint Frank to the municipal bench. Thereafter, Frank was known as I'll-Take-That-Under-Advisement Morrissey, because he would not make a spot decision. With that background, he was nominated to be a federal judge, an appointment promised by Joseph Kennedy as a reward for faithful service. The U.S. Senate, in an attack led by Everett Dirksen, refused to confirm him. Morrissey said it was just politics. Dirksen said it was just patriotism.

"God bless you, Bill," Frank said. "How's the world's greatest legislator?"

I was not overwhelmed. Frank had a comparable form of address for everyone he met. When it came to greetings, his was the gladdest hand of all. He would grip your arm or shoulder in fulsome bonhomie. He was a tubby man, irrepressibly cheerful, with frenetic energy and a face like a round red moon, and seemed to love everybody.

"Ted needs your help," he told me, using his sincere voice.

I tried to say I was committed to Eddie McCormack, but stopping Frank Morrissey was like dimming the sun in the Sahara. His conversation was rich in conjunctions, bereft of periods; it gushed and flowed. There was nothing to do but wait until he ran out of breath. I waited. We were standing on the corner of Beacon and Bowdoin Streets and it began to shower. The rain was very light, but it *was* rain. He went on unperturbed.

I wondered whether Ted even knew of Frank's approach. At the time I doubted it. I knew Frank as a trusted messenger for Joseph Kennedy, nothing more. He was often sent on what he described to everyone, in the *deepest confidence*, as vital and extremely delicate negotiations for the ambassador. Some of the alleged details were shocking, to anyone who believed them. But he *was* a messenger: he was always catching a plane or train. I know he did pick things up for the ambassador, he did deliver things, but what those things may have been I have no idea.

Frank boasted that he spent very little on expenses — which was probably true and would have pleased his parsimonious employer. He didn't need expense money. He was a master at finding people who fell over one another trying to wine and dine him, men who thought he might be a conduit to advantage through Joseph Kennedy or Jack, or even through Bobby, who had become U.S. attorney general.

Frank lived at other people's expense. He did not do it cunningly, but more like a child who expects to be liked and taken care of.

"I don't want to be a millionaire," he would say, "I just want to live like one."

He came pretty close to doing it. He was especially fond of a sponsor who would lend him a car and chauffeur when he was in New York. This friend would give Frank charge privileges at the posh New York Athletic Club, and Frank would hold court there. He didn't drink alcohol, but he could eat like a Roman emperor, and at the NYAC, he did. He would also use the occasion to telephone former hosts and invite them to join him. The munificence of his hospitality — on his sponsor's club account — was legendary. That treat of course obligated his guests to reciprocate in the future with comparable generosity. It was a remarkable system.

Morrissey performed some services for the Kennedy brothers, but neither Jack nor Bobby trusted him. They thought he spied on them for their father. Frank insisted he never did, but he often appeared on the scene suddenly and without apparent purpose, such as the national convention at which Jack won the Democratic nomination. He certainly wasn't there at the behest of either Jack or Bobby. Jack considered Frank's gaiety meretricious, but did not abuse him. Bobby, being pugnacious by nature and more than a little nasty, was overt in his animosity.

All of these things were running through my mind as I stood in the rain that day listening to Morrissey and waiting for him to give me a chance to speak. Finally he gasped for a breath and I hurriedly said, "I'm with Eddie."

Frank, rain dripping from the end of his nose, said, "Don't forget Ted, Bill."

I doubt he had even heard me.

A few others spoke to me on Ted's behalf, and then Ted himself called. He asked me to have lunch with him at Locke-Ober, then the best-known and probably most pricey restaurant in the city. I had never been to an eatery as grand as Locke-Ober, and the prospect of going there was appealing. I told him I'd check my schedule.

While I was thinking about it, I ran into Bill Carr on Boston Common. He was a school committeeman and former representative, and I had served in several of his campaigns. I told him of the invitation.

I remember saying, "I'd love to go, but I can't. It wouldn't be right."

"And why not?" Bill asked.

"Well, he's going to ask me to be with him."

"You were with his brother Jack," Bill said.

"This is different. McCormack's from South Boston and I'm pledged to support him."

Bill told me that Eddie was going to lose, and I said I thought that likely. He reminded me that some of those who had pledged to McCormack were changing their minds. I told him I was not among them.

"You're new to politics and you don't understand," he said. "Ted's got a right to ask you to help him, you've got a right to refuse. His father's got a pile of money, and you should go to Locke-Ober and order lobster Savannah."

"What's lobster Savannah?" I asked him.

"It's lobster stuffed with lobster, and everybody orders it the first time they go to Locke-Ober."

So I went. We were led up two flights of stairs and ushered to a private room — which cost an additional 25 cents per person. That convinced me Bill Carr had been right when he said the Kennedys didn't care what the luncheon cost. The prices shocked me, and I later obtained a copy of a menu to show friends who thought I was exaggerating. Steak was about $6. Trout was almost $2. A cup of coffee cost a quarter. But the jewel in the culinary crown was lobster Savannah at an incredible $10 — about what food then cost me for three days. I had never seen anything like it.

There were perhaps a dozen people at the lunch. I have forgotten most of them, because my mind was entirely on lobster Savannah.

There was a Yankee type, a handsome man who exuded a tweedy charm and enthused over what he described as Ted's commitment to liberal social theories balanced by conservative economics. He seemed a bit gushy, but a decent sort. There was a stubby man, an adenoidal type with a permanently open mouth. I thought him unctuous, buttery as an English butler. I don't recall the reason for *his* presence. The others were mostly politicians or businessmen. The ubiquitous Frank Morrissey was there, of course, and Gerry Doherty, now a lobbyist and consultant, but then a recent Harvard graduate with a touch of Charlestown in his speech. Doherty was a linguist — which he proved a few months later when, to everyone's astonishment, he spoke fluent Russian to members of the visiting Ballets Russes.

Everybody ordered soup (30 cents) or a tuna fish salad ($1.85). No one ordered both. When it came to me, I ordered lobster Savannah. I was conscious of a reaction — brief, but tense while it lasted — and of being stared at. I assumed it was because everyone was amazed by my knowledge of cuisine.

Doherty said Ted had the votes to defeat Eddie McCormack at the convention. I said nothing, but I thought Doherty was probably right. Frank Morrissey reminded us all that Ted's brother was president and that Ted would therefore be able to do more for Massachusetts.

"And he has international experience," Frank said.

"How so?" I asked.

"He was at the Court of St. James's for two years while his father was ambassador to Great Britain," Frank explained, holding up two fingers as though I might find it difficult to comprehend a number so vast.

I was about Ted's age, so I realized Ted must have been six or seven years old when getting international experience. But I wasn't there to argue.

I loved the lobster. I had never tasted anything so exotic. Everyone else was finished before me. While I was still eating they began counting heads, going around the table asking who would be with Ted. Everyone was eagerly pledging support. When it came to me, I said — between bites of succulent lobster — "I can't be with you, Ted. The McCormacks are my neighbors."

There were a few moments of silence. I began to suspect that perhaps Frank had given Ted an unrealistic report of his meeting with me that day in the rain.

Then Gerry Doherty said, "Could you at least stop eating for a minute so we can talk with you?"

Ted was very unhappy. "I don't know whether we *should* try to persuade him," he said. "I don't think we can afford to feed him."

"Well," I said, "I just came to be sociable."

Later, walking up Winter Street, Doherty asked me, "How the hell could you do that? You walk in there, you order more food than everybody else combined, then you tell the guy you're not with him."

"He asked me to lunch," I said. "If he'd said he'd buy my lunch if I'd double-cross McCormack, I wouldn't have come."

"Well," Doherty said, "you embarrassed me and Frank. We'll never understand why you accepted the invitation."

I explained that it had been my first chance to go to Locke-Ober, and that I might not get there again. "Gerry," I said, "I could have gone the rest of my life and never tasted lobster Savannah."

As we parted, Frank clasped my hand in both of his and said, "God bless you, Bill."

It was just habit that made him do it, but it drew some startled looks.

A few weeks later, Ted arrived at the South Boston Yacht Club to take a boat to Thompson Island, about a mile off the Boston shore. Just across the street was Knocko's house, and Knocko was standing inside his fence directing a group of men who were hammering "Vote Edward McCormack" signs into his front lawn. Somebody suggested to Ted that it would be gracious if he were to say hello to his opponent's father.

Ted crossed the street and extended his hand — which Knocko pointedly ignored.

Never one to clutter his conversation with synonyms, Knocko asked, "You hear that banging sound from them guys banging?"

Ted, lowering his hand but maintaining his composure, nodded.

"Every one of them is another nail in your coffin, Kennedy!" Knocko roared. Charisma was not a word you associated with our campaign manager.

That year, there were more than thirty in the Suffolk County delegation to the Democratic state convention. Knocko was the monitor — we had at least achieved *that*. Some worried about the impression he might make on the TV audience when he rose to announce our votes. Never a subscriber to *Gentlemen's Quarterly*, Knocko wore work pants and a T-shirt, and no barber would have boasted about his shave.

Originally, the delegation had been entirely committed to McCormack. Now it included a half dozen who had been won over by the Kennedy camp. Such defections left Knocko alternately furious and disconsolate. "Anyone who changes sides after he's pledged himself is a liar," Knocko said. "A liar and an ingrate," he added, "because there isn't a one of them wasn't helped by my brother, the Speaker."

When Frank Quirk, a delegate from South Boston, said he was switching to Kennedy, Knocko said, "Can you believe that? That mug owes the McCormacks for everything he has." Then he asked in a distressed voice, "Bill, how can anybody *do* that?"

Surely there are some who jump political ship after they have signed on because they are impelled to do so by principle. But that is more often a rationalization than a reason. Usually defections of this sort arise because a political goal, however desperately sought at some time in the past, does not, once achieved, measure up to its anticipation for very long. The prize begins to lose its luster almost as soon as it is attained. It becomes stale. Ambition covets the next rung of the ladder, and supports whoever will make it reachable.

That was clearly the case here, where some were persuaded the Kennedys could help them more in the future than could the McCormacks. It was my first exposure to the phenomenon, and it taught me the danger of expecting alliance as a *quid* for a *quo*.

There are some in public life whose loyalty is not fixed by what was done for them yesterday, but only by what can be done tomorrow. With such people, it is not *attainment* but *expectation* that motivates them. The McCormacks never learned that, and they paid dearly. I resolved never to make that miscalculation.

The situation within the delegation was predictably lunatic.

Occasionally one of the dissidents would approach Knocko, and the conversation would go along these lines:

"Knocko, I want to be sure I'm recorded for Kennedy."

"Forget it."

"I have a *right* to be recorded for Kennedy."

"The entire delegation is votin' for *my* kid."

The disenfranchised milled about in the rear of the auditorium. They conferred with Kennedy people, who were carrying little phones or radios and seemed very agitated. A strategy at last evolved, and one of the delegates approached Knocko. It went, as I recall it, like this:

"Knocko, the convention has a special committee of monitors organized to settle disputes."

"That's a very good idea."

"Well, they're in the back of the auditorium. If you'll come back for a few minutes, we can get everything worked out."

"I'm not goin'. I got nothing to do with those people."

When the distraught member finally left, I told Knocko, "You can't get away with this. He'll grab the microphone and demand a polling of the delegation."

"They can *have* the microphone when I'm done," Knocko said. "Won't do 'em any good." He reached in his pocket and drew out a wire cutter. "That microphone won't be working," he said.

Long before the roll call reached our delegation, Kennedy — as most of us had anticipated — had the necessary votes for nomination. Eddie conceded the convention endorsement, saying he would take his fight directly "to the people." He fared no better with the "people" than he had with the convention, so he left public life. But Eddie was successful in the private practice of law, quickly reaching that degree of affluence in which one begins decanting the wine.

But poor Knocko . . . Until that concession, Knocko had sat there unperturbed, stubbornly insisting his son would win. He seemed genuinely astonished at the outcome.

He was ever resilient, however. I knew his spirit would not sleep for long. I could remember watching him harangue a crowd on the corner of Dorchester Street and East 8th, saying, "I want you all to vote for Edward C. Carroll, and if anyone here doesn't support Edso Carroll, then . . ." There was a pregnant pause before he added, "The doors of the House of McCormack are closed to him *forever!*"

It had a stern Levitical ring to it. Even more, one thought of God delivering judgment to Adam and Eve.

But that day at the convention, with Eddie's campaign in shambles, Knocko was, at least briefly, confronted by truth. And at the end, he was no longer playing a part. He seemed pathetically alone. He looked like a man waiting in a station for a train that had already gone.

4

I WAS RETURNED to the House four times in the 1960s, a
decade of easy elections in increasingly complex times. As
ever, Massachusetts politics was a repertory production
in which adventure, melodrama and tragedy alternated with the
theater of the absurd.

There were achievements. There were defeats. There were scan-
dals. Our collegial exchanges in debate at times became bitter and
acrimonious. For leavening, there were droll interludes and the
usual supply of sad or comedic characters with their surreal behavior or exigencies. Over all, like an ominous thunderhead, hung
the gathering threat of discrimination against the children of the
poor.

It was, in the main, an uncomfortable era, a fervid and timorous time. It was rather like being on a speeding train — making
progress, enjoying the club car and the passing scenery, but at the
same time sensing somehow that up ahead a bridge was out and
disaster waited.

The essential learning process continued. I found I had a knack
for debate and enjoyed it. I was able to shepherd a number of laws
to enactment and participate significantly in supporting the initiatives of others. There were new friends to meet, new foes to add
spice to life.

In my first term our young president, John Fitzgerald Kennedy, visited the Massachusetts House, where he spoke movingly of the ideals of public service in his famous "city on a hill" speech. Later generations may find it impossible to appreciate the degree to which he kindled optimism and set young men and women afire with a zeal to bring purity and effectiveness to government. In some magical way that had nothing to do with his politics or his personal acts, he became a symbol.

Then, toward the end of the first year of my second term, the mere thought of him shook our lives like a force of nature. That was on November 22, 1963, when an obscure and enigmatic man aimed a mail-order rifle from a window in the Texas School Book Depository in Dallas. The assassin drew a deadly bead on the handsome head of the first Catholic president — and shot most Americans in the heart.

Like so many others, I was sickened and stunned. I regarded with horror the news photos of his bereft widow and fatherless children, made more terrible perhaps by the calm dignity of their demeanor. Above all, I was devastated because a beau ideal had been reduced to its pathetic human remains.

In time there would be a more detached assessment of his administration and its accomplishments. Exploration of his private life would reveal personal flaws, but none of that lessened those golden first impressions. None of it diminished his true status in our history — a status created not by anything he did or failed to do, but by what he made others aspire to. That gift to us remained as it does still, impervious to the abrasions of time.

It is a cliché that everyone remembers the moment he or she heard that Kennedy had been shot. Like most clichés, it is true. I remember vividly that Mary and I had been awake most of the previous night because our children had been restless. I was late leaving for the statehouse and heard a radio news bulletin of the president's death while driving to my office. I recall striking the steering wheel with my fist and saying aloud, "Oh my God!"

I cannot express how deeply shaken I was.

At the statehouse that morning people milled about, talking in hushed voices with the rapt solemnity of mourners at a hero's wake. There was a generally elegiac tone and a sense of inexpressible sorrow for that which is irrecoverably gone. There were at least two prayer services. Testimonials began haltingly and then swelled into competitive rhetoric, some of it moving, some of it moistly sentimental. A few men and women became completely carried away and unashamedly maudlin.

One young representative standing by my side and speaking softly, as though to himself, spoke the words of Horatio: "Good night sweet prince, and flights of angels sing thee to thy rest!"

The allusion to royalty was too much even for me. I went home.

In 1962 self-styled reformers created something called the Massachusetts Crime Commission. The Republican administration appointed Alfred J. Gardner, a Yankee lawyer from the seaside town of Marblehead, to lead it. It sat from July 30, 1962, until June 10, 1965, and during that period no Democratic politician's reputation or career was safe.

The commission's inquiries were supposed to be as secret as those of a grand jury; in fact, they were as confidential as the window displays at Bergdorf Goodman. As a fount of rumor, it rivaled the lurid tabloids whose grotesque exposés startle or titillate customers in today's supermarket checkout lines.

It was popular wisdom that the Crime Commission had been formed to explore allegations of corruption against one or more members of the Executive Council (often referred to as the governor's council). The council, an independent administrative adjunct that dated from the eighteenth century, was empowered to approve or disapprove appointments by the governor to the judiciary and other important positions. But media reports gave the impression — with a knowing journalistic nudge in the ribs — that the commission was stalking much bigger game than the Executive Council.

"Inside information" surfaced constantly to the effect that many prominent Democrats would be indicted. Unnamed "knowledgeable" sources confided that evidence of crime was so overwhelming that the miscreants would be speedily convicted. The public was led to expect fleets of tumbrels packed with Democratic felons being carted off to stern punishments richly deserved. The situation prompted the chief justice of the Supreme Judicial Court to express "grave concern." In a classic of understatement he said that "there is a strong inference that many of these rumors were deliberately instigated."

It was as though a latter-day Robespierre were loose in our midst issuing daily rosters of the condemned for the guillotine of the media. And the tenure of this Terror was such that years must drag slowly by before the truth, whatever it might be, could emerge to sustain or refute the dreadful rumors. By the time that happened, of course, any who had been wrongly accused would be irreparably harmed. Meanwhile, the ordeal went on and on, its miasmic stench of innuendo shaping political events. John Volpe, for example, leader of the Republican Party, identifying himself as "the man who created the Crime Commission," ran a successful comeback campaign for governor.

I was thankful my name was never among those bandied about. I did not delude myself that the omission was so much a tacit tribute to my probity as it was a judgment of the comparative unimportance of a newcomer.

In 1964 my father died. It was evident he was having difficulty breathing one blustery evening in early March of that year, and I took him to St. Elizabeth's Hospital. It was pneumonia. It was called by many the old person's friend, but he battled it for three days with all the strength he had left and went not gentle into that long night. I was with him as his life slowly ebbed away. He wanted to speak, but could not because there was some type of medical apparatus in his mouth. So I sat with him on that last day until he closed his eyes and it was over. It occurred to me that I had never heard him cry out or complain from my earliest memory of him until the end. I did not mope — he would not have wanted that.

That year — 1964 — did not merely bring grief to me personally; it was a difficult year for everyone in public life. And the media, which had been judicially empowered to defame falsely with impunity, made a difficult time almost unbearable.

The media have always criticized those in public office. There is nothing wrong with that now, nor was there then. Indeed, all save those public servants with extremely delicate sensibilities recognize that as the necessary role of a vigilant press. And it is unimportant if the criticism be ill founded, for a free media must be free to make errors.

There is, however, a hierarchy of error. There is the groundless statement that a certain political figure is stupid, incompetent and cursed with bad judgment. That sort of thing, however untrue, must be borne in a democracy. Then there is the instance when the media falsely allege specific personal conduct so defamatory that the publication destroys a reputation, ravages a family, ends a career.

For almost ninety percent of our existence as a nation, a public officeholder, so injured, had the same remedy available to other citizens. He or she could sue in libel, and the publisher was required to prove the truth of his statements or pay damages. The value of the law was not the money received in judgment — for it never fully atoned for a shredded reputation — but the fact that liability for false defamation fostered responsibility on the part of the press. Under that law of libel, our press was able to function so freely it became the envy of the civilized world.

In 1964, while rumors of the Crime Commission's findings were proliferating, the Supreme Court of the United States decided the case of *Sullivan v. The New York Times*. Appeasing the press lobby that had been hammering at its doors for a generation, the Court held that persons in public office could not maintain a suit for libel unless they could prove actual malice. The court then went on to give those words — actual malice — a meaning they had never held in law before. *Henceforth, a plaintiff would have to prove that a traducer knew he was lying, or was reasonably sure he was lying, at the time he published falsehoods.*

Thus the Court shifted the burden of proof, placing on the

victim the duty of proving he was not guilty. *He was required to prove a negative.* And before he could even get an opportunity to undertake that bleak task, he would first have to satisfy a court that he could prove the publisher knew he was lying, or was pretty sure he was lying, at the time of the publication. *That made it necessary for the plaintiff to read the secret mind of the publisher and prove its contents within the rules of evidence.*

As a practical matter, that is extremely unlikely — unless the publisher is willing to testify truthfully against himself, which has not proved to be a common experience. The progeny of the *Sullivan* decision extended the rule to amorphous "public figures."

It was a shifty and dishonest decision. The Supreme Court did not hold that it was lawful to damage or destroy public officials with false defamation. The Court simply made it virtually impossible for the victims to do anything about it.

How many speeding drivers would be fined if it were necessary first to prove that the accused *intended* to break the law?

The media, granted such immunity, were given *a license to lie.* It is a power that exists in no other civilized nation.

The American media have used it routinely, without conscience and with impunity, to destroy the innocent and to punish political foes — and to make a great deal of money from the carnage. Some elements of the media have used it, and currently are using it, against the timorous to extort favors and to blackmail men and women to violate public trusts.

Our first exposure to this judicially sanctioned tyranny was in connection with the Crime Commission rumors. Those of us in public life have since seen such abuse become ever more savage and insidious. In time that would embroil me in controversy with the press.

Meanwhile, more immediate battle lines were forming over alleged segregation in our schools, a struggle that would almost literally tear our city apart for decades.

School segregation had been found unlawful by the Supreme

Court in the landmark case of *Brown v. Board of Education of Topeka, Kansas*. There the power of the state had been used deliberately to compel attendance at racially discrete facilities. Egregious racial bias had been effected by statute, and the Court struck it down.

There was no resemblance in Boston to the legally mandated color separation of the old South. But the Boston School Committee's policies — which it said, truly or falsely, were based on residence, not race — had resulted in a concentration of black children in inferior schools in the district of Roxbury. Irrespective of intent, the situation had to be alleviated.

The National Association for the Advancement of Colored People had its solution: forced busing of all the city's schoolchildren. I believed, as did my neighbors in South Boston, that busing would bring nothing to our city but misery. I wondered whether the NAACP was giving any thought to the quality of education at the end of the bus ride.

Even if busing could rescue black children from schools they did not want to attend — which was doubtful — would it not drive the white children of the poor into schools *they* did not want to attend? And would it not do so on the basis of *their* skin color? Moving children to a safer area made sense; but busing children from a safe community, such as South Boston, into a high-crime area made none at all — and busing would do that. In addition, those of us in the city's old ethnic neighborhoods opposed any scheme that would take our children out of the local schools their antecedents had attended for generations.

We perceived busing — not desegregation, but busing — as a danger to our children and a threat to our cultural integrity.

At first, the prospect of forced busing did not alarm — because, I suppose, it did not seem probable. I and others believed a more rational and less draconian process would be found. But busing proponents were adamant and evasive. They spoke in slogans. Coming to grips with their argument was like trying to grasp a handful of mist. Slowly, slowly, the imposition of their "solution" became more apparent, drifting upon us softly, as menaces so often do, like Sandburg's fog approaching on little cat feet.

I began to realize the immediacy of the threat.

It was impossible, notwithstanding the media reports of Crime Commission activities, to believe that so many of those I knew in public life could be criminals. Some, I suspected, might be ethical nightwalkers who operated on the shadowed edges of propriety, but proportionately few, very few.

As far as the Executive Council — the commission's initial target — was concerned, I had no basis for judgment. Most of the members were virtual strangers to me. Legislators usually have contact with that body only to offer testimony on the character or competence of nominees appearing before it. And my initial experience with the council had been distasteful: I had telephoned to support the nomination of somebody — I don't recall who it was — and had spoken to Councilor Ray Cremmins.

"Wait a minute," he said. "First I want to go to my records to see how you voted on our bill."

I suggested where he might go, and it wasn't to his records. I suppose my pique did not help the nominee, but it was one of those instinctive responses to which I suppose I am prone too often.

However, I knew and liked one councilor, the colorful Patrick J. "Sonny" McDonough. He was my senior by more than two decades, but we were fast friends. I had childhood memories of him in Columbus Park in his native South Boston, laughing his robust laugh and tossing cardboard cups of ice cream, called "frozen Hoodsies," to the children.

In the rough and tumble of those days, he was a formidable debater. His favorite targets were Henry L. Shattuck and Robert Cutler, two socially conscious millionaires who were active in city government. Curley had described Boston's city hall as the place where Shattuck and Cutler kept their Irish mayors — and Sonny kept up the assault.

In a campaign against John Kerrigan, Sonny appeared on the

corner below Kerrigan's house. He began shouting: "Where is he? Where's Johnny Kerrigan when there are things for him to explain?"

Kerrigan was inside the house with a group of supporters, peeking out from behind a curtain. One of his aides said, "Johnny, you've got to go out there and debate him."

"I won't do it," Kerrigan said. "He's got the meanest tongue in Boston."

"You can't hide if you want to be elected," he was told.

"If I have to debate Sonny McDonough," Kerrigan said, "then I don't *want* the damn job."

Meanwhile, Sonny was haranguing the growing crowd. "I'll tell you where Kerrigan is," he said. "He's down at Boston harbor on Henry L. Shattuck's yacht. He's down there getting his instructions."

Sonny, barrel-shaped and usually jolly, had a whipsaw temper. He was muscular and tough. Once, in a private confrontation, when the Iron Duke — Speaker John Thompson — made a menacing gesture, Sonny picked up the larger man and casually tossed him over a table. But Sonny was rarely physical. He didn't have to be. He had a quick laugh, a quicker mind and an acid tongue. Few could stand up to him in a no-holds-barred debate. Absolutely no one intimidated him.

Sonny's wit was stinging and irreverent — appalling at times — and he often got away with it. When he applied for a job organizing New England for the Congress of Industrial Organizations, he was interviewed by a group of hard-eyed labor professionals. Sonny's only credentials were Massachusetts-oriented.

"Not enough," he was told. "We're looking for someone who knows his way around in New Hampshire, Vermont and Maine, someone who can really move around in those woods up there."

"Why don't you hire a reindeer?" McDonough asked.

They liked his irreverence. He was hired.

He never changed his style. In politics, Sonny described one opponent as being unable "to organize a two-car funeral." He called the Massachusetts Youth Service Board "a crime school" and referred to the powerful League of Women Voters as the "League of Women Vultures." Yet he was doggedly compassionate toward the underdog. "I love anyone who helps the poor," he used to say. "I was brought up in a house held up by a clothesline."

It was rumored that Sonny had avoided military service. A committee representing veterans' organizations was formed to explore the matter. The members asked him what role he had played during World War II.

"I followed it very closely," Sonny assured them.

"But did you have any active role?"

"Oh, yes. I cheered our lads when they went away and I cheered them when they came back. I was one of their biggest rooters."

"Are you saying you never served in the military?"

"No. I stayed home."

"Why, Mr. McDonough?"

"Well, you see, I wasn't mad at anybody," Sonny explained.

He had an incredible circle of friends: President Harry S. Truman — and several Boston cab drivers; Bing Crosby, Bob Hope and Jimmy Durante, whom he would visit in Palm Springs — and a group of blue-collar cronies who went fishing with him on his forty-foot yacht, *Galway Bay*. He was friendly with dozens of the judges he had helped confirm — and with some of the ex-convicts he had helped parole, and for whom he had found jobs.

Sonny was a wealthy man. He had left high school to help support his family, and by the time I was born he had a successful beer distributorship. He owned five package stores. When he left the liquor business — at about the time I was finishing high school — he went into insurance in Boston and real estate development in Florida, and prospered in both ventures. He had a house on Carruth Street in Dorchester, a summer home in Scituate — a South Shore community known as the Irish Riviera — and a winter home in Marathon, Florida. In time he sold his Scituate property, to escape "all those young politicians that are moving in," and resettled in the town of Plymouth.

Sonny ran unsuccessfully for mayor of Boston and failed to win nomination as governor, but he held his seat on the Executive Council for thirty-three years. He was the dean.

Yes, I liked Sonny, and if the Crime Commission was finding evidence of wrongdoing on the part of council members, no rumor could make me think Sonny was part of it. And that was not merely because of his affluence — I had noted that truly dedicated thieves were usually wealthy — but because he had a stubborn pride in his public trust. He had a Jacksonian view of political spoils and a hearty appetite for fundraising, but it was all within the law and openly done. There were no shadow areas. His code of honor was rough-hewn and brash, but it was pure where it mattered, and I was convinced he lived by it.

We who had grown up in a society primarily concerned with duty now found ourselves in one increasingly preoccupied with rights. The transition brought much good, in that it enhanced human dignity by overdue codification of civil rights, but it quickly deteriorated to a do-your-own-thing philosophy that fostered a bogus sense of self-importance and a concomitant "right" to deny the legitimate rights of others. Nowhere was that behavior more evident than in the antics of student activists who were disrupting our colleges and universities.

At the University of Massachusetts it was a common experience for students to rush into a classroom, bring instruction to a halt and make wild speeches about the glory of socialism. Administrative officers were harassed. School property was occupied, damaged and at times destroyed. The educational process was stopped. The same things were happening at private institutions, but my concern was properly with providing protection at publicly supported facilities for those students who wanted to study. The tuition in the various state institutions at that time was $200, only a fraction of the actual cost of education. Taxpayers made up the difference.

I filed legislation designed to prevent spoiled and selfish children from treating our academic facilities as political sandboxes in which they could play some silly game of revolution. The bill would have required any state-supported college to suspend, for varying periods of time (depending on the severity of the offense), any students convicted in court of unlawful conduct that interfered with the normal activities of the institution.

"This bill," I explained, "will guarantee, for the student who is serious about learning, an opportunity for purposeful study. For the taxpayer, who is paying the enormous cost of higher education, it will give assurance that he is not subsidizing a disruptive mob. Students have a right to speak freely," I added, "but that right does not entitle them to trample on the rights of other students by interfering with their studies and forcing them to be a captive audience."

Representative Michael Paul Feeney cosponsored the bill. Most of the Boston delegation supported it, but it clashed with the permissive passions of the moment and was defeated.

Usually the Boston delegation voted together. But we were a small minority in a House with more than two hundred members. We were weakened further, at least temporarily, when we lost the active day-to-day participation of three stalwart allies: Feeney, Herbert Cantwell and Charles Patrone, all from the city's Hyde Park district. They found themselves fighting for their political lives in a difficult election because of an incredible woman named Katherine Craven.

Of the small number of women on the political scene in those days, some with evident capabilities simply could not abide the Shootout-at-the-OK-Corral style of campaigning; others — tough, brainy, resourceful — could hold their own with the most chauvinistic of their compatriots; and then there was Katherine Craven, brash, brassy and unique.

Katherine, who had a large family living in Hyde Park, had a smashmouth style and a meat cleaver for a tongue, and her vocabulary was scarlet. She was rarely quoted verbatim, because the newspapers then did not publish the nouns and verbs Katherine often relied upon to articulate her views.

After she was elected to the city council, it was rarely possible for any of the other members to speak without interrupting her.

The sheer staying power of her larynx was awesome. Councilor Bill Foley of South Boston, the mild-mannered son of a former Boston district attorney, dared to differ with Katherine one day.

"Shut up, cement head," Katherine said. "I don't want to listen to you."

Poor Foley, bald as an egg and painfully conscious of it, knew that the allusion to what was inside his head was only a warning shot. He had no intention of inviting a broadside of epithets about its hairless exterior. He seemed to become engrossed with something in the middle distance, said no more and henceforth left the field to Katherine.

And now she was running for state representative against the incumbents Feeney, Cantwell and Patrone. Three seats were open to the four aspirants, and Katherine ran as though she wanted to win all three of them. She began referring to Feeney, Cantwell and Patrone as Kukla, Fran and Ollie, after an early children's TV program — and that was one of her more genteel forays. She went on to attack them with startling allusions to intelligence, conduct, genealogy, even personal hygiene. Katherine was at the top of her form.

Feeney, who first had been elected in 1939, had never seen a campaign remotely like it. He was stunned. Then he said, "I guess we have to do something about this." Toward the end of the campaign the district was flooded with a bit of anonymous doggerel entitled "The Viper's Tongue: An Ode to Katherine." The verse attracted much attention, and Katherine said she would dispose of it in a manner highly disagreeable to Feeney, Cantwell and Patrone. She also promised to perform atrocities on their anatomies in the election. To her opponents, she seemed to be sweeping through the campaign on a broomstick.

But Katherine, brashness aside, was an astute politician. When election time arrived, she was ready. She had an army of drivers assembled to take people to the polls. She had ads prepared for the weekly papers listing phone numbers to call for a ride.

The weeklies were published on Thursday. When election day arrived the following Tuesday, Katherine's phone numbers appeared in the real estate sections of the *daily* papers. This time, they were advertised as the numbers to call if one wanted an apartment with a modern kitchen, two bedrooms, two baths, a host of other amenities and a spectacular view of the sea — for $100 a month. This was at a time when rents were soaring and apartments hard to find.

The ads brought a tidal wave of responses.

Katherine's phones began ringing in the early morning and never stopped. "Is this where I get the apartment?" a caller would ask. Or, "Hello, I'm answering your ad in the paper for an apartment." On and on it went all day. No one could get through to ask for a ride. Meanwhile, Feeney, Cantwell and Patrone were driving their voters to the polls.

A radio talkmaster named Jerry Williams was a devoted supporter of Katherine Craven's — she certainly could be counted on to spice up a show — and she kept calling him all evening. Williams sounded panicky. You would hear him saying, "Where's Katherine Craven? Is she on the red phone? Try the red phone."

Finally Katherine's voice came through. "Goddammit, Jerry," she screamed, "I've been shafted by those bastards . . . shafted . . . shafted . . . shafted . . ." The voice faded out like the whistle on a train in the distance.

And so did Katherine.

Now there was increasing evidence of the dismay brought by the threat of forced busing to areas that would be adversely affected. On one occasion, eight thousand junior high and high school students boycotted classes. They protested that forced busing would destroy their communities.

Busing advocates ignored them. They did not, or would not, understand that local schools, like libraries and churches, were institutions essential to a neighborhood. It was not bringing children *into* communities such as South Boston, but taking them *out* that endangered our diverse identity. The architects of forced busing either didn't believe that or didn't care. Many suggested the city would actually be better off without ethnic communities.

The immediate problem was that we who opposed busing had no specific counterproposal to the busing "solution." I knew we had to develop one, and soon.

It was a perplexing dichotomy. Roxbury parents wanted their children to attend schools outside their residential area. Parents in other communities, such as South Boston, East Boston, the North End and Charlestown, wanted their children to attend schools within their residential areas. My visceral feeling was that both groups were right, both were making reasonable demands. I wanted to find an answer that would be equitable to both sides and that would be practical. I struggled in my mind for weeks to do so. At times it seemed impossible.

I was still a young man, and it is in the nature of youth to agonize over its problems. The cooler deliberative techniques we develop in later years evolve through experience. In our greener days, before we have endured the gauntlet of the years, we search for answers in a labyrinth of mental paths that stop and start and often lead nowhere. It is an enervating process, but inescapable — unless one is possessed of genius or preternatural vision — and I was blessed, or cursed, with neither.

Accordingly, as I did so often when troubled and perplexed, I went walking one late evening on Castle Island and onto the beach, where a misty sea wind was graying in from the northeast. I sat on the sand looking out toward the limitless ocean. It was a lonely vista, with the sea heaving in slow sullen swells like the flanks of some great, panting, lead-colored beast. It was very still except for the susurrant sound of the incoming tide. There was no moon, an overcast hid the stars, and shifting patches of fog scudded across the water — not the sort of night to attract many. But it was conducive to meditation, and I sat there in the quiet dark with a galaxy of complications raised by the busing issue roiling through my brain.

All the questions coalesced to form a single enigma: since the views of the black and white parents toward busing were opposite, how could they be equally valid, equally reasonable, as to me they seemed to be? The riddle haunted my mind like a restless ghost.

I had been schooled by Jesuits, an order of dogged logicians with a knack for reducing problems to their constituent elements. I tried to recall distant lectures on the ordered search for truth itself. That process, I felt, might reveal an algorithm for coping with such complexity. I sought to simplify, simplify.

It was not possible to do that while I allowed my thoughts to turn from one side of the argument to the other as though I were watching a tennis game. When I looked at the demands of the black parents, I concluded they were right. When I looked at those of men and women in threatened neighborhoods, I concluded *they* were right. That distracting process compounded confusion instead of dispelling it. What was necessary, if I were to make any progress, was to get away from the respective arguments and precisely identify the particular *thing* the two sets of parents were arguing about.

Marcus Aurelius wrote that for each particular thing we should ask, What is it in itself? What is its nature? That advice helped me to recognize — gradually — that the problem did not consist of reconciling opposite views. There was no argument to resolve. The parents, black and white, were in their separate ways all saying the same thing!

Both groups of parents were insisting that the state not interfere with their right to choose desirable schools for their children. Both were saying that the state must not deny the natural rights of parents to supervise the education of their young. Thus the true issue was not between black parents and white parents, it was between parents and the state.

The true issue was over the natural rights of parents.

That was the particular thing in itself. That was its nature.

That definition of the issue seemed to me to compel an obvious solution: give all parents a genuine opportunity to choose a school for their children. The goal, after all, was to rescue children from undesirable schools, not to evict them from desirable schools. Those ends could not be achieved by wielding the hammer of the state in the form of forced busing.

I believed I had arrived at the truth, but trying to communicate it was vexatious. The collective mind of the busing zealots and the media was made up. My words were often tortured from context. I repeated my position in hundreds of statements, speeches and debates. I assured all who would listen that black children would be welcomed in South Boston — if that was where they wanted to attend school — but that we wanted our children there, too.

I thought we were on the way to a rational solution when Frederick Gillis, superintendent of the Boston School Department, announced an "open enrollment plan." His proposal would have permitted parents who would provide transportation to send their children to any school in the city.

One problem remained: some parents would not be able to afford transportation. The simple answer to that was to subsidize transportation where necessary. That would let all parents select schools. It would end any appearance of coercion. And the costs of transportation and even of enlarging some schools would be less than that of massive forced busing.

Surely, I thought, that solution should satisfy everyone.

Often, though, we assume a danger has passed when in fact it has not yet arrived. That thought brought a sense of foreboding, knowing as I did that a patina of fanaticism clings to many plans of social engineers. I hoped, yes . . . but still I wondered whether the menace of forced busing really was all so soon and safely over.

My doubts were well founded. Proponents of forced busing were not interested in any alternative. They were not even interested in discussing it. They dismissed Gillis's plan and my suggestions abruptly and with scorn. They clouded the situation with inflammatory statements. They repeated relentlessly that we were involved in a black-white dispute over desegregation. Race! Race! Race! It was repeated like the incantation of a holy mantra. South Boston residents — who physically drove Ku Klux Klan white supremacists out of the community — were nevertheless portrayed as a constituency for segregation. It was a cruel falsehood. The issue was not race. *The issue was misuse of the state's power, and forced busing was its icon.*

The promised quick fix of busing — busing of poor urban children only — enjoyed noisy support from millions who lived in the all-white citadels of the suburbs. It was endorsed by affluent citizens of Boston who could afford to send their children to private schools, and who did so. None of them was affected. Only the intended victims resisted — only those in the targeted communities, primarily urban ethnic Catholics with thin pocketbooks.

Unrest was growing. There was talk of another day of school boycott. State Attorney General Edward W. Brooke warned that any such action would be unlawful. Two weeks after his ruling more than twenty thousand students defied him and boycotted school. More than two thousand parents marched on city hall.

I tried talking with some of the leading proponents. They seemed bored. It has been said that anyone's troubles are tedious after fifteen minutes. From my experience, that is an exaggerated attention span.

Some I spoke to were personally abusive, displaying those startling flashes of vacuity that often and perplexingly characterize the True Believer. Others were impatient, simply too infatuated with the intellectual exotica of their theories to countenance another view. Some of them just sat there waiting for me to finish what I had to say, regarding me with an expression of world-weariness. Most of them listened politely — listened, but would not hear. They stared at me, their faces closed and hard, as though coated with some impermeable varnish.

When I had talked myself out, some would merely shrug. Some would shut off further discussion with a statement such as "Well, we disagree." Those more loquacious spoke in a coded language. They recited numbers and statistics and used such slogans as "Times are changing, and your constituents must change with them" or "You cannot stop progress." That sort of thing.

The cold aloofness of such people in doing what they thought was good for us, their self-righteous indifference to human concerns, made me think of John Boyle O'Reilly's description of the organized charity: ". . . scrimped and iced / In the name of a cautious, statistical Christ."

On occasion I was advised, "There are two sides to every argument." How absurd! What is the positive basis for barbarous behavior from rape to genocide? Such inanity merely identifies those who find simplicity altogether too complicated to comprehend. I have always been leery of psychiatrists because of their penchant for this attitude; I have always wondered whether in knowing too much they understood too little. For, notwithstanding intervening gradations, there *are* polar extremes to human conduct: there is good, there is evil. They exist. They are identifiable by the conscience. Carried to the imaginative extreme, indiscriminate broad-mindedness must result in a head so flat no room is left to house a brain.

"What makes you think parents will surrender their natural right to supervise the education of their children?" I asked Jack Davoren of Milford, Speaker of the House from 1965 to 1968.

"I assume they'll obey the laws of Massachusetts," he said.

"What of their natural rights?" I asked.

"No one has a natural right to disobey the law," he said.

I was stunned by that response. It was inconceivable to me that anyone could assert the right of the state to coerce conduct in conflict with natural law. That would mean the state could outlaw behavior appropriate to being a human being. It would mean citizens were duty bound to obey duly enacted positive laws requiring them to embrace religions in which they did not believe; to abandon to the state their wives, husbands, parents . . . or children; to *murder* one another, in fact. And so on through a litany of comparable atrocities.

Was not such a response a repudiation of thousands of years of civilization? The Judeo-Christian ethic was grounded in natural law. Those whose writings were central to the substance of our polity identified limits on positive law. Our Declaration of Independence proclaimed mankind's "unalienable rights," each of them an explicit repudiation of existing positive law. Philosophers have explained that positive law is conterminous with the condition it addresses, so that a law limiting commerce on Sunday perishes when the popular concept of sin changes. But a natural law common to the collective conscience of humankind — such as a parent's right and duty to care for a child — can never lose significance, can never change.

What so clearly describes the primacy of natural law as the assertion of a duty to strike down positive law when it "shocks the conscience" — *which is the precise language applied by our Supreme Court in myriad cases?*

Obviously, those who would not even discuss the efficacy of busing were not disposed to listen to the philosophical infirmity of any law that would establish it in the situation then existing in Massachusetts.

The staggering irony of the whole thing was that I was unable to find among our elite opponents any parents who did not insist on *their* right to supervise the education of their children. We noted that teachers in affected schools were sending their children elsewhere, as were the police who tried to terrorize us. Politicians from Ted Kennedy to Mayor Marion Barry of Washington, D.C., supported forced busing — and sent their own children to private schools. Academics such as Dr. Kenneth Clark saw nothing wrong with busing our children, but took his own children out of the public schools in New York City. "These are my children," he said. "They go through school once in this lifetime. I don't intend to shortchange them in any way."

The same was true in the media. *Boston Globe* reporters, editorial writers and columnists who savaged us for resisting busing kept their children away from it. Robert Turner, a *Globe* columnist who was particularly vitriolic toward us, enrolled his own children in Milton Academy, an outstanding school. Tom Wicker of the *New York Times* was asked, "Why is it you advocate forced busing for our children but then put your own children in private schools?" He answered that he would not sacrifice his children for his political beliefs!

All of which made one thing very plain: the right of parents to supervise the education of their children was asserted by everyone — but routinely available only to those who had the money to buy it.

I asked Ann Wyman, director of the *Globe*'s editorial page, "Why are you for this?"

She answered, "We are trying to accomplish something of historic importance."

"But," I pressed her, "if you believe forced busing is the way to accomplish something of historic importance, why don't you include the adjacent suburbs?"

"We would be mixing the classes," she said.

The answer left me speechless. Finally I managed to ask, "Why should only the children of the poor be chosen?"

"Because their parents *have* to comply," she said. "They can't afford to do otherwise."

Her words aroused in me a set of clamorous alarms, a premonitory shudder. My hopes for a rational and compassionate outcome withered completely.

It was becoming clear that forced busing was the creature of an alliance of zealots suffering from a messianic delusion of social purpose. They hoped, without examining the likelihood of success, to redistribute children among schools so that each facility would have a student body balanced to reflect the city's racial composition. Their minds were aflame with that chimerical vision and locked against the intrusion of argument. They saw busing as a step toward the eventual racial balancing of society in all its several pursuits — which they perceived as an achievable goal of "historic significance." Their pursuit of so doubtful and diaphanous an end, by using children as guinea pigs, excited their fancy . . . but it shocked *my* conscience.

The tortuous wait for the Crime Commission to report its findings at last came to an end. Their range and severity were stunning. In substance, they amounted to a charge that the state Democratic Party was ravaged by corruption. The Republican-dominated commission sent its findings to the Republican attorney general, and indictments began to roll. There were 473 of them against 96 defendants!

Four Democrats who had served on the 1960 Executive Council were indicted. They were finally charged with conspiring to solicit bribes, of $5,000 each, to approve the reappointment of Democrat Anthony DiNatale as state commissioner of public works. A fifth member of the council, Democrat Edward J. Cronin, made a deal with the prosecutor and turned state's evidence.

Speaker Thompson and a former Republican Speaker, Charles Gibbons, were indicted, as were the commissioner of public safety, a former commissioner of public works and a number of lesser state officeholders. The former chairman of the Massachusetts Turnpike Authority, William Callahan, the state's legendary builder of roads, was accused of criminality. This was somewhat bizarre, since Callahan was dead.

The most spectacular indictment accused a former Democratic governor, Foster Furcolo, of conspiring to bribe the indicted members of the Executive Council. Furcolo thus became the first governor in Massachusetts history to be indicted for a crime allegedly committed while in office.

There were a few Republican targets, most conspicuously Gibbons, but the overwhelming number were Democrats. To Massachusetts Republicans, the charges and the avalanche of indictments promised to produce results in Massachusetts not unlike those of the elections of 1994 which, for very different reasons, wiped out Democratic control of Congress. Some pundits foresaw the decline if not the demise of my party. Even those of us who had been left untouched felt devastated by the enormity of the denunciation.

It was a media Mardi Gras. Radio talkmasters were ecstatic. TV commentators virtually danced at our funeral. Papers dragged the accused onto the killing fields of their front pages under lurid headlines appropriate in size for declarations of war.

Slowly, the dirt storm ran its course. When the dust settled, it became evident that the greatest corruption had been on the part of the Crime Commission itself, which had misused its power and trust to destroy innocent victims for partisan purposes.

Furcolo was found innocent by a directed verdict. Others were acquitted by jury. Some allegations vanished en route to court. Three men, none of them in elective office, were convicted. Aside from that, *the 473 indictments against 96 individuals resulted in a total of four members of the 1960 Executive Council being jailed for brief periods.*

Felonious misconduct by four councilors was of course outrageous, but all the rest — the allegations of widespread corruption infecting a host of Democrats in elective office — had been sleazy defamation. And that, too, was outrageous. It would have been fitting if someone had gone to jail for *that.*

The pivotal testimony against the councilors had been that of Cronin, the former councilor who turned state's evidence. In fairness, it should be noted that Cronin was later removed as a clerk of the Newton District Court for falsely testifying under oath during two appearances before a grand jury.

My friend Sonny McDonough, the lion and luminary of the Executive Council, was not accused of wrongdoing. *That* was no surprise to me.

Sonny had bashed and lacerated the Crime Commission almost from its beginning. He had referred to the chairman as "the poor man's Cotton Mather." He had scoffed at commission investigators, saying, "They couldn't find a Chinaman on Tyler Street" — the main thoroughfare in Boston's Chinatown. He described the commission itself as an alleyway in which Democrats were mugged.

Now, after seeing the prosecutorial fiasco, he was particularly scornful of the attorney involved, former Assistant Attorney General Walter Jay Skinner. When Governor Francis W. Sargent nominated Skinner for a superior court judgeship, Sonny fought against confirmation — and won. Skinner later made it to the federal bench through the sponsorship of Republican Senator Edward W. Brooke, but that was accomplished in Washington, not in Massachusetts.

The state Democratic Party was still intact, but there was a clamorous demand to abolish the Executive Council. That demand grew more strident when Sonny was asked whether politics played a role in confirmation proceedings, and he answered, "Well, you can always pick a well-qualified friend for a job as easily as a well-qualified enemy."

The League of Women Voters was horrified. Its members came by the busload to support a bill that would have eliminated the council. They invited Sonny — in fact they practically dared him — to speak to them in Gardner Auditorium, in the statehouse.

Remembering his description of that organization as "the League of Women Vultures," I cautioned him to be restrained. "I don't think they'll appreciate much more of that humor, Sonny," I said. "They won't understand you mean it in fun."

He said he'd be careful, although it was not in Sonny to be careful. When he addressed them, his opening words were "There must have been a terrible storm in the harbor, because I see all the gulls have taken refuge here."

I left the auditorium as unobtrusively as possible.

Sonny went on to battle a coalition including the Women Voters, the Junior Chamber of Commerce, the Massachusetts Federation of Taxpayers and a panoply of self-styled civic groups. They all demanded laws that would bury or neuter the council. Sonny called on all his wit and savvy and defeated every legislative foray. Eventually, the powers of the council were somewhat, but not significantly, reduced by voters in a referendum. Years later, Sonny defeated another effort to abolish the council, this one shepherded by Governor Michael Dukakis. The council, on which Sonny sat for more than thirty years, still survives.

Political power in Washington abides to a great extent in what are called the memo writers of every administration. Their ranks grow each year with recruits from prominent universities — Yale and Harvard conspicuously — men and women burning with social purpose and willing to work in obscurity for low pay to advance it.

They abound in the regulatory agencies, where they generate memoranda "analyzing" and "interpreting" laws and regulations from the slant of their social and political bias. By the sheer volume of their output, they come to be regarded as "specialists" in the areas of their preoccupation. Their work product shapes or reinforces the decisions of superiors who share the same prejudices — or who are too indolent or befuddled by detail to argue. Such "specialists" have managed in many instances to subvert the intent of the national House and Senate, rewrite the decisions of the Supreme Court and frustrate the will of presidents. Few know their names, but they constitute a shadow government within the United States.

It was anonymous specialists in the Department of Health, Education and Welfare, for example, who rewrote the definition of segregation. They were not satisfied with striking down laws or policies that intentionally segregated schoolchildren by race. They proceeded, memorandum by memorandum, inch by inch, to interpret the Civil Rights Act as calling for a rigid racial head count in each school.

They were indifferent to the fact that Congress had specifically stipulated that the law could not and would not be used for that purpose. When the Civil Rights Act was being considered, Senator Hubert Humphrey of Minnesota had assured his concerned compatriots that the act would merely desegregate schools. He noted that the courts had held that desegregation meant that children could not be prevented from intermingling because of race or color — not that there must be such "intermingling" in all schools.

But the regulations promulgated by HEW sought an unattainable racial balance to promote an undefined — and probably undefinable — ideal called racial understanding.

This was the seed and root of the Racial Imbalance Law. The Massachusetts legislature, driven by the doctrinal climate then prevailing, adopted such a law. It was the seminal basis for forced busing. The memo writers of Washington had even shaped sociological conceptions in Massachusetts.

I fought the Racial Imbalance Law on the floor, to no avail.

John Brooke, a Boston lawyer, told me that I was making powerful enemies by appearing inflexible in opposing forced busing.

"I *am* inflexible," I said.

"You can't stop it," he said. "It's going to come. All you're doing is getting opinion makers and the media mad as hell at you. You're charging windmills, and you're destroying yourself."

I appreciated his concern, but I had been cautioned on other occasions, with respect to other positions I had taken, that my future in politics was in jeopardy. I was getting used to being warned that I would become politically homeless. But our convictions, whatever they may be, place us all in danger. The only way to avoid that is to have none.

Brooke groaned and shook his head when I went on to file a bill to repeal the Racial Imbalance Law.

I was a terrier harassing a bull, but I kept at it. I remember going to Gardner Auditorium, with thousands of people standing around outside because there was no place to seat them. I urged the Committee on Education to help repeal the Racial Imbalance Law. "Affluent parents," I told them, "will send their children to private schools. They are like those in the Civil War who had the money to buy out their children's duty to serve in the military." That meant, I said, that segregation could be ended in our public schools only by attendance of the children of the poor and middle class. "And they won't be available if you drive them from the city with forced busing," I warned. "All busing will do is to segregate our schools by economic class — and that will color them black."

The crowd cheered, but the bill languished.

One evening a month or so later, when the House was scheduled to reconvene for a night session, I went to dinner with Paul Feeney. We were hungry and drove several miles out of the city, planning to go to Valle's Steak House on Route 128. Suddenly I had a notion, totally inexplicable, that we should forgo dinner and get back to the statehouse. Feeney logically asked why.

"Our repeal bill is coming up," I said. "I don't want to be eating a shrimp cocktail when that happens."

"It wasn't on the calendar," he said.

"I know. I still think it will come up."

He looked at me a little strangely, but turned the car back toward the city — for which we were both later thankful.

I have had many similar experiences in politics, moments when I knew what I should do without knowing why. How are such things explained? Some call it extrasensory perception, an answer I find uncomfortable, if not absurd. Most of us say we acted on a hunch — whatever that is. I suspect the answer is more complicated.

Deep commitment to any cause or project, like my involvement in the busing issue, has sensory results. Faculties are sharpened. You tend to hear and see an extraordinary number of small things that might otherwise pass unnoticed. You do not carry them consciously in your mind, but they are with you, cloistered in some closet of your memory. Then they are awakened, mysteriously excited by some recent perception — in this case perhaps a slight nuance of speech or expression or even body language that I had noted before leaving the statehouse for dinner. When that happens, as it plainly had with me, you are prompted to take action you feel certain is appropriate, without at the time knowing why it is so.

In any event, we returned to the chamber and lined up our floor captains for the debate, should it arise. Standing there, I remembered Julius Ansel explaining floor strategy to me at dinner by moving a salt shaker, a teacup and a butter plate about the table to represent the various divisions. The memory helped to lighten the tension: I thought, "I'm by the salt shaker, Feeney's got the teacup covered, Murphy's in place by the butter plate. We're ready."

It was fortunate we had returned. Speaker Davoren, a timid man, winced and rolled his eyes toward the ceiling when he saw me on the floor. I knew then my instinct had been sound and that he had hoped to move the Racial Imbalance bill through without serious opposition. That wasn't because he was sly, it was because he dreaded controversy of any sort.

During the year, while the House was still in session, Davoren had been called away to attend to a pressing personal matter.

Within a few days it became generally known that Davoren's crisis consisted of the danger of sunburn on the Florida beaches. Bill Moran of Somerville, a man of modest means who considered anyone who ventured south of Nantasket to be a jet-set wastrel, began to berate Davoren for "luxuriating under a foreign sun." He continued to boom away to the delight of the media. By seven that evening, Davoren — splendid in a white suit, but looking like a burnt offering from exposure to the sun — was back in the House.

"No more noise," Davoren pleaded. "I'm back! I'm back!"

But he could not avoid controversy this night. He brought up the Racial Imbalance bill with the opening crack of his gavel, and we went on the attack. We fought a protracted losing battle to keep our repeal efforts alive, but at least we were there to be heard.

In the long view, that was essential. We knew we were in for a drawn-out struggle. We had to fight for every inch. And we had to be ready — as we were — to lose every battle but the last, because we knew that in a war of principles, losers lose all.

It was during those troubled sixties that I came into contact with Alan Sisitsky, a cryptic man with obscure motivations. He was a Yale Law School graduate who served two terms in the House representing the western city of Springfield before going on to the Senate. He would have a depressing influence on my life for many years, one that in some respects lingers even to the date of this writing.

Alan was heavy in girth, ponderous in manner. He had a quick mind, but there was a distant expression on his round, purse-lipped face, and his eyes often seemed oddly unfocused. To me, he didn't compute. Something seemed missing or incomplete, as though he were in some peculiar way . . . unfinished.

He found little merit in my views, or what he considered my views to be. When we argued privately, which was often, his smile would be beatific, his manner benign. He would lecture me with pedantic self-assurance, as though he were standing at a blackboard with chalk in his hand. He was also given to sudden emotional storms: if I posed a question he found difficult to answer, something within him would flare and then die, like a star going into nova. On such occasions he would flush and respond with suggestions ranging from the merely prurient to the anatomically impossible. It was startling bathos, like Hamlet segueing from soliloquy to raunchy rap music.

He had a quaintly formal manner of speech, and his soft white hands would sometimes flutter gracefully like a descending bird when he spoke.

"I feel anger toward you," he told me, "because you are opposed to the Racial Imbalance Law, which is a good civil rights measure. You have made me very angry."

I argued that the Racial Imbalance Law was not an extension of the civil rights struggle, which I had always supported and still did. It was a device to accomplish forced busing. It was dressed up with a deceptive title to make opponents of forced busing look like opponents of civil rights. I said it was a fraud.

"The only basis for opposing the law is bigotry," he said.

"Alan, the title suggests that desegregation and forced busing are the same thing. That's dishonest."

"I'm very angry at you," he said and floated away, like a cloud that had dropped its acid rain on my head and was moving on.

I was too puzzled by him to dislike him.

On another occasion he began a conversation by asking me, "How are all your Boston bigots doing?"

I assured him he would not vilify us if Springfield were faced with the threat of forced busing as we were — a prediction that later proved wrong in a perplexing context.

"Why are you against the NAACP?" he asked.

"I'm not. I'm against its support of forced busing."

"You believe black children should be ghettoized," he said.

I told him that was contrary to everything I believed. "Alan," I said, "the NAACP was *right* when it opposed having black children shipped about on the basis of skin color. It's *wrong* when it wants exactly that done to the children in my district."

"You people just hate minorities," he said.

"You know that's ridiculous. You're too intelligent to argue by calling people names."

The face flushed. The storm broke.

"Screw you, Bulger," he said. "You hate every one of us. Why don't you just go and — "

It was a brief flare-up, but the vehemence and his scatological rhetoric were annoying.

David Bartley, a House member for thirteen years, Speaker from 1968 to 1975 and later president of Holyoke Community College, was a "westerner" like Sisitsky. He told me, "Alan's a nut. He's unscrupulous."

"Do I detect a certain coolness on your part?" I asked.

"Damn right," Bartley went on. "That guy told William Putnam at Channel 22 that I disliked Yankees. Putnam, as you know, is a Yankee. Then he told David Starr at the *Springfield Union* that I hated Jews. Starr is Jewish. Sisitsky's a liar and a backstabber."

The intensity of that language surprised me. I knew Bartley as a proud and sensitive man who refrained from *ad hominem* attacks. For years he was cruelly abused by a *Globe* statehouse reporter, but he saw it as a point of honor never to tell the paper she had an intimate relationship with the press secretary of then-Governor Francis Sargent.

The reporter, like Bartley, was of Irish descent, and followed the great tradition of Irish renegades: she sought to find a place where she did not belong, by means of savagery toward those from among whom she came. She seemed to emulate Boston's Yankees in everything except their tribal loyalty.

The *Globe* always provided a special niche for such people. A former priest, James Carroll, is a blatant example. As of this writing, he "reports" on the Catholic Church like a crime reporter assigned to the Mafia beat. Carroll may think his Faustian bargain has bought him security and even importance. The *Globe*, however, knows what it has. Should Carroll's views change, there will always be someone to take his place. As one prominent Catholic layman expressed it, "They can always find such a creature among us."

Bartley was not "such a creature." He was a fair, decent and honest man. I could understand it if he merely disliked Sisitsky — Alan was a living antonym for charisma — but Bartley's words were harsh.

I knew — how well I knew! — that Sisitsky was given to wild and at times malevolent hyperbole. However barbarous his rhetoric, though, he had always, as far as I knew, spoken to my face, not behind my back. I respected that. I told Bartley, "Alan loses control when he argues, but I think his problem is emotional, not ethical. I think I understand him."

"I don't think so," Bartley said, and we left it there.

He was right.

I learned *how* right he was when the state's Board of Education ordered the city of Springfield to end racial imbalance in its schools or lose state funds. Anthony Scibelli, a veteran Springfield legislator, promptly filed a bill suspending the Racial Imbalance Law *as to Springfield!*

Representative Royal Bolling Sr. of Roxbury, a black legislator, led the fight against Scibelli's measure. Bolling and I disagreed where forced busing was concerned, but he too was an able and decent man, and a friend. I respected him greatly.

I was urged to vote against the Scibelli bill.

Jim Craven of Jamaica Plain asked, "Bill, why should Springfield be exempted from forced busing while our city is victimized?"

It was a reasonable question, but I could not vote to bring agony to the parents and children of Springfield. I just couldn't do it. I voted against forced busing for Springfield and waited for another lecture by Sisitsky.

It never came.

Amazingly, Sisitsky voted against forced busing *for his city of Springfield!*

Suddenly representatives from communities outside Boston saw that busing could become a danger to *their* areas. The Springfield delegation, with Sisitsky in full voice, prevailed upon the House to pass their measure. The following day, Bolling lost a motion to reconsider, with Sisitsky again opposing him. Finally Sisitsky and others voted down Bolling's effort even to postpone the matter for a week.

Through it all, Sisitsky never condemned forced busing for any other "racially imbalanced" school system, only that of his own city. He continued to tell me I was a bigot for resisting busing for my constituents. At a time when everyone else was taking sides for or against forced busing, Sisitsky was managing to remain both inscrutable and deeply involved. I thought of the Shakespearean description of Caesar's epileptic fit, which we are told caused Romans to hazard opinions while Cicero, ever cautious, spoke Greek.

"Alan," I said, "I thought you favored forced busing as a matter of principle. What happened to the principle?"

His response, *sotto voce,* again was to suggest an anatomical impossibility.

It seemed to me that the only one who saw nothing astonishing in the man's opaque political agenda was Sisitsky himself. I thought of Hawthorne's words in *The Scarlet Letter:* "No man, for any considerable period, can use one face to himself, and another to the multitude, without finally getting bewildered as to which may be the true."

The Real Paper, a left-leaning publication that had cherished Sisitsky as a model liberal, began to cool. It opined that "Sisitsky's convictions have softened." It quoted a liberal legislator as saying, "We can no longer count on Alan as a crunch vote. When there's pressure, we don't even go to him anymore." It quoted House members who said that Sisitsky had been among "the most eager" in lobbying for approval of what was described as a "lily-white" redistricting plan.

Sisitsky was among the missing when liberals sought support for a gay rights bill. But he did join in sponsoring a bill to legalize all forms of sexual activity between consenting adults — until it was rumored that a newspaper columnist intended to attack the measure. When he heard that, Sisitsky repaired to the clerk's office and had his name stricken from the bill.

I no longer believed his problems were purely emotional. Yet I could not easily dismiss him as a foul-mouthed fraud. He struck me as the weirdest human being I had ever met, but his strangeness roused in me an inexplicable sympathy — why, I did not know.

There came a day when a young man in South Boston named Tom Nee faced what for him was a difficult choice. He was in his neighborhood pub on D Street trying to decide whether to have one more beer before going home. For some sad reason he decided, uncharacteristically, to abstain, and walked out onto the sidewalk — and into the festering busing controversy.

Had he lingered in the pub even for one more minute, matters would have been profoundly different. Instead, he was out and crossing D Street just as a car passed by, almost hitting him. Nee shouted angrily after the car, which then came to an abrupt stop. A group of black men, including one, James Cooper, emerged from the vehicle. Cooper walked toward Nee, who put his hands up, anticipating a fight. It is quite possible Nee had been partly or even totally responsible for the near accident by failing to look where he was going. It is almost certain he welcomed a fight: he was tough, he was angry, he was drunk, and he knew he could hold his own in a brawl.

What he didn't know was that Cooper was carrying a linoleum knife.

Cooper began slashing Nee, inflicting wounds that required 141 stitches. A bystander ran into the saloon and shouted that Nee had been killed. A group emerged from the bar, and a man named Paddy Linskey, seeing the bloody knife in Cooper's hand and Nee lying on the street, charged at Cooper. They fought all the way down D Street until Cooper was stabbed with his own knife.

Nee recovered. Cooper died. Linskey was arrested, and I was retained to defend him in superior court.

The violence was of course deplorable, but I did not believe Linskey should be held criminally responsible for Cooper's death. Even if it were true, and there was no evidence it was, that Nee was wrong in shouting at the occupants of the car, it is settled in law that mere words do not constitute an assault. Also, it was Cooper, not Nee and not Linskey, who carried a deadly weapon, and who used it to attack. As far as Linskey's conduct was concerned when he came to Nee's defense, I reminded the jury of the language of the Massachusetts Supreme Judicial Court to the effect that calm deliberation cannot be required in the face of an upraised knife.

Linskey was acquitted. I was deeply concerned, not because I doubted that justice had been done, but because I knew the ugly incident would be represented by some as more evidence of racial hatred in South Boston. It was nothing of the sort: blacks were in our community every day without incident, afoot and in cars. And Nee's angry shout had been a spontaneous — and perhaps drunken — reaction to what he saw as the recklessness of the driver, not a racial polemic.

None of that appeared to matter to those who seized on the incident as an illustration of Boston's black-white schism. Obviously their message, endlessly repeated as it was, could prove self-fulfilling and create a *real* racial polarization. That, in turn, could lead to violence. It seemed incredible those making such statements could be so ingenuous as to be blind to the danger they were brewing with their alchemy of hate, or so rabid as not to care.

I knew there were hotheads in both Roxbury and South Boston and wondered how we might restrain them if once they came to believe they were being challenged to a racial confrontation. It did not occur to me, as perhaps it should have, that there were also a few among us disturbed with wild imaginings and irrational fears who might be more dangerous than their merely pugnacious neighbors.

In South Boston, for example, there was the Griffin family. I knew them well. They had resided across the hall in the Old Harbor project, in apartment 755, when we lived in 756. They were still there when we left in the 1950s. One of them would, with tragic innocence, bring much agony to our area.

The father, Joe Griffin, had a drinking problem. Mrs. Griffin was a good woman and a devoted mother, but her life was bleak. A baby boy was born to the Griffins, and they named him James. I recall that my father — thinking of his own life and that of my older brother — considered James a hard-luck name and wished they had chosen another. One day the infant became sick, and Mrs. Griffin took the child to City Hospital, walking the many miles. She brought back an empty carriage. Two days later, the child was dead.

The Griffins were always behind in paying bills. Creditors hammered on their door. They never answered. The creditors kept returning. Finally a bill collector knocked on our door and asked my father what he knew about the family in 755.

"I don't really know anything," my father said.

"Well, do they still live here?"

"I don't know."

"You mean," the creditor shouted, growing angry, "that you live across the hall and don't know —"

He never finished. My father was out in the hall like a shot. "Don't cross-examine me," he said in a voice that sent the creditor scurrying down the stairs. "Don't knock at my door again," my father called after him. He never did.

"That poor woman," my father said of Mrs. Griffin, a quiet sorrow in his voice. "One child dead. The other boy, Joseph, a worry to her. Why do people like that have to suffer so?"

For her son, Joseph, was indeed a worry. He was a morbid teenager who would not leave the house for long periods of time. He imagined that others were "after" him and would beat him if he went out. Then he began fearing that someone would come after dark to do some vague mischief to him. He would lock all the windows on the hottest summer nights. His hair grew long and he became increasingly fatter and more timorous and morose. He lived in an isolated world filled with the menacing shadows of imagined terrors.

When the papers insisted there was growing hostility between the races in Boston, that did little to calm Joseph's apprehensions. But no one took him seriously.

In 1970 I decided to run for the Massachusetts Senate. It was a busy political year for others from South Boston. It was the year Speaker John McCormack reached the age of seventy-nine and resigned from Congress. Joe Moakley vacated his state Senate seat to run for the national House. Louise Day Hicks, a member of the Boston City Council and a former School Committee member, also ran for Congress and was elected.

My fight was with Patrick J. Loftus. He was a Moakley lieutenant who had indicated to me several times that he might not run. But he had gathered signatures and was on the ballot. He seemed unable or unwilling to make up his mind.

Finally he asked me to meet him on Northern Avenue near Anthony's Pier 4 restaurant.

"Why are we meeting out here on the street?" I asked him.

"Well," he said, "I wanted it to look accidental."

"It looks like we're a couple of Russian spies," I said.

"Bill," he said, "I'm not going to run."

I sensed he had more to tell me, so I said nothing.

"Without me running against you, things should be easier," he said. I nodded. "And all I want," he said, getting down to it, "is that you get me an upgrade in my job."

I knew he had a state job, but I didn't know where, and I didn't care. "I don't make that kind of deal, Pat," I said. "I'm never going to get into that sort of business."

"Well," he said, "think about it, because I'm not going to run against you. I'm going to leave my name on the ballot, but I'm not going to run. I'm leaving you a clear field."

I went back to my office and told Stephen Mulcahy, an aide, that we had better gear up for a serious campaign.

It annoyed me that Loftus thought me naive enough to believe his assurances. I knew I had angered him by the abruptness of my refusal to buy him off, and I knew that the old disdain of the Moakley men toward me was strong. I was still very much a loner, and though ten years had elapsed since my victory in that first campaign, there had been no warming in the relationship between us. To them, I was still an upstart, still Same Suit Bulger. Déjà vu.

Moakley was busy with his congressional bid. Both of us knew the best course was to concentrate on our own races and not interfere with each other. We correctly trusted each other to do that. Most of the Moakley campaigners were too busily occupied in Joe's race to do much for Loftus.

Pat ran a furious but shameful campaign. In the black community of Roxbury, he distributed a picture that suggested he was a buddy of Robert Kennedy's. It was a doctored photograph in which the head of one person had been pasted on the body of another. He distributed flyers in Roxbury indicating his support of forced busing. He then distributed flyers in South Boston inveighing against it. It was the crudest and most brazen duplicity I had ever seen in politics.

Some alert residents of South Boston, whom I did not discourage, collected copies of both sets of flyers. They distributed the South Boston publication in Roxbury, and the Roxbury flyer in South Boston. Both communities were incensed.

We probably already had Loftus defeated, but the evidence of his chicanery made it a certainty and I was elected to the Senate. One of the first to congratulate me was a constituent named Arthur Driscoll. That went a long way toward spoiling the day for me. I dreaded the sight of him. He would open every conversation by asking me how I felt. His relentless solicitude for my physical condition smacked of the curiosity of a mortician in a period of slack business.

Most of those who grab you by the lapel seeking personal help, however irritating, are not obnoxious. Arthur Driscoll was. He was constantly asking me for things I could not or would not do.

He stopped me one day on Broadway and asked me if I would get some contracts for his son, who was a printer.

"How can I do that?" I asked him.

"Well, Bill," he said, "I think you could get him some business from the South Boston Savings Bank."

"How can I do that?" I repeated.

"By putting a little pressure on them," he said.

"A little extortion?"

"Dammit, Bill," he said, "I'm not talking about extortion and you know it. I'm talking about a little political pressure."

I suggested he look the word up. He walked away in anger.

Arthur, infuriated by what he considered my indifference to his concerns, spoke harshly about me to several of my friends. He was angry, too, because I had not invited him when Mary and I celebrated our wedding anniversary.

"You know I've always been a friend, Bill," he said.

When I didn't answer, he said, "You know I've asked you for things a hundred times, and you know what I got?" To answer his own question, he formed a circle — a zero — with the thumb and forefinger of his left hand. "But," he said with the sigh of the oft-betrayed man, the archetypal victim, "I still go on being your friend."

On Secretary's Day, I took my secretary to lunch at Dini's seafood restaurant on Tremont Street. As we left, I spotted Arthur's angry face in the crowd. I heard him yell, "Look at him with that woman — and he's got nine kids!"

Arthur should have come along years later. He had the natural feral instincts of a radio talkmaster.

He tried to stay hidden in the crowd, but I saw him. And that voice that had deviled me for so many years was unmistakable. Instead of being amused, I was annoyed — which made me realize I needed a political holiday.

I had managed to arouse good-government groups by siding with Sonny McDonough in the Executive Council fight. I had alienated student activists by my efforts to restrain their disruptions at tax-supported colleges and universities. The whole ar-

ray of social engineers — academics, editorial writers, columnists, commentators and special-interest groups — as well as civic
leaders and other pliant tools, were outraged by my resistance to
forced busing. I had missed few stops along the way. Everyone
kept reminding me that I had a lot to worry about. I lost no sleep
over that, but I thought it might be a capital idea to get off and let
the merry-go-round spin without me for a while.

For so many years I had been hearing people who asked me for
help saying things like "Paul Feeney would do this for me in a
minute if I could find him" or "John McCormack is my love, but
this is not the kind of thing I would bother *him* with." I wanted a
brief but complete respite, not just from Arthur Driscoll and his
ilk, but from the unrelenting problems and demands of constituents in general, even those of whom I was fondest.

So I went three thousand miles away, to Ireland, an idyllic place
of uneventful misty mornings and long languorous afternoons.
When I arrived it was raining lightly, what the Irish often call a
soft day.

For two reasons I went north to the remote wilds of Connemara: it was the ancestral county of a great number of South
Boston's residents, and its thatched cottages and rutted roads
seemed frozen in an ancient frame of time, a far remove from
politics.

Americans are very popular in Ireland. If your surname is Irish,
the villagers will recite from memory the genealogy of your family,
often telling you of relatives unknown to you. The welcome is
warm for anyone who does not behave like a lout. Ancestry and
religion are not material factors. Ireland is a Catholic nation, but
none of its recent politicians was more popular — and more routinely reelected — than Robert Briscoe, the second generation of
Jews to be lord mayor of Dublin.

At the same time, many of the country folk consider Americans
to be . . . not exactly daft, but a bit strange. They are too polite to
mention it. They don't hold it against us, but at times you can see
it in their eyes. I think I contributed to the notion.

The night I arrived in Connemara, I was invited to a "singsong" in a local pub. I had a glorious time joining in the chorus of Irish songs. In time there came a lull. An elderly man, who had been reading an Irish newspaper while the singing went on, looked up and, speaking around his pipe stem, asked, "Are you a real senator?"

I assured him I was.

"And would you be knowing Senator Kennedy?"

"I would."

"How far away from him do you sit?" he asked.

"About six hundred miles," I told him.

I waited for the question that would allow me to explain my little joke, but it never came. He nodded a couple of times, as though my answer confirmed something in his mind, and I saw that look in his eyes that seemed to say, "Strange, very strange." He went back to reading his paper. I thought, Please, won't *somebody* give me a chance to explain? No one did. For perhaps a minute no one said anything. Then the singing started again.

By the next morning, I had gotten over it. I rose after a grand night's rest, wonderfully refreshed, filled with a singing joy. I had found in Connemara, I thought, a tonic for the soul!

I set out for a stroll in the lambent dawn, exhilarated by the chill, crisp air. There was a pink glow opening like a rose in the nacreous sky. The fields of stiff weeds and thistles glistened under a silvery dew. The heady fragrance of gorse and the smoky tang of peat were everywhere. I listened, totally charmed, to the anguished yearnings of some morning bird. All about me was the peace of a rugged countryside where no one aspiring to a career in garbage removal lay in wait.

Approaching through the morning haze was a shawled countrywoman, like an impressionist figure daubed in by an artist painting the pastoral scene. She looked at me intently as I tipped my cap and passed by.

"Bulger," she called after me.

I stopped as though I'd been shot.

"You're Bulger, aren't you?"

"I am," I said.

"You must know my sister, Rose Cleary," she said. "She lives in South Boston."

"Ah, I'm sure I do — I'll tell her we met."

"Never mind *that*," she said. "Tell me how she can get into the Foley Apartments."

Already a grayness seemed to be dulling the day. The air had a sudden chill.

"The Foley is senior-citizen housing," I said. "There's a waiting list. Besides, it's a city project, and decisions are up to the mayor."

"Don't duck the issue," she said. "*How can she get in the Foley?*"

I had taken ten days off from such questions. But here they were, waiting for me at dawn on a lonely lane in distant Connemara. I knew then that I had a job from which there were no vacations.

5

THE AGING granite building in which the federal court is housed in Boston is a dingy Euclidean complex, poorly illuminated and full of sharp angles — as are some of the judgments that emanate from it.

Nothing better illustrates the latter fact than Judge W. Arthur Garrity's stewardship of school integration in our city. He brought to that — his most important case — the sensitivity of a chain saw and the foresight of a mackerel.

He belonged to that breed of men who go through life getting themselves appointed to things. Presumably he accomplished Holy Cross College and Harvard Law School on his own. But thereafter he stood in line, as it were, waiting for someone with political power to call his name.

He landed a political appointment as an assistant U.S. attorney.

He went to work for the Kennedy family and was rewarded with an appointment as U.S. attorney.

Later, after the Kennedys were unable to get Frank Morrissey on the federal bench, they plucked W. Arthur out of the wings and got that post for him.

Rung by rung, in accord with established principle, he was appointed up the ladder until he arrived at his level of incompetence.

He demonstrated that to my satisfaction when in 1974 he chose the Racial Imbalance Law to "desegregate" Boston public schools. That brought forced busing to our city. It led ineluctably to a mandate that our children be taken from good schools in the city's safest community and be sent to inferior schools in Boston's highest-crime area.

To accomplish all this, it was first necessary for him to find certain facts requiring remedy. But the statute he selected neither addressed the facts he had found nor provided the remedy he sought.

The problem before him was to end unlawful racial segregation in any schools where it existed. Instead of doing that, he pursued the quixotic goal of establishing rigid racial ratios in *all* schools. In a situation calling for deft surgery, he chose a meat ax.

He was asked why. Why the Racial Imbalance Law?

"It's the only wheel in town," he said airily.

His statement was the first of many judicial jewels of dubious provenance he bestowed upon us.

A federal court in Michigan had rejected a racial-balance scheme almost identical with the one Judge Garrity embraced. The Detroit judge had seen no merit in a plan treating children like pigmented pawns to be shuffled about to achieve an abstraction called "racial mix."

But this was at the height of capricious judicial legislation, and Judge Garrity was indifferent to dissenting counsel.

Over a period of years, he ignored the fact that the U.S. Senate, the House of Representatives and the Massachusetts House and Senate all went on record against forced busing. When President Gerald Ford said he did not think forced busing would accomplish desegregation, Judge Garrity was unimpressed. When Robert Coles, a hero of the civil rights movement, urged proponents of forced busing to examine their own motives, Judge Garrity wasn't listening. His deafness persisted when the secretary of health, education and welfare — the federal department that administered the Civil Rights Act — said, "Social engineering such as forced busing may destroy personal freedoms."

The instances of school segregation in Boston — existing, in fact, only in Roxbury — could easily have been corrected while preserving our city's high academic level. But a manicured mob of iconoclasts wanted revenge, not reform, and that's what it got.

The court's action was not corrective, it was punitive. And it didn't punish the Boston School Committee, which was responsible for the situation, it punished parents and children who were innocent bystanders.

It was an improvident decision, stupid and cruel, and its results were predictable and uniformly execrable. In the years that followed, our school system, once highly regarded, became a scandal. Children were left functionally illiterate in an educational vacuum rife with drugs, violence, crime, teenage pregnancies, truancy and dropouts. Graduates, some of them literally unable to read their diplomas, were disposed of into a society where they were unqualified except for the most menial jobs. Communities that had enriched the city's character were devastated.

It brought nothing, absolutely nothing, of value to our city.

Kevin White, who was mayor through most of it, said, "There were three extraordinary periods in the city's history: the Revolutionary War, the abolitionist time before the Civil War — and busing. From the first two, we grew and prospered. We're still dealing with the aftermath of the third."

Today, more than two decades later, we still are.

That was almost inevitable, because while busing was an issue in many parts of the United States during the 1970s and early 1980s, it was most intensely so in the city of Boston.

Ours was a city of old communities, low in income, rich in cherished traditions of a vigorous culture, none more so than my district. And thus the tiny enclave of South Boston became in time, not just in Massachusetts but nationally — and even abroad — the symbol of resistance to busing.

We were the lightning rod.

The fiercest struggles are always those fought over ideas. No lust for power or greed for riches can evoke the intensity aroused by philosophical disputes. And that is what this was:

The state and federal governments fought for the power of the lawmaker to regulate society. We fought for the right of parents to supervise the care and education of their children. It was, in microcosm, the classic clash of positive and natural law — ancient as Antigone, modern as Mandela.

We found ourselves defendants in a court of public opinion, facing the complaint of an aroused and powerful collective of forced busing votaries. If you believe you are right, as surely we did, you do not shrink from such confrontation. But when only the plaintiff is given a meaningful opportunity to be heard, while you are told to be silent; when the jury is drugged by media reports prejudicial to your cause; when the judge — the referee, if you will — gets his advice from the plaintiff! . . . prospects for a fair trial significantly diminish.

We saw the whole architecture of deception on display. The thirst for bad news about South Boston became unquenchable. The media drummed up pro-busing comments from politicians, from civic and academic spokesmen, from religious leaders. The surest tactic for instant, prominent and laudatory publicity was to support busing and condemn its ignorant and evil opponents, namely us.

The gaudy media mythology about us, rampant in America, was replicated in the foreign press, attracting unique attention to our controversy. Remote areas, previously unaware of our existence, read and heard of this barbarous outpost of racial bias called South Boston. Magazines fantasized that blacks feared for their lives on Boston streets because of our sanguinary bigotry. Editorial writers, columnists, television and radio commentators all joined in trying to browbeat us into submission with that scalding epithet — *racist!*

That hurt as any injustice hurts. It wounded as only a lie can wound. But it never made us think about abandoning our children. And while South Boston was caricatured as the home of hate, the media fastened on me as its dark spirit incarnate. My lifelong aversion to political tact no doubt facilitated that choice.

I had always spoken extemporaneously in the past, but now

found it advisable to use a written text to provide some safeguard against distortion. I also learned the unwisdom of confiding in reporters who were seeking not information but ammunition. Members of my staff became similarly cautious, none more adroitly so than my campaign treasurer, John Sullivan.

John owns a tavern across from St. Augustine's Church. He never went to college, but is possessed of great natural wisdom. He was tending bar one day when a woman reporter and two cameramen walked in and began setting up.

"Hi," said John — which is a pretty long speech for him.

"Mr. Sullivan," said the reporter, "we're from Channel Two. I have some questions for you about Senator Bulger's campaign account."

John raised one huge red hand as though he were stopping traffic, closed his eyes, and with the air of one declaring a mighty principle, said, "Hey, if there's one thing I *never* answer, it's questions."

Judge Garrity announced that he had assembled a group of distinguished experts to counsel him. They were distinguished, as far as I could see, only in the sense that not one of them was the parent of a child who would be affected by forced busing.

They were a well-educated, articulate assemblage of prejudiced and occasionally venomous activists. Thomas Atkins, then president of the local chapter of the NAACP, met all those criteria. It is one of life's great injustices that men like Atkins are not required to suffer the results of all the bad advice they give to others.

Atkins was a former Boston city councilor, former state secretary of communities and development, and former general counsel of the NAACP. Like Judge Garrity, he was a graduate of Harvard Law School. We who represented South Boston found him to be bright, but flawed by a veiled desire not merely to advantage blacks but, in the process, to revenge them on whites, irrespective of the innocence of his targets. Louise Day Hicks, James Kelly of South Boston — a vigorous opponent of busing — and I had many meetings with Atkins.

Louise was formidable. A descendant of Irish immigrants, she had graduated from law school at a time when few women did — especially a thirty-six-year-old mother of two. She fought busing throughout her public career and was dubbed the Iron Maiden by busing proponents. She endured constant harassment and was unfazed by it. Once she was surrounded by a group of angry students who thrust a wooden swastika in her face. Louise struck it to the street and ground it under her heel. She never backed down. Never.

Kelly could never be intimidated. He was arrested frequently because he insisted upon his right to speak out against busing. I remember the day when I saw two police officers holding Kelly's arms while one of them reached inside his shirt and tore the hairs from his chest. Kelly didn't flinch.

We were fortunate to have hearts as stout as Hicks's and Kelly's.

Our meetings with Atkins were icily polite sessions, but strained. He was dealing with three combative personalities who found his condescending air irritating, but we were determined to remain calm. When we differed over the meaning of one of Judge Garrity's opaque statements — as often happened — Atkins would say smugly, "Well, I'll speak to the judge about that." He implied constantly, truly or falsely, that he had immediate access to the judge. Atkins's views *did* seem sinuously to find their way into judicial orders.

Atkins's vindictiveness frequently surfaced. I remember one incident when I reminded him we were not opposed to having black children come into our schools. "You know, there were black children in South Boston schools before anyone ever mentioned forced busing," I said.

He stared at me without answer.

"What we object to," I went on, "is having our children shipped into a high-crime area and having their education savaged. Why would you want to do that simply on the basis of their skin color?"

"You didn't complain when things were tough for black children," he said in a hard tone. "Now things are tough for white children. That's good." He thought about that for a few seconds while we stood staring at him. Then he added, "Yes, that's good. In fact, that's fine by me."

I recall that exchange clearly, but there were other times when the substance of his remarks conveyed a similar thirst for vengeance, though I do not remember his words. Of course there was no hint of revenge in his public speech, but he seemed to enjoy revealing it to Mrs. Hicks, Kelly and me.

That mind-set was not limited to Atkins. There was Sandra Lynch, one of the judge's advisers, who contacted me years later when she was seeking a judicial appointment. She asked me to speak on her behalf to Senator Joseph Biden of Delaware — asking him, in turn, to speak to Senator Orrin Hatch of Utah, who was hostile to her because of her support for forced busing. She told me she believed the drastic effects of busing on white children were deserved because their parents had elected a recalcitrant school committee.

I found it grossly offensive to hold voters answerable for the conduct of elected officials. Such logic would justify jail terms for those who voted for someone who proved to be corrupt. But it was the blinding immorality of her position that was appalling. She deemed it proper to get even with adults she thought culpable *by punishing their children!*

How many of the judge's advisers shared that depraved doctrine with Thomas Atkins and Sandra Lynch and how many merely pursued an end and ignored the means is a distinction without a difference. The salient fact is that the judge formulated his plan with only the dim half-light of their biased counsel to guide him.

Judge Garrity announced that each provision of his plan would be the *law,* superseding any power of the school committee. He issued some four hundred rulings on student assignment, composition of school staffs, distribution of resources and virtually every other aspect of public school management. Some of his edicts sought to keep South Boston silent, if not acquiescent. Later, as he became more inebriated with power, he hinted that he might jail some of our wives and mothers. He talked of putting the entire school system in receivership and running everything himself.

And the *Globe,* the loudest voice for forced busing, cheered the judge on through it all. It mattered not that school enrollment of whites plummeted to a level that changed the goal of racial balance from the improbable to the impossible.

It seemed to me our Neighborhood had become Judge Garrity's white whale, and that only its destruction would bring him peace. The advisers would advise and the judge would act, and each ukase would bring a tremulous chill to us. I complained that the court would not even listen to us. The judge, living in the remote and posh town of Wellesley, insisted he was not insulated from our concerns.

"I know what's happening in Boston," he said. "I read the *Globe* every day."

Among the many things he would never read in the *Globe* was the fact that he would not and could not intimidate South Boston. He might flood it with riot police — as he did. He might drive many out of their ancestral district — as he did. He might damage the ambiance of the area to some extent — as he did. But the great power of the federal court, in combination with the coercive might of police, marshals and the National Guard, could not break the district's spirit.

The continuing vigor of that *geist* was made evident when Jim Shannon, who was running for attorney general, told me he would like to campaign in our area. I suggested he come to a rally scheduled for the South Boston Social Club. He was delighted.

"Now Jim," I warned him, "these people are very outspoken."

"They're loyal Democrats, aren't they?" he asked.

"Yes," I said. "They're Democrats — but *very* democratic."

"That's fine," he said. And I could see he did not know what I meant.

So he came. I introduced him and urged the audience to support his candidacy. Shannon began to speak and was cruising along when suddenly a man and a woman stood up in the aisle.

"You're no good, Shannon," the man roared. "You voted in Congress to cripple Ireland. You're a traitor."

Then the pair walked out. Shannon turned to me and asked, "What are they talking about?"

I told him I had no idea.

"But you asked them to support me," he said.

"Well, I did," I agreed. "Jim, these people will listen to suggestions, but nobody can tell them what they must do. Nobody."

"Is it always like this?" he whispered.

"Not infrequently," I said. "That's why we have an entrance to the fire escape right behind the speaker's platform."

Shannon looked quickly over his shoulder, as though he wanted to make sure he knew where the fire escape was, and then went on speaking. No one in the audience acted as though the slightest thing untoward had happened.

Father Paul Donovan, who was in a church in Hyde Park at the time, and who got most of his information about busing from the media, had doubts about our attitude. He telephoned me and seemed upset because he thought I was orchestrating South Boston's protests.

"I've never called for a demonstration," I said. "Never. Not once. I attend them to show solidarity and because I hope I can help prevent things from ever getting out of hand."

"Well," he said, "why don't you say something that might help with this situation?"

I think he meant, Why don't you quiet your neighbors? But his words reminded me that those of us who represented the people of South Boston, who understood their anguish, had an unsleeping duty: we must keep on trying — again and again and again — to articulate their view, however many times we were ignored, whatever the cost.

I said, "Fine. I will."

Very much in my mind at the time was something my father had said to me: "Bill, people can stand unhappiness. They can hang on

Jean and James Bulger, my mother and father, circa 1950.

Note the alert look on the faces of Joe Quirk (*left*) and his lifelong pal Bill Bulger in 1939. A pair of natural rebels, we were probably poised to flee the social worker who kept trying to line us up and march us around.

In 1949, as a fifteen-year-old second baseman for St. Monica's, I was one of the rich kids of South Boston. We had close families, loyal friends and a strong sense of community — everything but money. Many youngsters at posh boarding schools were impoverished by comparison.

Mary and I at our wedding in 1960. I thought I loved her with all my heart then — but somehow I have grown fonder of her with each day since. (Sharon's Studio)

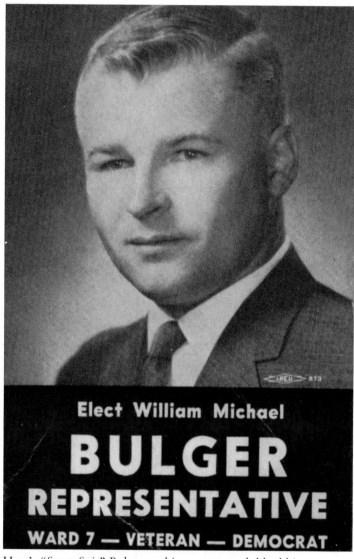

Elect William Michael

BULGER

REPRESENTATIVE

WARD 7 — VETERAN — DEMOCRAT

Here's "Same Suit" Bulger, as his opponents dubbed him, wearing that precious suit and trying desperately to look mature as a candidate for state representative in his first campaign, in 1960.

It was a great boost to a Boston politician — especially one in his first term, in 1962 — to be greeted by U.S. House Speaker John W. McCormack. I was smiling then, but I wince now to see how shamelessly I played to the camera.

Edward J. "Knocko" McCormack, brother of John McCormack, was a big man in the Neighborhood and loved to ride his horse, Jerry, in the St. Patrick's Day parade. Knocko once rode the horse into a bar — but then, he did a lot of unusual things.

In 1971, when I began hosting a St. Patrick's Day breakfast, the event was held at the old Dorgan's restaurant. *Left to right:* Patrick J. "Sonny" McDonough, City Councilor Louise Day Hicks, Senate President Kevin Harrington, Governor Frank Sargent, me and Raymond Flynn.

Luciano Pavarotti greets me with characteristic restraint on a visit to the statehouse. When Governor King asked me to sing for the great Italian tenor, Pavarotti clapped his hand over my mouth in a stunningly swift move for so hefty a man.

Boston Mayor Kevin White reacts to gentle needles applied by his St. Patrick's Day breakfast host. The jolly bystander is Representative Michael Flaherty. (John Blanding, *Boston Globe*)

Singing "The Isle of Innisfree" with John Williams and the Boston Pops. Jackie Kennedy told me that the song had brought tears to her eyes, and later wrote me a touching letter, which I framed. "Don't get carried away," Mary said. "When you sing, Bill, you make a lot of people weep." (Eric Roth)

The Boston Symphony Orchestra toured in Europe in 1982, and Mary and I went along. Here's Mary at a sidewalk café in Paris — where, to her delight, nobody was talking politics.

My most loyal constituents check out my office at the statehouse. *Back row, left to right:* sons Jim, Dan, Bill and Pat. *Front row:* Sarah and Chris, Mary and I, and daughters Mary and Kathleen. In the foreground is Brendan, our youngest. (Fayfoto)

Morley Safer of *60 Minutes* comes to my home in South Boston to do a
segment on me in 1992. After the show was aired, I received mail from
around the world. Strangers in distant airports would stop me and say,
"Hey, I saw you on TV!"

Harvard law professor Alan Dershowitz (*far right*) is unhappy with my description of him as a "murderer of reputation." The confrontation took place before the Executive Council, which was considering the confirmation of Paul Mahoney to a district court judgeship. Between us are Ed Phillips (*left*) and Richard Hayes. (Jim Davis, *Boston Herald*)

Waylaid by the media in a Senate corridor in the early nineties, an oft-repeated scene. Most of the journalists were decent, but that never made it easier to run a gauntlet where an ambiguous word, if misinterpreted, might do damage. (John Tlumacki, *Boston Globe*)

At the Democratic national convention, in New York in 1992, where Bill Clinton was nominated for the presidency. I was a delegate, Mary was a sightseer — which means she probably had a better time than I did.

Ted Kennedy and his bride, Victoria Reggie, attend my St. Patrick's Day breakfast in March 1994. The visitors are laughing because I have just told Ms. Vicki how good it was of her to take him in. (Harry Brett, Image Photo)

Democratic Senator William Keating, the leader of what he perceived as a Senate rebellion, takes his BEAT BULGER campaign to Boston's "cradle of liberty," Faneuil Hall, in 1994. (Bill Brett, *Boston Globe*)

JOHN F. KENNEDY SPOKE FROM THIS ROSTRUM
TO THE MASSACHUSETTS GENERAL COURT ON JANUARY 9, 1961
I carry with me from this state to that high   Colony and the Bay State–the qualities which

Presiding at a joint session of the House and Senate on the occasion of Governor William Weld's second inaugural. Behind me, left to right, are Lieutenant Governor Paul Cellucci, Weld and Speaker of the House Charles Flaherty. Whatever I said couldn't have been too partisan, because they all seem amused. (Gail Lewenberg)

Sinn Fein leader Gerry Adams, visiting the United States in his quest for a peaceful resolution of the troubles in Ireland, finds time to drop by our home in September 1994. (Harry Brett, Image Photo)

A fundraiser for U.S. Senator John Kerry in 1995. *Left to right:* Teresa Heinz Kerry and Senator Kerry, President Clinton and the Bulgers. I told John I might run against him, and promised I would take no money from my wife if he would make the same pledge. (Fayfoto)

through almost anything as long as they don't stop thinking there is a possibility of happiness sometime."

I knew that was what I had to try to keep alive, a belief in the possibility of happiness.

I drafted a "Declaration of Clarification" which noted that repairmen, utility workers, taxi drivers, even doctors and firemen, had all refused at one time or another to venture into Roxbury, yet Judge Garrity was demanding that our children do so on a daily basis. He was insisting we act against the best interests of our children.

The declaration added: "If parents seeking to regain control over their children flee this city, as indeed so many have been doing; if communities such as our own are systematically dismantled simply because federal judges are unwilling or unable to recognize the value of such communities, then all who live in this City are the losers. We will be a Newark or a Detroit — a tragic result for all people, white or black."

Jim Dahill, a good friend, read the declaration and said, "Forget it, Bill. It won't change anything. The dice are loaded against us. All it will do is start another firestorm in the press."

"I can't argue with that," I said.

He looked at me for a few seconds, and then he said, "You're going to do it anyway, aren't you?"

"You're damned right I am."

It was contemplated that Mrs. Hicks and the two South Boston representatives, Michael Flaherty and Raymond Flynn, would join with me in signing the declaration. Mrs. Hicks, Flaherty and I signed and then looked for Flynn to get his signature. We pursued him. He was not to be found. He returned no phone calls. He was elusive as smoke. People would report seeing him enter his office, but when we called, we were told he had not been in all day.

My associates were puzzled and annoyed. They knew Flynn had been elected because he had campaigned against forced busing, and they expected he would call. I thought we should not go without food or water until he did. Flynn, it seemed to me, had made it clear he wanted no part of the declaration. Since he said he opposed busing so vigorously, one had to assume he was hiding because he was fearful of renewed media abuse. That was consistent with my appraisal of the man.

I had long been aware that nothing terribly exciting went on between the ears of Raymond Flynn. But the fact that you might not want to be snowbound in a cabin with him — and no one else to talk with — did not mean he lacked political skills. He lived by instinct, which he obeyed with a degree of cunning — a combination that seemed effective. He won election as a state representative, then as a city councilor, and then for several terms as mayor of Boston. At the time of this writing, he is United States ambassador to the Vatican. I always thought each political uniform he wore was a little too large for him, but he works hard at what he does and is possessed of almost legendary physical stamina.

I sensed in him a certain fluidity of principle, however. I considered him a political surfer, one who seeks to ride the waves of public opinion, which is difficult to do against the wind — and Flynn could read the wind like a wolf.

At the time of the declaration, he was where he wanted to be. He had surfed all the way to the statehouse on the flood of anti-busing sentiment in his native South Boston. I had no doubt his instinct told him not to irritate the media further.

No — it did not surprise me that he had not called back.

Police Commissioner Robert diGrazia, whom busing was making a media celebrity, called our statement inflammatory. At that time, Judge Garrity and diGrazia had South Boston policed by more than one third of the Boston force — which apparently was not supposed to inflame *us*. DiGrazia was a posturing, crafty man who built his career, bus by bus, during that troubled period. He was literally the strong arm of the judge. He pleased the media. Sometimes he went beyond all that, as when his Tactical Police Force, for which he was responsible, administered gang beatings to quiet bystanders for no apparent reason. At such times I wondered if he was satisfying some dark need within himself.

We challenged the *Globe* to publish the statement on page one, where attacks on us were routinely displayed. The newspaper printed it, but on an inside page. Editorially the *Globe* denounced our declaration as being too strong.

Flynn told the press he had not signed the declaration because he considered it too strong, the same words used by the paper. His statement reveals much about the man, when one considers that he had not read the declaration until after it was published.

While all this was going on, I came home to find Mary annoyed because a group of representatives of the Boston Bar Association had been to my home. They told Mary they believed that as a lawyer I should not be criticizing the judge's orders. They asked her to tell me that. Mary, while characteristically unfazed, thought their manner subtly threatening.

I called the bar association to say I was saddened to learn the First Amendment had been repealed. I called around town to find out who had been to my house, and then left messages for them to stay away from my home and family. I never heard from any of them.

Later, a huge crowd formed on Beacon Street in front of the Boston Bar Association building to protest an award to Judge Garrity by the association, which was then headed by Edward Barshak and Edward Masterman. Both men were residents of Brookline, an area unaffected by the busing decree.

Many well-intentioned men and women disagreed with our position because they simply didn't comprehend the issue. Senator William X. Wall of Lawrence told me he could not understand our upset; hadn't parochial schools been busing students for years without complaint?

I spent hours with him trying to make the distinction between busing with parental consent and busing forced on children against the will of their parents. I thought that if I could clarify our position to Wall, I could do it with most if not all of my compatriots.

That was not because Wall was dumb. He wasn't. But he had an innocence that made him incapable of believing that other well-intentioned people could mistakenly do evil. He was a character, but he was a deeply caring man, gentle, compassionate, thoroughly good. He had a monumental conscience that never spared him: were he alive today, he probably would feel responsible in part for global warming and any problems with the ozone layer.

Wall knocked at a priest's door late one night to assure him he had solved a passport problem for a parishioner.

"I'll tell her the good news in the morning," the priest said.

"Why don't you call her now so she can sleep comfortably?" Wall asked.

That is the way he was.

Wall was a striking man, tall, angular and bald as an oyster. He carried a heavy burden of service to his constituents: he would run errands for them, deliver their packages, do their shopping. People would call him from Lawrence and ask him to pick up a white dress shirt, or a blue wool skirt, or whatever, at Filene's Basement "before the sale ends." He would write down particulars of size and style, use his lunch hour to get the merchandise and deliver it to the caller's door that night. It was antic behavior, but there seemed a kind of grace about him as he took his ritual turns among the department stores for his constituents.

He belonged to everything, including the Knights of Columbus. Once, caparisoned in his splendid Knights uniform, with plume, ribbons and sword, he accepted Governor Furcolo's invitation to accompany him on an inspection of a mental institution. The tour director unobtrusively asked Furcolo for the identity of his companion. Furcolo, an inveterate practical joker, whispered, "I don't know the man. He was in the lobby when I got here."

The director asked Wall who he was.

"I am Senator Wall. Call me Bill."

"Do you wear a sword in the statehouse?" the director asked.

"This is a uniform of chivalry," Wall explained.

The director spoke quietly to an aide, who asked Wall to follow him. Wall said he would prefer to inspect the asylum. Help was summoned and he was led away — pleading with Furcolo to speak up for him. Wall was detained for hours until he was able to prove his identity. He left in a car Furcolo sent back for him. He was never able to see humor in the event, but he bore no malice.

I was always fond of him, but I gave up trying to win him as an ally in the anti-busing effort. He seemed incapable of indignation or anger. After he thoroughly understood our position, he would express sympathy for the unhappy parents and their children, but then he would add with a smile of apologetic deference that he believed busing proponents meant well.

"My God, man," I said to him, "so did Torquemada."

But he was not deeply conversant with religious history.

In a further effort to force the media to report our position, I canceled for one year the St. Patrick's Day breakfast I held annually for constituents and guests. I said I was doing so as an action of protest against the assault on our community.

The breakfast was a popular event, a good-natured roast. Local television stations covered the event, and national TV at times aired excerpts. In 1992 the CBS program *60 Minutes* devoted one of its segments to the breakfast, and I received an incredible number of letters from around the world.

Hundreds of South Boston guests always attended to enjoy the traditional corned beef and cabbage while national and local politicians, and occasionally celebrities from motion pictures and television, baited one another. A typical exchange involved the late U.S. Senator Leverett Saltonstall of Dover and the ubiquitous Sonny McDonough. The senator was introduced as "the Yankee with the South Boston face." Sonny quipped, "Yes, Salty is Irish on the chauffeur's side."

The senator, who had a wonderful sense of humor, borrowed Sonny's words and repeated them at many functions.

One of my favorite guests was U.S. Senator George Murphy. As far as I know, he was the first prominent actor to have a successful political career in his later years. He first attended our breakfast when he came to Boston for the making of a film — I think it was *Walk East on Beacon*. We became friends.

George was a successful actor, but at heart he was a song-and-dance man. He told me how hard it had been to get started in show business. He said he had decided to try Hollywood because he had become almost penniless in New York City.

"The kiss of death, Bill," he said, "was for people to think you were idle and needed work." George said he avoided that by smearing a bit of makeup on his collar to give the impression he might be a careless — but was certainly a busy — actor.

Murphy and I did a skit. He would strut to the tune of "Me and My Shadow" and I would follow behind, singing with him, imitating his movements, simulating his shadow. We did the skit often — the last time was in Washington on his eightieth birthday, when George revealed that he had been married the night before to a pleasant woman he had met during his campaign.

The *Globe* was unhappy about the breakfast cancellation and told its readers I had acted from fear of violence. That falsehood was repeated for years afterward, no matter how many times I denied it. "What violence?" I would ask. "Violence by whom? My constituents? My guests? Judge Garrity or his advisers? The allegation is absurd on its face." But it did no good. "Violence," like "racism," had become synonymous with South Boston in the media.

Globe editor Thomas Winship telephoned Flynn. It was reported to me, by what Winship would call an informed source, that the editor had said, "Bulger is a quitter. That's not like the Irish. Irish don't quit. Why don't you take it over and host your own breakfast?"

I believe the report of that conversation to be substantially correct, though of course I was not party to it. There can be no doubt whatever that Winship knew the right person to call.

Flynn telephoned me and suggested it might be a good idea if he were to hold a breakfast in Roxbury with Senator Royal Bolling. It was obvious Flynn was transported by the thought of standing up before all the cameras with the black senator at his side.

I told him I had no objection, but doubted he'd have many guests from South Boston, since they understood the cancellation was a protest with which the community sympathized.

Flynn said he would think about it — which I knew was an extravagant commitment. Someone must have done it for him, however, because he did not try to hold the breakfast. It may well have been that Senator Bolling was not keen on the idea. Royal was an old friend of mine, and I know he resented efforts to pit our communities against one another. At all events, he did not appear with Flynn and continued to be my guest on St. Patrick's Day.

Mayor White, another well-intentioned man, tried to create an impression of normality during the crisis. He craved peace. Like my own cousin in Rockport, White never seemed to appreciate the extent of our suffering nor grasp the fact that the busing decree itself was an injustice. "Please," White would say, "let's just keep everything friendly and quiet."

In an effort to keep things friendly and quiet after I had canceled the breakfast, he presided over a St. Patrick's Day parade that wound through South Boston. It lacked local flavor. It had the hollow gaiety of a public relations event and featured a marching unit from the First Cavalry Division of Fort Hood, Texas!

Meanwhile, the political parade never ended. The Fourth Councilor District was redrawn, and Sonny McDonough lost several wards in Boston as well as Revere, Chelsea and Winthrop. In their place he was given such South Shore communities as Cohasset, Weymouth, Brockton, Hanover, Hingham and Marshfield. To Sonny, those were frontier outposts endangered by tribes of Republicans brandishing political tomahawks.

"I'm going to have to get out and hustle," he told me. "Maybe you can help."

I did my best.

His opponent, whom he referred to as "the kid," was twenty-five-year-old James Hunt of Dorchester. Hunt had been a Democrat, but he was running as an Independent. He claimed Sonny was in Florida half the time he was supposed to be serving on the Executive Council. Sonny explained that he kept in close touch — by phone.

"I can be there in three hours by plane," Sonny said.

Mike Barnicle, a columnist for the *Boston Globe,* asked him about the expense to constituents who could reach him only by telephoning Florida.

"*My* constituents," Sonny said with a superior air, "use slugs."

Asked if he was worried about his first serious challenge for reelection in years, he puffed on a cigar and said, "I've never worried as long as I get up in the morning and don't find my name in the death notices in the newspapers."

I decided to leave the quips to Sonny while I tried to carry a more serious message of his qualifications to voters. There was much material. He had fathered the first Fair Employment Practices law in Massachusetts and the Fair Educational Practices program. His efforts lowered telephone rates, raised workers' compensation to a decent level, created benefits for the aged and better treatment for the mentally ill. He won passage of the "loanshark" bill that established legislative control of interest rates in small loans, saving millions each year for borrowers. He supported economy in government and brought about major reforms in the correctional system. And it was Sonny — not any civic group — that made the Executive Council open its sessions to the public.

It was a difficult campaign, but Sonny won.

Sonny liked to say, "I'm a bit of a rogue." In his next campaign, he proved it by being guest of honor at a $100-a-plate "Appreciation Night." Only Sonny could have carried it off. He was running unopposed. He was wealthier than most of his contributors. But he thanked them all — the governor, the judges, the legislators and all the others who had donated — and with a straight face added, "Thank God, now I will never have to be on welfare."

We would urge one another not to talk incessantly about the busing threat to our community. We would advise one another to try to keep away from the subject for at least one night. We would say let's go out to dinner or take a walk or see a movie — anything — but let's not stay in and talk about *it*. Let's not talk about it on the telephone. Let's not spend tonight writing to relatives about it.

But we could not escape those doleful nocturnes. Night was the season of reveries, and ours were troubled. Our problem was like a gun pointed at us. It was not possible to look away from it.

A deep and growing hostility festered in us. It was not directed against the parents of Roxbury, but it *was* aimed at the entire pro-busing apparatus, at those who would lie about us and represent us as being against desegregation or even characterize us as racists. It was directed against any blacks who, angered by the racial rhetoric in the media, attempted to act violently toward us.

But we held together. If anything, we shared a closer intimacy than ever, born of the loneliness of our cause.

I met Joe Stafford one morning on Castle Island. He told me he had been "walking and walking and walking," trying to decide what to do.

I asked him what he meant.

"I went up to the Tynan School, where my daughter is," he said, "and I look in one class and here's this big guy. He's got a pool stick in his hands. When anybody gets near him he starts swinging it and swearing at them, and everybody is scared of him."

I asked him how they brought the student under control.

"I don't know," he said. "Maybe they didn't. Maybe he's still down there swinging that damned stick or braining somebody with it. I left and went down the corridor to my little girl's class."

"Was she all right?" I asked.

"Nobody was hitting on her," he said, "but when I looked in, she was sitting next to this pregnant girl who couldn't have been more than fourteen. I thought, My God, this is a bloody nightmare. I don't know how to deal with it, Bill."

I didn't like what I saw in Joe's face. It upset me. I wondered how long we could keep a lid on this boiling pot.

Soon after, there came the day when André Jean-Louis, a Haitian taxi driver, wandered into an anti-busing demonstration. A young man suddenly began punching Jean-Louis and had to be restrained by the demonstrators.

The assailant turned out to be Joseph Griffin, the disturbed youth who had cowered in his home, hiding from imagined foes he feared would climb through the windows to beat him. He had picked the worst possible time to venture forth, and had attacked a man who posed a threat to no one. Surely the media's insistence that there was a growing black-white hostility had done nothing to calm Griffin's apprehensions. Except in his confused mind, he certainly needed no protection from Jean-Louis.

We knew all about Joseph Griffin. We knew his mental stability had always been precarious. However, we were sure our foes would make no allowances for any of *that*. The media made it sound as though the entire population of the area had attacked the Haitian. Humberto Cardinal Madeiros told us the incident had been reported that way around the world.

Griffin was not the only mentally or emotionally disturbed person we saw in South Boston. I recall seeing one stoop-shouldered old man who wore a long army overcoat. I had never seen him before and never saw him again. I don't think he lived in our district. He was huge and had the wild white hair, the explosively whiskered face and the obsidian eyes of an Old Testament prophet who had been struck by lightning and survived. He carried a sign reading BOMB THE BASTARDS. People looked at him, shrugged and went about their business.

There *were* scattered incidents of violence in South Boston. In a community of many thousands, with emotions running high, there are always a few who enjoy violence and seek any excuse for doing it. We had some among us, ranging from the simple-minded to the bully, who occasionally attacked blacks on our streets, but they almost always found themselves confronted by their neighbors. The overwhelming majority of our people deplored such conduct. They knew it was not only wrong in itself, but that it also provided our opponents with opportunities to fortify their criticism of us with selective evidence, inevitably exaggerated.

There were also attacks by blacks. But if white-on-black violence was reported in lurid headlines and amid shrieks of civic outrage — and it was — black-on-white crimes were not. And the latter were much more violent.

In one case, a white man took a wrong turn in his car and went down a one-way street in Roxbury. No one alleged that he had done or said anything to incite violence, but he was attacked and severely injured by a black mob.

There was Ludivico Barba, who was standing in the water at Carson Beach, fishing. A gang of black thugs approached him from behind and stoned him to death. They also stabbed him. Reading accounts of the incident, I had the impression the victim had shown extremely bad taste in dying and "possibly" exacerbating matters.

A white woman whose car ran out of gas in Roxbury walked to a filling station and purchased a gallon can of fuel. While returning to her car, she was forced into an alley by black youths, who poured the gasoline over her and set her afire. She was horribly burned and it took her five hours to die.

White-on-black violence was almost always considered racially motivated. Much worse violence by blacks on whites was very rarely considered to be such. In several cases, blacks armed with knives held up whites — which cannot be said to be racially motivated crimes. Frequently, however, after collecting all the cash or jewelry, they proceeded to stab and slice their victims viciously. It is difficult to imagine a reason for that other than racial hatred.

The head of the Community Disorders Unit of the Boston Police, a resident of Cohasset, hardly ever saw it that way. He didn't explain. He simply declared what was racially motivated, and what was not.

The *Globe* reported a clash between black and white students at South Boston High School. We said the troublemakers, whatever their color, should be expelled or in some way removed from the school. We proposed to Judge Garrity that they be sent to a special course in behavior at an institution on Thompson Island. As the evidence came in, however, it clearly showed that black students had been the attackers, and the judge responded, "They cannot be sent to an educational Siberia because they are aggressive. Aggressive students are often the future leaders of a community and may be the ones to benefit most from a normal education."

We knew full well what happened to any of our "future leaders" who got aggressive: they were dragged, often beaten by police, to the Siberia of a cellblock — and the education they received there was not of an academic sort.

The *Globe* editorial writers were in lockstep with the judge. An editorial explained that a clash between students was "not necessarily unproductive, if an education in living and working together is the result."

Not only was the logic insane, but even the facts were wrong. It had not been a clash between students. It had been a gang of black students attacking a smaller group of whites.

Throughout the period of forced busing, not a single black was seriously injured or murdered because he was black. Whites *were* seriously injured and whites *were* killed because they were white.

Any conclusion that the criminal misconduct by some black youths was condoned by their community, or that it was indicative of any racial proclivity, would be unjust and absurd. It would be the same as suggesting that all whites endorsed the violence by white troublemakers and shared their instincts. In each case, the faults were the faults of individuals, and it would be factually and morally wrong to imply or infer otherwise.

The myth of incipient violence in South Boston resulted in huge overtime-pay allowances for Boston's police. Commissioner diGrazia kept stirring that pot of gold by warning of dire plots by South Boston residents:

Police units were placed on alert to guard against a planned attack on Roxbury — which never happened and was never planned. Then diGrazia had information that we were planting bombs, which sent squads of police searching under bridges and elsewhere on overtime pay. No bombs were found; there weren't any; the only time I knew of the word being used was on a sign carried by the strange man in the army overcoat whom everyone thought crazy.

The fewer the dangers, the more sentries diGrazia posted.

Mayor White was cautioned that he was marked for assassination by my brother, James, who was described by an anonymous police source as an anti-busing extremist!

The police warned vaguely of "snipers." No resident ever fired a shot in South Boston, but someone *did* fire a rifle at a window in the *Globe* plant. It was not lost on the people of our district that the only ones who benefited from that shot were the police, who were then assigned in force to see that it didn't happen again.

The extra pay from such assignments created a feeding frenzy. Officers, most of whom lived in suburbs where their children were in unaffected schools, doubled and in some cases tripled their income by trying to keep our children in Judge Garrity's buses. As busing costs soared, their overtime pay reached record highs. They enlarged their homes. They bought new and better automobiles. They purchased yachts and with a grim humor named many of them *Phase I* or *Phase II*, referring to the phases of the busing plan. To us, they were a hostile army of occupation.

Before the schools opened in 1974, diGrazia said 1,400 Boston policemen would be available for school duty. That left less than half the force for the safety of the half million or more uninvolved citizens of the city. A year later he had 1,600 police officers on duty in South Boston. There were supporting contingents of Metropolitan District Commission officers and state police as well. There were 100 federal marshals and 50 FBI agents. Some 600 National Guard troops were in ready reserve. Judge Garrity was in command of a virtual invasion force and seemed delighted with his role.

Stirred up by all the police reports of our nonexistent plans for violence, Governor Francis Sargent called out the National Guard. Troops were gathered at the Fargo building, a sprawling structure operated by the U.S. Navy. They were on television, wearing combat gear and carrying shields and clubs as well as their rifles, and going through crowd-control exercises in the area in front of the building. The spectacle was amusing in a terrible sort of way, because we knew — as did those who called them out — that there was nothing for them to control.

However, it infuriated the people of South Boston. The sight of the armed soldiers was more than they could bear. Hundreds from our district converged on the Fargo building and began throwing stones at the guardsmen who, after a brief show of menace, thought better of it and ran into the building.

I told the leaders of the attack that they might feel better but they had solved nothing, while providing further ammunition for those who were trying to depict us as ravening animals.

It was the women of South Boston who saved us from what otherwise might have degenerated into an extremely serious confrontation.

They simply took charge. It was not planned. There was no formal declaration. They were mothers protecting their young — and the anger of the men was as nothing compared with the intensity of the women. It was an intensity that came, I believe, from the womb, and it was enough to awe any man.

Firmly and quietly they formed what must be one of the most formidable grassroots movements in the history of urban American politics. The men sensed what was happening, sensed the right of the women to seize the initiative, and accepted their leadership.

New rules were emanating from Judge Garrity's court with dizzying frequency. The people of South Boston were forbidden to gather in certain areas of their district. In some areas, two could gather, but not three. In other areas, even two could not be together. It was permissible, the judge ruled, for residents to speak to one another on the street, provided they kept moving in opposite directions as they did so!

The women seemed to thrive on the adrenaline of crisis. They defied him immediately. Six of them gathered on a street corner, where diGrazia's troops arrested them for praying against busing.

In district court we argued that the First Amendment says Congress shall make no law abridging freedom of speech or the right of the people peaceably to assemble and to petition the government for a redress of grievance. I argued, "No law means *no* law."

The court agreed and the women were found not guilty. Judge Garrity had no comment, but kept on issuing new rules.

I recall mothers who carried signs on their backs listing the crime statistics for Roxbury — highest in the city and some eight hundred percent higher than South Boston, the city's safest neighborhood. Beneath the statistics were the words "This is where they want to send my children."

I saw indications of the growing involvement of women in my own home. Michael Dukakis, a candidate for governor, strongly supported Judge Garrity's busing plan. Mary pointed out a photograph in the morning newspaper showing Mrs. Dukakis taking their children to a neighborhood school in Brookline.

"Why," Mary asked, her eyes flashing, "can't I take *my* children to our neighborhood school?"

When Dukakis became governor, I tried hard to work with him, and we got along well. But I could never quite get over the pain of knowing that he harbored such contempt for me and my family that he would want my children shipped to inferior schools. I wondered what the reaction of Dukakis and his wife, Kitty, would have been if told that their children were to be bused into a high-crime area.

No, I didn't wonder. I knew what it would have been.

Women organized meetings. They lobbied at the statehouse. They organized the Women's Auxiliary, a group that went out on assignment to print the word NEVER! in bold red spray paint on walls and bridges and fences throughout our area.

I recall one day meeting a member of that contingent, Fawnie McDonough. She looked exhausted.

"Fawnie, what's wrong?" I asked.

"I was on graffiti until four o'clock this morning," she said matter-of-factly. "I'll be fine after a bit of a lie-down."

When busing proponents tried to divide the women's front by offering well-paid jobs at South Boston High School, the answer was a pamphlet urging: "Sign Up for a Job at South Boston High

... Send a Neighbor's Child to Roxbury ... The Pay Is Good ... Praise Is High ... All You Have to Do Is Betray Your Neighbors. Hurry!"

The women developed an intricate informational system that would be the envy of any political campaign. The *Globe* treated it as though it were a subversive activity. "The system of spreading news in Southie is now clear," the paper revealed. "Two 'informationists' each call four 'coordinators' who each call six 'area captains' who each call 'block captains' who each call about a dozen neighbors. Within three or four hours, the network can have everybody in South Boston ... out marching."

Rita Graul and Virginia Sheehy were typical of many. They lived on Grimes Street, a small way behind St. Augustine's Church. No one could intimidate them. They were unfailingly courteous, but determined, tireless — and tough as tenpenny nails.

I recall them clashing with Thomas Atkins of the NAACP.

"Who are you that you can tell us what to do with our children?" Rita asked him.

"It's the court that's telling you," Atkins answered.

"Well, we'll take no orders from the court that are against the best interests of our children," Virginia said.

When their words were reported to Judge Garrity, he ordered the women to appear in court.

"Tell the court that we're not appearing," Rita told Atkins.

"We'll see about that," Atkins said — but the judge backed down and we heard no more of it.

It was another illustration of the power of the women. It also served to identify them clearly to the entire pro-busing apparatus as the primary force that must be reckoned with.

When Judge Garrity would attend the Clover Club banquet at the Park Plaza Hotel, there was concern about the fact that most of the waitresses were women from South Boston. A special waiter was engaged to attend to the judge's needs. That may have been one of Judge Garrity's more judicious decisions.

The Protestant Council of Churches — which condemns Catholic clerics who become involved in current affairs — plowed

into the forced-busing issue. They released a statement supporting
the judge's actions and telling those who opposed it to comply
peaceably. This from a group that sympathized with those who
burned draft cards, occupied college facilities violently and even
rioted in the streets. But the women of South Boston were dis-
turbers of the peace when they wheeled baby carriages down the
main street of their community bearing signs protesting forced
busing.

I repeatedly challenged the clergy — Protestant, Catholic and
Jewish — who criticized us from afar. I would say, "To show your
sincerity, urge your parishioners and congregants to place *their*
children at the disposal of Judge Garrity." I know of none of them
whose "sincerity" went that far. In any case, no one answered my
challenge.

A group of mothers decided to wheel their carriages from Farragut Park at City Point to the Broadway subway station. When
they reached the corner of G Street and East Broadway, they were
met by a phalanx of the Tactical Police Force. This was a paramili-
tary force of men selected on the basis of their size, strength and
appetite for combat. They wore helmets and special jumpsuits.
They were armed. And they carried clubs and other instruments
for coping with frenzied crowds.

In front of this martial array, lined up on G Street, stood Commissioner diGrazia, arms locked behind him in a chesty parade-
rest position, facing the mothers with their baby carriages. The
mothers stood there in silence. They had broken no law. They had
covered most of their planned route peaceably and could see the
termination point from where they stood. They felt threatened by
the show of force, but they didn't retreat. They showed not the
slightest sign of fear.

I asked diGrazia which mother or child he intended to club
first. He told me pompously that he was keeping watch to make
certain we behaved. I thought at once of the ancient question
"Who will watch the watchers?" As a deliberate and, I suppose,
petty means of aggravation, I put the question to him in Latin:
"Sed quis custodiet ipsos custodes?"

His eyes squinted and he looked as though he were trying to decide whether I had said something vile to him.

"You got a big mouth, Bulger," he said. "Why don't *you* try something."

"All right," I said. "I'll try explaining to you why you're a disgrace to this city and to your uniform."

"You and these damn women get off the street," he said. His mouth was trembling with anger.

I told him, "These women and I will walk down this street long after this city has gotten rid of you and your storm troopers. That's a promise, diGrazia — and I keep my promises."

I did ask the mothers to avoid confrontation. I had not the slightest doubt diGrazia's uniformed hoodlums would use their clubs on them.

Virginia Sheehy said, "Tell diGrazia we'll be back."

I said, "I think he knows that."

The incident was a terrible reminder that a government will always be able to find men ready for such work. There is a breed that has always surfaced when any government wanted their kind. Make no mistake about it: they are available today and will be whenever needed in all the tomorrows. They enjoy their work.

One late afternoon Henry Roberts — known for some reason lost in history as The Good Robb — came to my home, his eyes shining with achievement, and told me he had great news. "Bill, there's a cop wants to help you," he said.

"Why would he want to do that?"

"Jeez," he said, "would you just meet this guy? He wants to have supper with you. C'mon, Bill, just as a favor to me."

I knew from experience that The Good Robb's advice was almost inevitably bad, but it seemed I was always saying no to him, and he was a loyal friend. I asked him when the man wanted to meet with me.

"Tonight. At eight o'clock," Roberts said, and gave me the name of a diner in the South End.

So I went. There was a tall, gaunt figure sitting at the counter and he waved at me. He was a wiry man with quick, cautious eyes, long of forehead and short of chin. He wore a shiny black suit and heavy-toed cop shoes, and he shook hands with his left hand.

I had a cup of tea and a dangerous-looking bowl of stew, and listened to him.

"I think you people are getting a lousy deal," Murphy said. "I can help you."

"How can you do that?"

"I'm in headquarters," he explained. "I know everything that sonofabitch diGrazia plans. I can keep you informed so you can do whatever you have to do."

"You mean you'll be a spy for us?" I asked.

"Well — I guess that's what it comes down to," he said, wincing a little as though he found my directness a shade uncouth. He sat there chewing slowly while he thought things over, and then he said, "You know something, I like you." He said this as though he found it remarkable.

But I didn't like him.

He smiled a lot but his face had a vulpine aspect, and the smiles did nothing to relieve it. He affected an easy, relaxed manner, but I knew that beneath it he was tense as a held breath. Watching his shrewd, hard face as he talked of spying, I sensed he had a strong natural inclination for that sort of thing.

"You know," I told him, "we're not big on spies in South Boston. It's a tribal thing, I guess. We'll pass."

The venomous look on his face as I left persuaded me that he was indeed a spy — one sent to spy on *us*. After I told that to The Good Robb, he went around the district referring to the officer as "the Judas cop" until I told him to drop it. Some mothers asked me and other South Boston lawyers to establish guardianships so their children could move in with others outside our community. We did so and wished them well, however sadly.

Many women returned to the workplace they had abandoned at the time of their marriage. They took almost any job they could get in order to raise the tuition to send their children to parochial school. This outraged activists, who asked parochial schools to close their doors to any who were using those facilities as an "escape hatch" to avoid forced busing.

South Boston's Gate of Heaven Church, not wanting to be drawn into the controversy, announced it would seal off access to its school. I went there and acknowledged that mothers — mostly Catholic mothers — were clerking, waiting on tables, washing dishes and scrubbing floors to rescue their children. I argued that it would be a terrible betrayal to tell them their children were unwelcome. "If there is no sanctuary in a church, then where?" I asked.

It wasn't easy for church officials, who knew they would be vilified if they admitted children from the affected public schools. Eventually they bit the bullet and changed their minds. They even agreed to create a new first-grade class, as I had implored them to do.

Some mothers soon began discussing the creation of private academies. That was brought to the judge's attention. He speculated on the possibility of draconian punishments. Busing, as an end in itself, possessed him. He was committed to it with an almost religious zeal. It seemed for him the ultimate goal, the Holy Grail, the New Jerusalem. He was, I suppose, as honest as his obsession allowed. But it has been said we are always most violent against those whom we have injured, and he was relentless against all those who resisted him. He kept turning the thumbscrew — turning it, turning it — and insisting there be no outcry from the pain. My youthful faith in the innate fairness of the judicial process, the wisdom and evenhandedness of all judges . . . goodbye to all that.

I was asked for legal advice, and I told my constituents that as long as the academies met academic standards, there were few sanctions available to the judge. It was not yet a crime to stay off his buses, so long as the children were not guilty of truancy. The only real punishment, I told them, would be the libel of the media who would accuse them of ugly motives.

South Boston's parents were used to that. Call someone a false name often enough, and the pain threshold rises until the victim no longer winces.

So they did not wince. The academies came into existence — and swiftly and dramatically outperformed the city's public schools in all desirable respects.

We had been condemned by Protestant spokesmen. Even some leaders in the Catholic clergy were disturbed by what they considered our stubbornness. Only one strong, clear voice spoke to give us strength: the voice of a Jewish academic.

His name was Oscar Handlin. He was chairman of the editorial board of WCVB-TV, a station whose news department had trashed us vigorously. In a broadcast editorial Handlin said in part:

> South Boston is probably the most cohesive, self-conscious and proud neighborhood in the city. In many ways, it is a perfect example of what Americans mean when they speak of neighborhood.
>
> . . . Nothing concerns South Boston more than education and the future of its neighborhood schools. State Senator William Bulger, who represents South Boston on Beacon Hill, says the threat of forced busing jeopardizes the very survival of his community . . .
>
> We view with tragic alarm the confrontation which may . . . grip South Boston. It is a great paradox of our modern urban existence that this neighborhood, with such tremendous desire and apparent strength to survive its other problems, may be torn apart to achieve the admittedly worthy goal of integration.
>
> We have no right to judge which is the greater good. We do believe, however, that the survival of Boston's neighborhoods is a matter of the greatest importance.
>
> The strength of any neighborhood lies in its sense of identity and its shared values. South Boston has, and will need, that strength.

Dr. Handlin could have won an election in South Boston the next day.

We found some of the strength Dr. Handlin had mentioned

when Dr. James Coleman of the University of Chicago announced he had surveys showing busing was causing whites to flee their cities.

We were aware white flight was a growing problem. Families were buying or renting homes, or moving in with relatives, in the suburbs or in unaffected cities. Men and women by the thousands were leaving Dorchester, Charlestown and East Boston. At the time there was a significantly smaller, but still disturbing, exodus from South Boston. But we knew our people would leave in droves if their community effort failed.

However, for Coleman to make such a statement was an extraordinary event: he was considered by many to be the father of forced busing. While at Johns Hopkins University, he had been the principal author of a report on educational inequalities that was routinely cited by courts to justify busing. It was known as the Coleman Report and had given the professor national prominence. Now, suddenly, he was speaking the unspeakable — finding fault with forced busing.

Dr. Ernest Q. Campbell, dean of the graduate school of Vanderbilt University, who had worked with Coleman on the landmark report, shared Coleman's concern. Campbell said, "The goals sought by large-scale busing are desirable, but the negative consequences . . . are larger than we thought."

Coleman was instantly decanonized. Those who had previously insisted his word was gospel now condemned his apostasy. It was a swift decline from social saint to social heretic.

Coleman would not retreat. He said that when court-ordered remedies went beyond redress of *specific* acts causing segregation, "they have exacerbated the very racial isolation they have attempted to overcome."

Coleman said a court should not attempt to assume the function of educators. Integration could not be accomplished by a court order seeking racial balance, he said; such efforts disrupted classrooms and stripped control from parents.

He visited me at the statehouse. I told him I was most bothered by the continuing effort of busing proponents to make me appear hostile to people because of their skin color. I assured him they would not intimidate me with that sort of thing, but it stung.

"The irony is that you and those you represent have done no wrong," he said. "There is the wrongdoing school department on the one hand, the aggrieved black parents on the other, and you people represent the innocent third party. You should not be shy about saying so."

I assured Coleman with a straight face that I would try not to be shy.

That seemed to please him. He nodded a few times and said, "Your critics who have chosen the racial isolation of suburbia are the true segregationists. They may not intend to be, but if you judge them by their acts, that is the course they have chosen."

Judge Garrity could not ignore Coleman's statements, but the judge's team of experts always had someone in the wings to tell them what they wanted to hear. This time it was a "demographer" at Boston University, Dr. Christine H. Rossell. She said there was no flight.

Dr. Coleman, unaccustomed to having his research challenged, made an affidavit and filed it with the court, swearing that forced busing was causing white flight.

Back came Dr. Rossell to tell us not to worry. "There is little or no white flight as a result of busing," she said.

That was what the judge wanted to hear. He announced that white flight was a fiction. He referred to reports to the contrary — including, obviously, Dr. Coleman's affidavit — as "wild estimates." The judge said white flight was all in the minds of those who opposed forced busing.

Unfortunately white flight was well under way, as later evidence would prove beyond question.

I remember one morning, driving on Atlantic Avenue, thinking of how much had changed in my life. The past came to my mind like a series of old snapshots in an album: Powers and McCann . . . the enigmatic Sisitsky . . . Speaker Thompson, the sad Iron Duke . . . the Crime Commission . . . friends like Moakley, Finnerty, Feeney,

Julius Ansel, and so many more. I thought, almost with nostalgia, of the days I had spent in the district court — I say "almost" because I was grateful to be free of that grind.

The rush of so many memories became oppressive, so I turned on the radio to hear the news. I heard the fluted tones of an announcer broadcasting from the Northern Avenue waterfront, where a huge British sailing ship had arrived.

"There is a woman being restrained by police," the announcer was saying. "I am told she is a state representative from Somerville named Marie Howe. I'll try to speak to her as she goes by."

I knew Marie well. She was a leader in protests about the situation in Northern Ireland. She was almost literally at war with the British government.

On one occasion Marie, theatrical as thunder and surrounded by a coven of her supporters, had boiled into the Prudential building followed by a battery of reporters and television cameras. She had come to do battle with the British consul. Her entrance suggested ruffles and flourishes. I could not recall the nature of her grievance, but Marie had descended on the consulate like an army with banners and stood in the corridor demanding confrontation.

The consul, Alistair Maitland, a slight and courteous man who seemed appalled by the spectacle, came to the door and invited Marie into his office.

"I will not set foot on British soil!" Marie said disdainfully.

That was vintage Marie. I wondered what she had done now.

I did not have long to wonder. The announcer with the mouth full of plums was back to explain that Marie Howe had been arrested for biting a British sailor. He said Marie, waiting on the dock with a group of women, had shouted something and the sailor had shouted back at her. "At that point," the announcer said, "Representative Howe ran up the gangplank and bit the sailor."

The poor woman, I thought, has finally gone round the bend. Then I heard the announcer calling: "Representative . . . Representative Howe . . . why did you bite that sailor?"

Back came Marie's voice, loud and clear. "I was standing up to the Brits," she said. "I am not worried about this case at all. I will get justice, real justice, in the South Boston District Court."

I shook my head in disbelief, and I could not resist smiling.

Marie's voice began to fade as the police led her away, but it was still strong enough for me to hear her parting words: "My lawyer is Senator William Bulger."

For a moment I found myself staring incredulously at the radio instead of the road. I pulled my car over to the curb and parked. I sat there wondering, Why me? Why do these things happen to me?

There was no way I could escape, though, without appearing to desert my fellow legislator and friend in her dark hour. So two weeks later there was Marie, demurely camouflaged in a shirt-waist dress with a Peter Pan collar, walking with me into South Boston District Court. We had to wade through reporters and cameramen. Inside, the courtroom seemed to be occupied by the entire British Navy.

The incident that brought us there, as described to me by Marie, was substantially this: She had walked up the gangplank behind the sailor, trying to reason with him. While she was speak-ing, he had turned suddenly, gesticulating with his hand, and in the process had struck her teeth, "because my mouth was open, you see."

"Marie," I said, "that's an improbable story — except for the part about your mouth being open."

A British sailor rose and addressed the court. "You wouldn't believe it, your honor," he said. "I was going down the gangplank when this woman who was down on the dock with a bunch of pickets began yelling we should get out of her country." He looked balefully at Marie for a moment and then went on: "I could see she was a wild one, your honor, so I turned around to go back on the ship. She come charging up the gangplank and she bit me. She *bit* me! Look at my hand, your honor, which was perfectly good till she got her teeth into it." He held the bandaged member out for inspection, adding, "How many countries do these people think they own?"

Judge Joseph Feeney's expression was glacial. Feeney had been born in South Boston but, when orphaned at an early age, had been sent to relatives in County Galway, where he had spent his youth. Galway is notably restrained when it comes to sympathy for things British.

The clerk was John Flaherty. Ralph Clougherty was the assistant clerk. Charley Gibbons was the court officer. All aggressively Irish. None seemed passionately distressed by the sailor's plight.

Judge Feeney stopped glaring at the complainant. His demeanor softened. Then, in a memorable demonstration of South Boston's tradition of impartiality in such things, he turned to Marie. "Now, dear," he said with avuncular tenderness, "why don't you tell us what *really* happened."

The court, after profound analysis of the evidence, was unable to discover clear criminal intent on Marie's part, and suggested that the sailor's remedy, if any, was a civil matter. All of which meant that Marie had been allowed one free bite.

It is undeniable that the British sailor was a victim of the deep-rooted South Boston bias against anything or anybody English. As the defendant's lawyer, I did not want to lose the case, but I felt uncomfortable winning it.

So she was innocent; I felt a little guilty.

The Boston School Committee was being stripped of all its powers. On the date when Phase I of the busing plan ended, the judge told the committee it was essentially out of business.

He impatiently ordered all busing-related bills to be paid promptly out of city funds. The city explained that in some things it could not go faster, because it was bound by laws governing bidding procedures. The judge was disdainful of such temerity. He told the city to forget its bidding procedures and get on with paying the costs of busing. He said he'd find the funds, if necessary. His manner made me think of Lady Macbeth's scornful words to her hesitant and pusillanimous spouse: "Infirm of purpose! Give me the daggers."

The cost of Phase I busing was estimated at $11 million. Ninety days later, the projection was revised to $24 million, not including building renovations and an additional $7 million for police overtime. The ultimate cost of Phase II is lost in a labyrinth of separate accounts, but two things are clear: it was much more costly than Phase I, and it included millions to pay for muscular monitors to deal with violence on the buses and in the schools.

Two days before Christmas in 1975, with Phase II in full swing, Judge Garrity announced that East Boston High School would not be a district school the following year. Beginning in September of 1976, he said, it would be a citywide vocational school, with three quarters of the seats reserved for students who did not reside in East Boston.

With his ready gallows humor he told the representatives of the Boston School Committee, "Go and spread the bad news."

The judge next drew a bead on Boston Latin, one of the nation's most prestigious public high schools and the jewel of our city's system. It was designed to encourage scholarship, and applicants were required to pass a stiff entrance examination. Thomas Atkins and his cohorts saw that if someone was able to pass the test, he or she could avoid forced busing. They told the judge that meant Boston Latin was another "escape hatch."

The judge moved mercilessly to close it. He did. He announced that more than a third of the seats would be reserved for minorities from underrepresented areas.

The headmaster of Boston Latin, Dr. Wilfred O'Leary, whose entire life was absorbed in the magnificent school he headed, said he hoped Judge Garrity's order was limited to minority students who could pass the entrance examination. "Otherwise," he said, "it's all over. It will all be lost. All the excellence. It will be gone, and we'll never see it back in our time."

The judge would have none of that. He said minority students would not have to take any examination. Had they taken one of the previous tests, he explained blithely, they might well have scored better than those who did take it. If that were so, of course, they could be admitted to the school without any help from the judge: Boston Latin had always accepted students on the basis of academic showing, not skin color.

What of those who had taken the examination? One third of them were displaced by the judge's ruling. My son James was one of them. He had worked hard to prepare himself and had scored well on the test. His place was now given to a person who had not qualified — simply because James was the wrong color.

This reverse Jim Crow law established iron quotas on Boston Latin. It has been the common experience that quotas, diluting admission policy as they do with a consideration other than sheer scholarship, militate against the preservation of academic excellence, however heroic the efforts of the administration and faculty.

As we neared the decade of the eighties, the Senate had an unusually strong leadership team. The media's political experts saw dazzling futures for all of them. Like the generality of such pundits, they were dazzlingly wrong.

So was I. It never occurred to me that, like characters in some implausible melodrama, most of them would become tragic figures — nor could I imagine how profoundly their destinies would shape mine.

The leadership included Kevin Harrington of Salem, the Senate president; Joseph J. C. DiCarlo of Revere, the majority leader; and James A. Kelly Jr. of Oxford, chairman of the pertinent and puissant Senate Ways and Means Committee. Harrington, canny and competent, had been a basketball player in his youth, and looked it: a husky pituitary prodigy with the easy physical grace of an athlete. DiCarlo was intelligent, articulate, very resourceful and extremely ambitious. Kelly was a doctrinaire liberal with robot-like obedience to editorial writers who portrayed him as the brain and soul of the Senate. Harrington and DiCarlo were occasionally admonished by the press, but Kelly could do no wrong.

I had an uneasy relationship with Harrington. At times he commended me for what he perceived as my skill in advocacy and in the mechanics of enacting legislation. At other times he railed at what he deemed my stubborn and unrelenting opposition to some measures he favored. He was particularly incensed when I chided him — as I did often — for his sensitivity to public opinion.

DiCarlo I found to be a pleasant man, less austere than Harrington, but more reserved with me than with other compatriots. Sometimes when I entered a room where Joe was talking with Kelly, their conversation would end and DiCarlo would leave as soon as he decently could. I assumed he found me too brash or aggressive for his taste. Nevertheless I wished him well, largely because while attending a dinner for DiCarlo in Tecce's restaurant I had been touched to see the pride and joy that lit the face of his father, an Italian immigrant. It made me hope that DiCarlo would achieve his ambitions, not only for his own sake but for the likable old man who so obviously idolized him.

I just did not like Kelly. My distaste was partly intellectual: he impressed me as a dutiful hawker of the social nostrums of his media masters, an unprincipled creature thriving in a spiritual wilderness. My aversion was largely visceral, too. I sensed in him a predatory cunning. His air of sophistication struck me as studied and absurd. His accent seemed contrived. Even his *gait* annoyed me — the way he would bounce along with his toes turned out. It was clear to me that the feeling was reciprocal: he avoided me as though I carried some sort of contagious disease.

One day, to my surprise, he stopped me in passing and, relative to nothing, began a rapturous account of a dish he had enjoyed at a newly opened restaurant on the south side of Beacon Hill.

"You must try it," he told me.

"It sounds too much like a medical condition," I said curtly.

He seemed offended.

I disliked being so spontaneously short, even rude, with a human being who had done no hurt to me, and I tried to overcome it. I was determined to do so. I resolved to do so. But I could not. Instead, to worsen matters, there was in me a growing but totally unsubstantiated suspicion that the man was a scoundrel. I felt astonished and ashamed that I could make a judgment so cruelly gratuitous, yet there it was, instinctive and implacable.

DiCarlo appeared to take a giant career step when he was named to head a joint committee investigating costs in connection with construction of the University of Massachusetts. It was a high-profile position. To begin, the target was a major New York construction firm, McKee, Berger & Mansueto, which had been selected to oversee construction in preference to two Massachusetts firms. There was, in addition, an element of great political significance: the MBM contract had been approved for the state by Donald R. Dwight, a Republican who DiCarlo was convinced would be his ultimate foe when he sought higher office.

That committee appointment did in fact prove to be an enormous step for DiCarlo — right off the edge of the political cliff. Allegations bobbed to the surface in the sewage of rumors, rumors to the effect that members of the committee had been guilty of grave misconduct. Then the media, attributing their information to highly placed but unnamed informants, reported that subpoenas had been issued. Having lived through the masquerade of the Crime Commission, I was dubious.

But the media were right this time. DiCarlo, Kelly and the minority whip, Ronald C. MacKenzie, a Republican from Burlington, were charged with political corruption.

The government's case rested on the testimony of Gerald McKee Jr., president of MBM, who swore he authorized the payment of $40,000 to MacKenzie in five installments, and even made one delivery himself. He alleged MacKenzie had said $30,000 or $40,000 more might be required "to change things."

Anthony E. Mansueto, MBM's senior vice president, backed up McKee's testimony and swore that Kelly had solicited $100,000 on behalf of DiCarlo. There followed a parade of MBM employees who gave damaging testimony.

Judge Walter Jay Skinner ruled that the prosecution had failed to link Kelly to the DiCarlo-MacKenzie conspiracy. He ordered references to Kelly deleted from the indictment. The trial was not

Judge Skinner's first experience with political corruption: he had prosecuted for the Crime Commission the decade before.

On February 25, 1977, DiCarlo and MacKenzie were found guilty on all eight counts of political corruption involving MBM. After losing on appeal, both MacKenzie and DiCarlo were sent to federal prison for a year. They later admitted having extorted $23,000 from MBM in return for a favorable legislative report.

DiCarlo said he needed the money for the unceasing financial demands on political candidates. MacKenzie offered a form of bizarre expiation when he expressed hope that his crime would prove the need for public financing of campaigns.

MBM is now defunct.

The Senate was paralyzed. No one wanted to act on anything substantial for fear of tainting the outcome. Finally MacKenzie resigned. DiCarlo, who refused to do so, was expelled — the first senator in that body's 126-year history to suffer that ignominy.

And still it was not over.

The press reported that the Senate Ethics Commission was considering allegations that Harrington and Kelly had received campaign contributions from MBM. It was revealed that a $2,000 check made out to Harrington had been cashed at his Salem bank. Harrington admitted that the endorsement on the back of the check appeared to be his, but insisted he did not remember either endorsing or cashing it. Privately, he decided his gubernatorial prospects were gone.

He had to make a hard decision: his successor.

I knew he agonized over the problem. Kelly had too much baggage from the MBM scandal. Other possibilities were eliminated for one reason or another. He told me he needed someone with leadership qualities whose behavior would not result in another corruption scandal. With evident reluctance, he said he was naming me majority leader. That meant I was one step from the Senate presidency.

Soon the word spread that Harrington would not run the following January for another term as president. Five members of the Senate, disturbed by my appointment, met with Harrington. The group consisted of Bill Owens of Boston, Jack Backman of Brookline, John Olver of Amherst, Chester Atkins and Alan Sisitsky. They made various proposals, but Harrington did not budge. Meanwhile, many aspirants for the presidency surfaced. Most conspicuous among them was Stanley Zarod of Springfield, a protégé of John Powers. Although Zarod was several years my senior, Powers would call members of the Senate, pleading, "Give young Stanley Zarod a chance."

Stanley had gone to Dartmouth and then had returned to Springfield, where he operated the cash register in his father's saloon. It was remarkable: he seemed more a product of that dark barroom than his prestigious school.

His face had a strange expression, a sort of puzzled frown. He always looked as though he had just heard something highly improbable and was thinking it over. He was concerned about his vocabulary, which he considered too limited — as indeed it seemed to be. He would collect new words that impressed him and write them down. I recall being in a group one day when a senator referred to language in a pending bill as being confusing and almost arcane. The adjective seemed to fascinate Stanley.

"Arcane!" Zarod repeated, choked with admiration.

Senators held many informal discussions about the choice of Harrington's successor. Stanley would tell them he entertained grave concern about my ability. He was constantly breaking away to go to a telephone, and everyone knew he was reporting to Powers. The senators wondered whose concern Zarod really was expressing.

A caucus was held in Harrington's office on July 30, 1978, to consider a matter relating to the judiciary. Harrington took the occasion to tell the caucus formally that he was ready to resign. He asked everyone to support me as his replacement.

One senator suggested I should be elected immediately, so I'd be in a better position to be reelected in January. It was known, of course, that the press was hostile to me because of my position on forced busing. Another senator argued that if the election was delayed, it would allow powerful elements in the media five months to bludgeon members into choosing someone else.

There were dissenters:

The door entering the president's office is in a corner of the room, and when open it creates a considerable shadow. There was a chair in the shadow. My old nemesis McCann had sat down in the chair, and he remained in that dark refuge throughout the meeting. At times his voice would emerge, always urging delay. Senator Backman agreed. Backman was a vigorous supporter of busing and a flaming liberal, but he did not have the personal bitterness toward me that the Powers group had. His differences were ideological, and I respected him.

The caucus voted McCann and Backman down. I was elected. McCann and Backman, bound by the caucus decision, then voted for me.

Zarod was not involved. His many problems included a chronic inability to get anywhere on time. Powers had relied on "young Stanley" to lead the opposition, but there was no Zarod in evidence. He was still on the road from Springfield. He never understood the rules of the Senate, among them the rule that a scheduled caucus begins on time whether you are there or not.

By the time Stanley arrived, it was all over. He received the news with that habitual puzzled look on his face and went to the telephone, undoubtedly to inform Powers. What Powers told him I do not know, but Stanley immediately called a press conference to inform a hostile press of my selection.

"This is like a coup," he told them.

Some of the reporters who knew Stanley's fascination for what he considered exotic language began chiding him.

He was asked, "What exactly is a coup, Senator?"

"Well, it's a coup," Stanley said.

"Is it a coup d'état or a coup de main?" one reporter asked.

Another reporter asked, "How do you spell 'coup'?"

"I don't know too much about coups," Zarod said, "but I'm telling you — this was like a coup."

Dartmouth!

And so I became the eighty-fourth president of the state Senate.

The *Globe* was not enthusiastic. "Bulger . . . has not always been on the best of terms with Harrington," one writer revealed. "A hot dispute over rent control in December 1975 left them not even on speaking terms for several weeks." Columnist Robert Healy wrote, "Not every member of the state senate is overjoyed at the prospect of William Bulger becoming the senate president."

There was speculation in the press that I would not last long.

DiCarlo and now Harrington were gone. Two of the brightest stars in our political firmament had burned out. Only Kelly remained, and his light was dimmed.

Two years later, a bit older but apparently no wiser, Kelly was again indicted for extortion. The charges were separate from the MBM scandal. This time he was convicted of accepting $34,500 in bribes from an architectural design firm in Worcester, Masiello Associates, in return for steering design contracts to that company. He was sentenced to two years in prison.

Harrington was, I think, a victim of the political climate. He was accused, at most, of bad judgment in accepting a contribution from MBM. He was never accused of extorting it or of doing or promising anything in return for it, and none of the battalion of witnesses ever suggested he even knew of the DiCarlo-MacKenzie conspiracy. But he was undoubtedly careless and his timing was bad — two often fatal mistakes for anyone in public life.

It is the harshest of truths to acknowledge that DiCarlo, Mac-Kenzie and Kelly deserved what befell them. It is factually undeniable that they betrayed their public trust and, in the process, tarnished the entire legislature. They contributed to the media's fiction of a universal venality among politicians. I do not know whether they were corrupted by the power they achieved or whether some warped template had been implanted early in life. One way or another, they were flawed.

Yet I grieved for them, even for Kelly, whom I disliked and had long distrusted. I grieved for such waste. So much had been given to them, such opportunity for service and even greatness, and they had sold it for a fistful of trash. Most of all, I thought of the adoring face of DiCarlo's aged father, so full of pride as he looked at his golden son that night at Tecce's. It made me wonder whether the knife edge of criminal justice did not strike down as many of the innocent as it did of the guilty.

It took a decade and a half for our opposition to forced busing to be vindicated. The Supreme Court of the United States, upholding a California referendum, made it clear that no federal law empowered a court to order busing to achieve racial balance. Thus, unlawful segregation in schools was distinguished — as we had insisted all those agonizing years it should be — from racial imbalance, which is an economic and cultural phenomenon violative of no law.

As of this writing, matters have gone full cycle. To some extent, the memory of the judge still broods over our lives, and we yearn for the community structure that was ours before it was to some extent hammered out of shape by his gavel. We are left with an almost ineffable nostalgia, haunting as the melancholy of youth. But we have survived and still share an effulgent faith in our future.

The judge and his anger — if that is what it was — are gone. Commissioner diGrazia is gone. The Tactical Police and all the marshals are gone. We are thankful for all of that. Even the *Globe* has acknowledged, in a circumlocutory editorial, that busing was indeed a failure.

Some sociologists mourned for their lost dreams of social engineering, like Niobe for her lost children. They made me think of Voltaire who, when dying and asked to renounce the devil, is said to have replied, "This is not a time to make new enemies." But most of those who had considered busing more important than the rights of parents to supervise the education of their children recanted. One of the more striking examples was Christine Rossell of Boston University.

Dr. Rossell, who had insisted that busing caused no white flight, and who had been a member of the coordinating council that helped implement Judge Garrity's plan, changed her views completely. She appeared before Boston's city council *and urged a survey to discover the needs and wants of parents!* Personally, she said, she favored "walk to" schools. Asked about her pro-busing past by the council president, James Kelly, she said, "I was wrong. Now I can say that was a mistake."

In our city, the effort to strip poor parents of any right to protect their children and supervise their education was defeated — mostly, I believe, because of the courage and spirit of the women of South Boston. Their battle involved no issue of gender or economics, so the nation's feminists ignored them. But their demonstration of the latent power of women in our society was magnificent. They devoted a major slice of their lives to keeping their children off Judge Garrity's buses, and almost all of them succeeded in doing so. They were determined to preserve the identity of their community, and they did that. In the process, they challenged city, state and federal governments, thugs in police uniforms led by a brutal commissioner and the unsleeping malevolence of a hostile press.

And they accomplished remarkable results. They did that against all those odds. They did that because they were *right*.

The price was high. Six years after Judge Garrity's decision, some eighty thousand people had left Boston. The city's neighborhoods were weakened: Dorchester had lost twenty-four thousand. South Boston had lost eight thousand. Others had suffered similarly. Most ominous, one third of neighborhood families with children under the age of eighteen had vanished.

When it all came to an end — as come it had to if Boston were to survive — segregation, as measured by any standard, including the judge's yardstick of the Racial Imbalance Law, was much greater than ever before.

With forced busing, the public school system of Boston — birthplace of the common school and ranked as one of the country's best only two decades ago — became an academic slum. Dropout rates soared as high as fifty-six percent. Violence was rampant: we read of a student shot, a student stabbed, a headmaster cowed in his office at gunpoint, a school forced to close down because of rioting gangs, both male and female.

To glimpse the actual extent of chaos and brutality, one had to talk with parents and with school personnel afraid to speak out publicly. They told of the daily threats and assaults, the abuse and humiliation and sexual harassment, the malicious damage to clothing and other property, the extortion of money. And — everywhere — the pervasive climate of terror.

Those were the conditions in the eighties. A 1993 study, reported in the Boston press, expressed fresh dismay at the level of drugs, drinking and promiscuous sex in Boston's public schools. Obviously, education is not readily absorbed by students who are drunk, drugged and disorderly — nor by their classmates.

Forced busing ravaged our schools, but it is a powerful lobby, ludicrously entitled the National Education Alliance, that is preventing their salvage. The NEA, a union purporting to represent teachers, has a membership in the millions. With its ample war chest, it has enormous political clout. Indeed, some men and women in public life might fairly be described as wholly owned subsidiaries of that organization's lobby. Most school administrators and teachers have expressed opposition to the politicized agenda of their union leaders. Because of NEA policies, administrators are not free to administrate, teachers are not free to teach. They, like their students, are locked into a system that too often stifles initiative and rewards failure.

Teachers actually make up a dwindling percentage of those employed in the public school system. That is because the system is now glutted with nonteaching personnel, a bureaucracy of men and women that proliferates regulations, sets guidelines, develops procedures and, in the process, causes the overhead to soar. Salaries for teachers have declined as a proportion of operating budgets — a result of developing the bloated apparatus to politicize public education. That is where much of our educational funding is being spent, while teachers complain that they need more textbooks.

The leaders and agents of the public education lobby are not focused. They do not dedicate their time and funds to improving the quality of schools. Instead, they involve themselves as political activists in an endless array of issues such as abortion, gay rights, statehood for the District of Columbia, nuclear energy, aid for revolutionary movements in Latin America, the fitness of judicial nominees — and all the stops in between. None of those intensive and expensive activities, whatever the merit of the NEA's position, has any direct relevance to the immediate crisis in public education in Boston or elsewhere.

The NEA *does* have a panacea for all school problems: money. For more than a decade they have been insisting that more dollars mean better education. But the worst educational decline in this nation's history has been financed by the largest increases in spending. America now spends more on education — in both absolute terms and in cost per student — than any other nation in the world.

There have been studies — 150 of them at my last count — and all of them agree: no consistent relationship exists between increased funding and improvement in the quality of education.

In Massachusetts we have increased spending for education year after year. We have reduced the size of classes and provided for a higher ratio of teachers to students. In Boston we have been spending some $8,000 annually per student. That is higher than the state or national average, higher than private schools that achieve outstanding results. Our efforts prove the findings of all those studies: you can't spend your way to educational excellence.

A survey conducted by the U.S. Census Bureau, released in February of 1995, revealed that employers now rate the importance of educational credentials near the bottom of hiring criteria. Their explanation is that our schools are no longer teaching necessary and basic skills to students. A diploma, by itself, no longer certifies more than attendance at school.

There has been heroism on the part of many teachers. There have been outstanding examples of serious and dedicated students. There have been isolated instances of individual schools —

mostly elementary schools — that have shown dramatic improvement. Our public education system as a whole, however, is in critical condition. The only hope for rebuilding from the detritus of that system is for the schools to recapture their plants from gangs and thugs and restore discipline and an orderly climate conducive to learning. Administrators and teachers must be free to design meaningful curricula, and to teach language and literature and science and mathematics — and the enduring values of Judeo-Christian culture. Schools must compete for students by providing a venue for quality education. Most important of all, parents must be given meaningful opportunity to participate in the education of their children, to choose better schools for them. At present, parental choice is too often a cosmetic fraud designed by the teachers' lobby to frustrate the purpose it is alleged to serve.

In the quiet that follows the busing storm, it is difficult not to wonder at times how much of a permanent nature was really accomplished. All the passion, the fury — all the pain and sacrifices — spent or suffered for the sake of our children, it's all history; yet now, as is the way with history, it must be repeated. Again we must fight for children at risk, children trapped behind the barbed wire of our school bureaucracy. Most of the victims today are black or brown or yellow — but precious to the whitest among us because they are *children*. It will be a long, bitter struggle to salvage them, but it is one to which all people of goodwill must be committed to the end.

Severe residual damage remains. We may do much for the future, but we cannot retroactively reclaim the minds stunted by poor schooling in the past. And each year more young people are being discarded into a society that has no place for them. Lacking skills, unable to express themselves except in street jargon, they are not only unemployed, they are unemployable. Huge numbers of them lack essential arithmetical skills. They don't read. They can't write a simple high school composition, and they can't spell "grammar," much less use it in their speech. Their agonies will afflict our society in many ways, all the days of their lives. And each of their empty days in each of their empty lives must seem to them to be a death of a different sort.

During the busing ordeal, I rarely saw a tear in South Boston. There was grief aplenty, but not tears. The pain was too great for tears.

Superficially, our lives seemed to go on as usual. Men and women went to work each day. Shoppers crowded our markets. Small children skated or played street hockey. Their elder brothers and sisters went to community dances or enlivened other social activities. Grandmothers played beano and met in ice cream parlors when the game was over. Old men fished from our bridges.

Each year we adjusted to the cadence of the seasons. Each day when it wasn't raining, the sun came up over our stricken community — red and splendid or yellowed by the city's haze or bleached white by the sheen of an approaching storm. On clear nights the moon still silvered the sea, and the salty ocean breeze was faithful as ever. In those respects, everything seemed to be as it always had been.

But there was an alien presence among us, and its name was fear. Through it all we lived with an almost palpable sense of impending calamity — another threat, another defeat, another reason why it was difficult to keep alive that essential belief in the possibility of eventual happiness.

Yet believe we did. Somehow, we did that. And I suspect the reason may be found in the words of an old Irish song:

> Oh, the strangers came and tried to teach us their way.
> They scorned us just for being what we are.
> But they might as well go chasing after moonbeams
> Or light a penny candle from a star . . .

6

MY FRIENDS in Boston's Chinatown, which was and is in my district, had small regard for the Communist government that had seized the land of their ancestry. Their sympathies lay with those who had fled mainland China and settled on the island of Formosa, now called Taiwan. Tourism was a growing industry on the island, and this prompted Bill Chin, a friend of mine and a leader of his community, to suggest that on one of my trips to Ireland I might "stop along the way" to visit Taiwan.

Bill is a man of erudition: he knew full well Taiwan did not lie "along the way" to Ireland. What he was really saying was "You know, we vote, too." But he was too polite to put it that way.

Finally I agreed to go. I persuaded Mary to go with me, promising her a vacation she would never forget.

In preparation, and so I might make Mary's trip more enjoyable, I spent three hours at the Boston Public Library researching the stops along our way. Meanwhile, Mary wrote instructions, sixteen pages of them, for the baby sitter. She handed them to me.

"Add anything I've forgotten," she said.

I wrote "Pray" at the end of the list.

Our first stop was San Francisco where, assuming my role as guide, I recited the flora and fauna of California until I perceived her eyes glazing over. Then, to liven things, I described the great San Andreas Fault. "Oh, yes," I assured her, "experts predict a horrific earthquake someday. A lot of this state may just slide into the sea."

Mary has the heart of a lioness, but the discretion of the wise. "My God," she said, "when do we get out of here?"

"Oh, it won't happen before the next century," I said.

"You have a really firm commitment on that?"

Obviously, I had not started off too well.

Our plane landed, if I recall correctly, near the city of Taipei. We were warmly welcomed. The young woman who seemed to be in charge of everything was amiable and appeared to know what she was doing, so we followed her to a crowded bus.

We were told it would take us to our hotel. A seat had been reserved for us directly behind the driver. The other passengers smiled and waved at us. The language barrier was impenetrable, but we all bounced along happily together until, after considerable time, we reached the foot of a mountain.

Our driver, a young man who wore black trousers, a white shirt, bow tie, baseball cap and wraparound sunglasses, looked surprisingly American. He crooned tunelessly through his teeth, seemingly oblivious of the complaining gears of the vehicle as it ascended the steep road.

Eventually, grinding and rattling, we reached a level stretch, a ledge actually, perhaps two lanes wide, near the crest. It was a breathtaking aerie. On one side of us was the stone wall of the mountain. On the other side, beyond the precipice, was a stunning view of green fields and tiny towns thousands of feet below.

The vista was made especially stunning by the fact that the only barrier between us and open space consisted of a few men and women shoring up the side of the road, which had crumbled in spots.

Once on that level ledge, the bus lunged forward, giving its all. The driver hunched over his wheel like a jockey urging a mount into the homestretch. It seemed to me we came within inches of being launched off the edge like a flying rock. I could not understand why the other passengers — completely at ease, chattering away, laughing — were so unaware of their proximity to their maker.

Mary, staring straight ahead, put her hand on mine and kept it there.

Finally, years later it seemed, it ended . . . in a roller-coaster descent that delivered us to a hotel on the coast. For what must have been a full minute, Mary and I sat still. Then we got off in silence.

I had a distinct feeling Mary had not yet started to savor our wonderful vacation.

The next day an American who introduced himself as Colonel Tom Marsh escorted us to a plane for a flight to the island of Quemoy, which had figured prominently in a Nixon-Kennedy election debate. The colonel was in mufti, and for some reason I cannot explain, I felt certain he was an agent of the CIA. I still do.

The surface of Quemoy seemed pastoral, but its flora concealed observation posts and weaponry; beneath the ground the island was a huge, sprawling fort. The colonel led us to a subterranean bunker and introduced us to a General Lee: tall, lean, handsome, very military.

The colonel translated for us. "The general welcomes you," he said. "He wants you to know the eyes of the world are on this spot."

"Why is the world looking at us?" Mary asked.

The colonel pointed through a narrow slit to a brooding gray promontory across the water. "That's China," he said. "That's the launching site for the invasion."

When he put it like that, it seemed disturbingly close.

"Invasion?" Mary asked. "Invasion of what?"

"Of us — of Quemoy, of course," the colonel said. "We're the steppingstone."

"When?"

"Could be anytime," the colonel told Mary. He sounded quite blasé about it all.

"You mean it could happen *today?*"

"Oh, I doubt *that.* There'll be signs of preparation, you know, and we haven't seen any yet. But of course," the colonel added, "you can never be sure. Thing about the Reds, they're very clever."

"Good God, Bill!"

Before I could think of anything calming to say, a soldier arrived bearing a tray. He gave Mary a cup of green tea while the general poured some colorless liquid for the colonel, himself and me.

It looked like gin or vodka, and my limit is an occasional glass of beer or wine. That is not a restraint born of moral strictures; I have little capacity for alcohol and dislike its electric impact on me. The drink offered by the general had a pleasant herbal aroma. There seemed no malice in it. So when the general held his cup aloft and said something that sounded like "Gombay!" I drank along with the others. It was warm and quite mild, very pleasant really.

Mary, who was still contemplating an invasion, said softly, "Bill, do you think . . . I mean, under the circumstances — "

"It's mild, Mary. Probably nonalcoholic. Very soothing."

"Oh, yes," the colonel assured her. "It's *very* soothing."

And so it went, on and on, with the colonel telling us of the industrial miracle of Taiwan and the general repeatedly urging us on from one Gombay! to another. As time wore on, I began to find the general increasingly fascinating. The colonel seemed to become more witty and likable by the minute.

When we had a brief opportunity to speak privately, Mary said, "Bill, I don't think the general is in a state to cope with any invasion."

But he looked fine to me, the very picture of sobriety. It was unthinkable anyone would disturb such conviviality with an invasion. All at once it seemed a capital idea to sing "The Wild Colonial Boy" for our new friends, and I did.

Mary looked at the ceiling, but Marsh and the general applauded lustily. So we enjoyed another Gombay! or two.

I sang "The Rising of the Moon" as an encore. Its martial

cadence transported the general; he drummed the tempo on a table with his knuckles.

"Well, it's been wonderful," Mary said, "but —"

I knew the tone, and it was fine by me. Everything was fine by me. So we thanked the general; the colonel escorted us to our plane.

When we were back in our hotel, Mary said, "We've survived a threatened earthquake, a suicidal bus ride and the danger of invasion. We must be doing something right."

I searched for something appropriate to say. All I could think of was "Gombay!"

It struck me as a dazzling response at the time.

Mary, wonderful Mary, never since has referred to the Quemoy incident.

I had promised her a vacation she would never forget. In a manner of speaking, I had delivered. But years passed before I could talk her into another.

Complete agreement on anything rarely, if ever, exists in politics. One of the closest instances in my memory was the view, after my election to complete Kevin Harrington's term as Senate president, that I should not and would not be reelected to a full term. The widespread hostility, rooted in my insistence that forced busing could not integrate schools, was exacerbated by undeniable evidence that I had been right.

I was the *bête noire* of many academics. The media had a profound lack of enthusiasm for me. It was as though, by some sort of convoluted rationalization, they all held me at fault for the failure of their improvident panacea for achieving racial balance.

They disliked me too much to be angry at me. That would have made me far too important. Their attitude fell somewhere between disdain and total contempt. They explained that my background and origins made me hopelessly insular — adequate, perhaps, to represent South Boston, but surely incapable of wielding power affecting the entire state. My horizons were cramped, my leadership talent nonexistent, and on top of all that, I was entirely too artful to be trusted. Finally, the state's electorate, which to an overwhelming extent considered itself liberal, was told that — notwithstanding my efforts on behalf of children, the poor, labor and the aged — I was that ultimate enemy of the people, a *conservative!*

Such political epithets, of course, have no enduring definition. The word "conservative" evokes an image, good or bad, that varies endlessly with the eye of the beholder. Similarly, the title "liberal" is applied to a Jefferson who valued property, a New Dealer who would tax it to the bone, a socialist who would like to do away with it entirely. Such labels represent a debauchery of our language. Still, we use these ideological incantations. They are the shorthand of politics. And we shall go on using them, because in our hurried era the public's attention span won't tolerate nice distinctions.

Coming as I did from a blue-collar background, my economic views were in many respects more left-leaning than those of my liberal detractors. It was my social outlook that distressed them. They bridled when I protested that tolerance of dissent extended only to special groups, that reasoned discussion was almost extinct. They considered my concern over the desuetude of good manners as an anachronistic preoccupation. Mostly, though, they winced when I said, for example, Woodstock was a squalid obscenity. They were amused — the ultimate degree of contempt — when I spoke of what I perceived as the disarray of our time, a precipitous decline in morality, in the quality of American life, in civilization.

It was my view that efforts to synthesize the libertine life and ethics — Sodom and Jerusalem — must fail: liberals ignore that there is, in the final analysis, a binary identity of right and wrong, the yin and yang limits of morality. It was not sin that I deplored — few of us are in a position to throw that stone; it was not *knowing* right from wrong that concerned me. A saint in his youth once prayed, "Lord, make me pure — but not yet." He did what he should not do, which is human; but he knew it was wrong, which is civilized.

In short, I was saying that it was recognition of objective standards of good and evil that mattered.

I believed that. I still do. The great strides made in technology and pure science have fostered in many the secular illusion that God has been displaced and the natural law repealed. But the heart abhors a vacuum. If you take God out of it, you must replace Him with something — humanism, relativism, socialism — *something*.

No way has been found to do that. Nothing has worked.

The currently popular substitute for a deity is worship of *la vita dolce,* a life of ease, permissiveness and promiscuous self-indulgence, an unending summer of milk and honey. If that in fact could be delivered — and it never has been, nor ever will — still it would be woefully inadequate. Shakespeare wrote of those who, "surfeited with honey . . . began to loathe the taste of sweetness, whereof a little more than a little is by much too much."

I not only believed all those things, I said them, over and over again. As a result, there I stood, a *conservative!* — by which was meant one out of step, one behind the times, an intellectual bumpkin, the droll totem of a small and barbarous tribe of urban dissidents. Mary, reading a paper at breakfast, said, "If I'd known you were so awful, I'd never have married you."

My predicament was clear. I knew I had the confidence of my colleagues, and that they would vote for me — if they dared.

That was the question: would they dare?

Many of them anticipated great pressure from the media. That prospect discouraged even my stoutest allies, and I was deluged with the dispiriting auguries of the disconsolate. I wish I could say I conceived a plan to salvage matters. I did not. I could think of nothing that might discourage the media from waging a determined campaign to prevent my reelection.

And I had no doubt such a campaign would be successful.

"When you can think of nothing to do," a wise man once advised me, "then that is the thing to do, nothing." So I did nothing — not because I considered it clever, but because I had no strategy at all.

Amazingly, a miracle was granted to me: the media also did nothing! Apparently, the press believed its own assessment that my deficiencies had destroyed me: I was a quaint political Neanderthal, an anachronistic embarrassment that soon would be fossilized by the election of one of my betters. The result was that I was ignored.

I counted each day while that lasted, wondering what would upset that complacency and awaken the sleeping tigers.

But nothing did.

Norman Lockman, a black reporter, thought I could not be judged on the basis of a truncated term. I was *such* a dead issue that he was able to express his view in the *Globe* magazine section. Lockman's article helped still fears of reprisal among my more nervous compatriots, and the election became routine.

I was elected to my first full term as Senate president. The media were horrified, but they awakened too late.

Sometime later, Lockman was discharged by the newspaper. I do not know whether the article about me was a factor in his dismissal. It probably did not help him.

"Well, you slipped in the door while the press wasn't looking," David Wilson, a long-time friend and *Globe* columnist, said. "I'll bet they regret that."

I'll bet they did.

And have for almost two decades.

It is thought that any legislative leader, state or federal, whether a House Speaker or a Senate president, is insulated from most of the migraine agonies that beset his colleagues. The truth is opposite. Surely, the patience needed to achieve consensus among members is less wearing, if less exciting, than the rigors of debate in the pit. And the power to select committee leadership can eliminate the personality cults that otherwise may delay or even throttle worthwhile initiatives. Finally, control of the gavel — that oaken hammer that commands silence with a few raps — is wonderfully better than trying to gain attention from the floor. But persuasion often requires compromise more enervating than combat. Appointing men and women to committee chairs, as I would learn dramatically, can lead to explosive reaction. Even the apparently simple power to maintain order can make the legislative leader wish someone else had the job.

There was the matter of Senator Alan Sisitsky, the bright, articulate and, to me, very strange lawmaker with whom I had clashed so often when we served in the House. He had always puzzled me, but I had enjoyed debating with him. Now, in the Senate, he puzzled me more than ever before, and I wasn't enjoying Sisitsky at all. His antics also disturbed many of his colleagues.

Never close to the cutting edge of fashion, he was now looking increasingly disheveled. He tended to ramble in his speech and mutter to himself. He brought constant vexation to our proceedings, where he would rage interminably — often incomprehensibly — about extraneous matters.

Senator Bob Cawley came to my office. "About Alan — " he began.

"I know, I know," I said. "Be patient. He'll be all right."

"He's dangerous," Cawley said. "I mean dangerous, as in he might hurt somebody. Or worse."

"He's a talker. He's not physical. I don't think he could fight a summer cold."

"He's walking around carrying a barbell. Hell, Bill, that can be a lethal weapon."

"So can a shoe," I told him. "Sisitsky won't run amok with a barbell."

Cawley said, "That nut came into my office, and when I bent over to pick up a piece of paper, his damn barbell sailed over my head. There's a two-inch groove in my wall where it hit."

I began to watch Sisitsky more closely, aware I was faced with a problem of maintaining order. When we were in recess, he would pace the halls, carrying his barbell and badgering members with loud argument. Often, when he returned to the chamber, he would go to his seat and begin reading newspapers while other members spoke. He would turn the pages noisily while debate was in progress. Sometimes he would just sit there, staring into space and tearing his newspapers into strips. He would throw the strips in the air like confetti and litter the floor about him. I vividly remember one night session when the members were arguing an involved bill — while Alan continued tearing, tearing, tearing his infernal papers until the sound seemed to roar in my ears.

I did not think him mad, but he seemed to be wandering in the penumbra of irrationality. He struck me as one suffused with an enormous loneliness of some sort. Disturbed, at times almost disoriented, he was certainly a consummate nuisance. But dangerous? No.

It was hard on all of us, but we tried to live with it until whatever afflicted Alan should pass. Against all my instincts, I opted for an experiment in benign neglect. Surely, I felt, it can't get any worse.

I was wrong. It *could* get worse. And it did.

One day Sisitsky told the senators, "The Senate president's brother, Whitey Bulger, is listening. He hears everything we say."

According to Sisitsky, Jim was operating from an instrument-laden truck parked in some hidden place. He was monitoring all that went on in the statehouse. The motivation for Jim's electronic invasion was not spelled out, but Sisitsky's voice and expression made it clear my brother was up to no good.

Other wild notions would occur to him when he was wandering the corridors, grotesque defamations of his colleagues, particularly of me. He would confide these to members of the press and was indignant when they asked for supporting evidence — which, of course, he could not supply.

He had an eager audience in a journalistic predator named Larry Collins, who lusted to get Alan's fulminations into print. Collins knew how to do that. He urged Sisitsky to repeat them on the floor of the Senate, which made them privileged and enabled the *Globe* to publish them, with an air of cutthroat piety, as routine reportage of public events.

Sisitsky was ecstatic. Thereafter, we would watch him traipse into the chamber trailed by the lupine Collins, notebook in hand. It meant the scene was set for another horror story. At first we would speculate whether one of us was about to be accused of the Brinks robbery, the Lindbergh kidnapping, the invasion of Poland, whatever. But the gallows humor soon wore out.

The media, which treated as infamous the memory of a senator from Wisconsin who had said the State Department was full of Reds, saw nothing wrong in Sisitsky's insistence that our legislature was full of crooks. Instead, he was portrayed as an eccentric maverick, even given the status of a legitimate critic of the political system.

And so it went on: no peace of any kind, no relief; members demanding that I act, the press enjoying the show, Sisitsky blasting away recklessly like a child with a shotgun.

All legislatures, federal and state, forbid *ad hominem* attacks by any member on colleagues. It is an essential rule designed to protect the privilege attached to comments on the floor, a privilege that might be narrowed if it were misused to air animosities. Collins was well aware of the rules, and knew Sisitsky could destroy himself by violating them. But Collins was in the scandal-gathering business, and practitioners in that line are insensitive to the body count resulting from their work.

As for Sisitsky, he appeared to be stupefied by his own rhetoric, to have lost all self-control. Now he was saying outrageous things anywhere, to anyone who would listen. Mary's pediatrician saw Alan on television and was alarmed. Mary, who always called Sisitsky "that man," told me, "He says the way that man looks and talks — his gestures and the expression in his eyes — all indicate he could be dangerous. He thinks you should be afraid."

"Afraid of what?"

"Afraid he might hurt you," she said. "The doctor said that man acts as though he has some kind of morbid hatred for you — I don't remember the medical term."

"Well, he might aggravate me into a stroke or bore me to death, I'll give him that."

But I remembered Cawley . . . I realized it was the second time someone had thought Sisitsky dangerous.

Soon after, I arrived home when several of the children were listening to a conversation on radio between the program host, David Finnegan, and Sisitsky. Alan was speaking by phone from O'Hare Airport in Chicago.

"Billy Bulger will be arrested tomorrow morning," he said.

"For what?" Finnegan asked.

"Federal agents will be waiting for him when he arrives at his office," Alan went on, ignoring Finnegan's query.

I never heard more about that. But I continued to hear from Sisitsky — endlessly:

When Senator Denis McKenna urged a bill to increase revenues to the city of Somerville from pinball operators by charging them for a full year's license even when they operated only for a few months, Alan was on his feet. "There we go," he said. "The same old story."

Obviously, Sisitsky had completely misunderstood the intent of the bill, and thought it was beneficial to the licensees when, in fact, it burdened them.

Alan turned to face a class of students seated in the gallery and told them, "This Senate provides the finest representation money can buy. And you are witnessing it right now." He went on to inveigh against political corruption and then said, "McKenna had filed this bill because he received money from the pinball machine operators. Now he is serving their private interest. That is what goes on around here."

McKenna was on his feet. Glaring at Sisitsky, he said, "Senator, taking this sort of abuse is not in my job description. And be advised that in Somerville, where I come from, when we have a nut we crack it."

I gaveled the chamber into silence and then told Sisitsky, "Senator, I have warned you several times, and I do so again: you may not impugn the motives of any member of this body."

The following day, one columnist accused me of muzzling a courageous senator. By now, though, most members of the press knew — as all the senators had known for some time — that we were dealing with a man out of control.

Sisitsky made a complaint to the attorney general's office accusing Senator Chester Atkins and me of grave misconduct. It was ludicrous, because even the most casual inquiry would have revealed that the charges were false. We were aware that Attorney General Francis X. Bellotti was a media acolyte, but he was also a lawyer of considerable ability. We anticipated a prompt, clear and public refutation of the complaint.

Bellotti was in no hurry. He allowed the complaint to sit in his office. The papers made the most of it: buried in story after story dealing with the Senate were words such as, "Criminal charges against Atkins and Bulger are under investigation by the attorney general's office."

The previous year, an amendment preventing politicians from keeping their campaign funds after they left office had come before the Senate. At the time, Bellotti had a war chest of some $400,000. He said publicly that he would not ask anyone to block the amendment, but privately he let it be known he would be very disappointed if the measure got through. I refused to block it. I doubt that improved his regard for me. In addition, he smarted from my refusal to aid him in earlier years when he turned on his governor, Chub Peabody, and tried to take over his office. I could not but wonder whether such things might have deterred him from seasonable action on Sisitsky's complaint.

The request for an investigation remained pending until Sisitsky, in a typical mood swing, wrote to Bellotti, saying, "I now believe that such an investigation is neither appropriate, nor necessary, nor justified." Nonetheless, the delay had been unaccountable and irritating. I have never looked at Bellotti since without thinking of it.

Now I realized *I* could no longer wait: I had to protect the members from Sisitsky.

"Alan," I said, "I have tolerated your attacks on me. I resent them, but I have tolerated them." He stood in my office, saying nothing, looking at me with a half-smile on his face. I went on: "But I won't tolerate one more instance of vilification of *other* senators. That's over. Sick or well, you can't do that."

But he did.

Senator Jack Brennan, who chaired the Banks and Banking Committee, was arguing his position on a bill when Sisitsky struck out, figuratively as well as literally.

"Brennan is co-opted by the bankers," shouted Sisitsky. "They gave him money. Now he does their bidding."

Brennan looked to the chair for reaction. I repeated my warning to Sisitsky, but he would not stop. Finally I named him personally — the ultimate censure.

Legislators are identified by the district they represent. Alan, for example, would be referred to as "the senator from Hampden." Under our ancient rules of procedure, when a senator is cited by name, he or she is, in fact, expelled and may not return unless the members vote to overturn the ejection.

Sisitsky, who had so frenetically sought distinction, became a historic figure: the first member in the Senate's long history to be named.

He rose to leave, his eyes bulging, his face red, but he could not resist the last word — and it proved to *be* his last word. "Being thrown out of this Senate," he cried, "is like being thrown out of a brothel."

"Just a minute, young man!"

The imperious voice came from the Republican side of the aisle, and its sharpness brought Sisitsky to a halt. The speaker was John Parker of Taunton, the leader of my legislative opposition and a noted historian of the Senate. Parker, a gentle, courteous man who looked like everybody's favorite grandfather, was deeply offended.

"A brothel indeed," he said, his voice resonating with reproach. "Have you no shame? Will you say *anything* — however cruel, however hurtful, however false — when this strange and disordered mood is upon you?"

Sisitsky was immobilized. He stood speechless while Parker went on to recount from memory the names and achievements of members past and present. Then there was complete silence. For a few moments the chamber seemed a frozen tableau, with Parker and Sisitsky facing one another and all the members staring at them.

Then Parker went on: "We are human," he said softly, "and therefore imperfect. But we are not what you say — and you know that as you say it. In your wanton efforts to shame us, you have shamed yourself."

Sisitsky stood there, his eyes fixed on Parker.

"I commend the members for their forbearance," Parker said. "It is a course I have long urged. But there comes a time when a stop must be put to misconduct, whatever its cause, and that time is now. There will be bipartisan support for the president's action."

There was — and it was overwhelming.

Sisitsky's mother, through Senator Martin Reilly, who, as did Sisitsky, represented Springfield, expressed her gratitude for our patience with her son. Columnist Abe Michelson, who worked for the *Berkshire Eagle,* a major newspaper in western Massachusetts, wrote that the Senate's action, while sad, was necessary. There were a few — most of them people without the foggiest notion of the facts — who disapproved. The sternest reaction came in a letter from one Harvey Silverglate, a Boston lawyer.

Silverglate wrote that my behavior in ejecting Sisitsky was outrageous. He said I was a disgrace. He said it was not clear to him whether "we are going to survive as a civilization," but that if we failed to do so, I would be substantially to blame. The Senate chamber would have benefited, he said, if Sisitsky had remained and everyone else had walked out.

I was relieved Silverglate didn't reside in my district. I would never feel I could really count on his vote.

After I expelled Sisitsky from the chamber, I took my children to the circus. Some fearless young ladies in white tights and ostrich plumes were flying about on galloping horses when I was distracted by a commotion in the aisle.

It was caused by a crew from Channel 4, armed with all the accouterments of their trade. Reporter Dan Rea told me, "We went to your house and Mrs. Bulger said you'd be here."

"How can I ever thank her?" I asked.

When the camera started, Rea wanted me to explain why I had

expelled Sisitsky. It was a difficult question: I had no intention of cataloging Sisitsky's acts of misbehavior at this difficult time in his life. I don't recall my exact words to Rea, but the substance of my answer was "Well, it seemed the thing to do at the time."

My apparent addiction to incendiary causes led me, from my first term as Senate president, to try to cleanse the Massachusetts constitution of an expression of religious bigotry.

The hope still lives with me.

My unsuccessful effort to end more than a century and a half of discrimination against Catholic schoolchildren has been the most painful failure of my public life. I have struggled tirelessly toward that goal and have achieved nothing, absolutely nothing.

This evil bias was enacted into law in the mid-nineteenth century when the Know-Nothing Party briefly controlled our state government. Its members, virulently anti-Catholic, inserted into our constitution code language barring any form of state aid to "private schools."

The Know-Nothings were quite honest about their purpose. They acknowledged that the words were meant to discriminate against *Catholic* schoolchildren. They said so. They bragged about it. Their speeches in the legislature are still available to anyone who doubts it.

The amendment had no real meaning: our federal constitution ordains separation of church and state, so denominational schools have no illusions of being supported by government. Repealing the amendment could not change that.

Thus the amendment does not deprive parochial schools of anything; it merely insults them. And that is the issue, the real issue. The Massachusetts constitution was stained by an amendment deliberately and avowedly reflecting hate toward a specific religious group.

The Massachusetts Teachers Association has lobbied fiercely against me in this matter. The MTA is routinely joined by a few men and women professing to represent non-Catholics. I question the bona fides of the former group; I doubt that the latter truly speak for any substantial constituency. But the coalition, by threatening to withhold campaign funds and endorsements, has been able to intimidate legislators who have told me privately they would prefer to support my position.

In the beginning, arguments were premised on vague references to separation of church and state. The opposition did not abate in the slightest, however, when I proposed replacing the amendment with the precise language of the federal constitution mandating separation.

Why? I believe the answer is somehow related to the view of union officials, often expressed, that parochial schools threaten public schools. I believe they fear parochial schools, not because they are *Catholic* schools, but because they offer an escape from inferior public schools. To suggest that such fear is the motivation for the MTA's support of the hateful amendment implies that it is acting irrationally — but many fears provoke irrational behavior, and I can think of no other respectable basis for the union's conduct.

As of this writing, Massachusetts still has a constitutional provision admittedly created to discriminate against one religious group. Happily, we have expunged all other enactments expressive of hate toward any other group.

I still fight the battle. I shall do so as long as I am in office. I hope . . . but things being as they are, I am not overly sanguine.

7

SOON AFTER Sisitsky's ouster, Israel's President Yitzhak Navon attended a dinner at Boston University Law School. We sat beside one another and got along famously, talking about the problems politicians face trying to make financial ends meet.

"We have terrible restrictions in Israel," he told me. "A plumber is allowed to practice his trade while in office, for instance, but a lawyer gets in trouble if he practices law. That's unfair."

I agreed with him and said there was no such restriction here.

"You have no restrictions?" he asked, surprised.

"We must be careful to avoid the appearance of a conflict of interest, but that's all."

"So you can practice law," he said. "That's as it should be. Are you free to borrow money?"

"Of course," I assured him, "so long as there is no conflict."

Navon was impressed. "In Israel," he said, "it is dangerous for one in politics to assume he has almost the same financial rights that other citizens enjoy."

"Not here," I said.

Not long after our discussion, Navon resigned from office to devote himself to writing, artistic interests — and earning a living.

I had liked the man immediately, and I felt a sad empathy for him, because by 1983 I had what is described euphemistically as a cash-flow problem of my own. I had severely reduced legal work after becoming Senate president in 1980, and my state salary wasn't enough. As the children grew, so did expenses — tuition, clothes, the rest. We needed to add to the house; they were sleeping in the cellar.

By then we had two houses — our home in South Boston and a cottage we had bought on Cape Cod when we were younger and more daring and when everything seemed possible. Paint and repairs were constant needs. I dreaded the burden if a roof suddenly wept in the rain. In addition, there were 100,000 miles on the car Mary drove to take children to school and to do her errands. We had a clothes washer that worked, but other appliances were moody and often required vigorous shaking before they would do their duty. The list of things we needed was long and growing longer. The only thing that wasn't growing was my income.

Mary, as always, worked miracles to budget our accounts, but more was going out than coming in. We were not broke, but we were not far from it.

All of that was painfully on my mind the day when the Quirk brothers, Robert and Bruce, came with the answer to our needs. They wanted me to represent them in a real estate dispute with a company called Data Terminal Systems over property in the town of Sudbury. DTS had made them an unsatisfactory offer for their land, and the matter was in litigation.

For me, there was no possibility of conflict, so the opportunity seemed providential. While I listened, visions swam through my mind: a new car for Mary . . . paint, repairs and appliances . . . a new roof . . .

I respected the Quirks. I admired the work they had done in building more than six hundred houses and industrial sites. They were capable and honest — but exceedingly cautious: they wanted me to handle the case on a contingency basis. I would be paid a percentage of any increase I could get them, but nothing if I failed.

I had never suffered from an overabundance of insecurity, so that arrangement — raising as it did the prospect of a substantial fee — was alluring. I did not want to appear unbecomingly eager, so I delayed perhaps ten seconds before agreeing.

The battle was waged in a succession of courts, in Cambridge, Concord, Marlborough, Woburn. I also represented the Quirks in a number of lengthy negotiating sessions.

The canny brothers were not easily satisfied. I went to them with several settlement offers, but they felt they were entitled to more.

"Somewhere along the line you'll have to authorize me to wrap this up," I told them. "If we draw it out too long, we may end up back at the starting line."

"Not yet, Bill," I would be told, time and time again.

Finally, in 1985, I worked out a settlement they liked. The case had dragged on for two years, while Mary and I went on eking out tuitions, rattling appliances, nervously watching the roof . . . somehow making do.

My fee totaled $267,000, but under our agreement it was payable after the settlement had been fully executed, which would be in the next year.

The fee solved all our problems. The delay aggravated them.

"Well," I told Tom Finnerty, my lifelong friend and former law associate, "I'll be in great shape next year when I get my fee, but until then I would describe myself as one of the impoverished rich."

Tom offered to lend me $240,000 against the Quirk fee. He said his office was doing so well that he had established a large rainy-day trust fund from which he could draw. "There's no risk to me," he said. "The fee is earned. The Quirks are honest and solid financially. And," he added with a grin, "I can make more interest from you than from the trust."

I was delighted, and for the first time Mary and I were, by our standards, secure. It had all been like the answer to a prayer.

Money is not happiness, yet for at least a brief time it can offer a satisfyingly close imitation.

But as a sainted woman once observed, more grief may come from prayers that are granted than from those that are denied. I soon learned how right she was.

That came about as a result of a conversation I had with Finnerty about one of his clients, Harold Brown, a man with troubles endless and contagious. Brown was an obscenely rich developer of real estate, mostly in Boston. How many millions he was alleged to have depended on which newspaper story you had read most recently.

I had never met him, but I had seen photographs of him in the press. In some, he might have been a character from an F. Scott Fitzgerald novel — smiling, holding a tennis racket, standing on the sunlit court of a country club. In others, published with stories castigating him as Boston's biggest slumlord, the face was saturnine, almost furtive. He was at times described as a donor to charity; he was also accused of using slugs to avoid paying turnpike tolls. He spoke against religious discrimination, but he settled out of court when sued for racial discrimination. He spied on his tenants.

I asked Tom when he'd become involved with Brown.

"Back in 'eighty-three," Tom said. "He was making plans to build that glitzy skyscraper at Seventy-five State Street."

Tom said Brown had approached Eddie McCormack to represent him before licensing and regulating agencies, but that the former attorney general's fee had been too high.

"Eddie recommended me," Finnerty said.

"I doubt Eddie did you any favor. Brown would make me uncomfortable."

"Bill, I already have a half million in fees from the man. He's a good client. I've built a healthy trust fund on his fees."

The words "trust fund" were like an alarm bell. "The money you lent me came from a trust fund."

"Right. The St. Botolph Trust Fund. I told you that. So?"

"What was the source of the corpus of that trust?" I asked.

"A half million Brown paid me."

"You didn't tell me *that*," I said. "I'm paying it back — and right now. I want no connection, however remote, with Brown."

Finnerty insisted there was no connection. He argued that the money had ceased to be Brown's when paid as a legal fee, at which point it became his money, not Brown's.

"Sometimes, Bill, when you get like this, I just don't understand you," Finnerty said. "What if I'd earned the fee representing a burglar? Would you think the money was contaminated?"

"It might depend on which burglar," I said. "At all events, I think Brown walks around under a private dark cloud — and I don't want any of his rain splattered on me."

Finnerty stared at me as though I had lost my mind. "I'll never forgive myself for telling you about this," he said. "I know you needed that loan."

"I would never have forgiven you if you hadn't told me."

Logically he was right, of course. But I might have been retired from public life on many occasions had I always acted logically.

I had received the $240,000 loan in late August of 1985. I repaid it in full, with interest, that same year. I was once again waiting for my fee from the Quirks. After a brief illusion of affluence, Mary and I were back facing a tidal wave of tuitions, and all the rest.

And we had paid interest to get back there.

I telephoned Mary and said, "You'd better put some of our plans on hold for a while."

My instincts had been sound. Brown was trouble. Within the next two years, Finnerty was complaining that Brown was behind in payment of fees — and Brown himself was answering criminal complaints. When questioned about a series of fires at properties he owned, Brown admitted he had employed a convicted arsonist. He had also made a loan to a member of the fire department's arson squad.

"Do you trust your client around matches?" I asked Tom.

"I just represent him in civil matters," Tom said. "I know nothing about his criminal problems."

I was relieved by Tom's words.

In May of the following year, Brown struck a plea bargain with U.S. Attorney William F. Weld's office. He pleaded guilty to bribery in connection with his dealings with the fire department, and was fined and given a suspended prison sentence. In exchange, the government dropped three perjury counts against him. Part of Brown's bargain was his promise to help federal agents collect evidence of misconduct by public officials.

Soon Brown, seeking admissions of wrongdoing, was bustling about the city initiating conversations with elected officials and with the heads of regulatory agencies. Since no one possibly could believe Brown as a witness, it was certain he had been equipped with recording devices. Sammy Kupchick, a statehouse hanger-on who, like all such people, pretended to an astonishing amount of information, said, "This guy Brown is wearing so many wires that no one wants to stand near him when it's raining — you could get electrocuted."

The thought of men and women fleeing from Brown's presence at the first sign of a cloudburst had a sort of bleak humor to it. I could afford to laugh: surely I had nothing to fear from the man.

At least that's what I thought. It would be a few years before I discovered the truth in Yitzhak Navon's words: "it is dangerous for one in politics to assume he has almost the same financial rights that other citizens enjoy."

While Finnerty was having his difficulties with Brown, and Brown was having his problems with the U.S. attorney's office, I had cause for particular joy. The John B. Hynes Veterans Memorial Convention Center — a grotesquely cumbersome but politically apt honorific — opened its tall brass doors in Boston. It was an event that capped more than a half decade of labor for me.

Back in 1980, I had led the campaign to bring us into the major leagues of modern tourism with a state-of-the-art convention hall. I proposed and lobbied it. I negotiated with Mayor Kevin White for an amicable takeover by the state of city property, including a decaying exposition center. The package for the newly created convention authority included a garage under Boston Common as an auxiliary source of income.

Who would direct the authority? That was a threshold question. It would take an enormous commitment to attract an established director from a proved and successful convention center — rather like a new baseball franchise trying to sign a highly regarded free-agent pitcher.

I thought I had the solution. Francis X. Joyce of South Boston was an extremely bright and principled young man whom I regarded as a protégé as well as a friend. He had been a mailman when I persuaded him to go to college. He had been working at a part-time political job when I persuaded him to go to law school. Now he was my administrative assistant, well regarded by House and Senate members, accustomed to analyzing budgets bigger than those of some nations. Fran was calm and self-contained; he had demonstrated to me a capacity for dealing with unexpected and complex problems.

He was my choice to head the Convention Center Authority. I knew, though, that if the media heard of it, the South Boston–Bulger nexus would trigger wild opposition. I wanted to avoid that.

A committee had been formed to find a director, and because of the role I had played in creating the center, I was asked whether I had a candidate.

"I do," I said, "but I'm not ready to name him yet."

Robert Q. Crane, then the state treasurer, was a committee member. I liked Bob, but I knew he was a conduit for his friends in the press. Old literature speaks of Turkish mutes, confidants whose tongues were removed to prevent betrayal of secrets. Clearly, the Turks carried matters much more than a bit too far, but a lack of discretion in government causes mischief and has always been a concern. Thus, when time and again Bob asked me to tell him the name of my nominee, I would time and again ask him to be patient.

On the day the search committee was to meet to decide on suggestions, Bob's patience was exhausted. He phoned and said, "We've got to know, Bill. We're meeting in two hours."

"I'll make my suggestion in plenty of time," I said.

"It's because of me, isn't it?" Crane asked. "You just don't want me to know. You think I'm a leak, don't you?"

"You're not a leak, Bob, you're Niagara Falls."

When the committee assembled, I made my case for Fran Joyce. Everybody seemed to think I had a good idea. Joyce was unanimously chosen to be director.

Oh, the thunder in the press! There were the usual distortions, which began on that day and continued. Under Joyce, it was said, construction costs were wildly excessive — actually, they were within budget; the center was a "patronage pit" filled with people from South Boston — actually, only three of the hundreds of employees came from that district. So it went, on and on.

Politicians leaped aboard the media bandwagon and denounced Joyce, me and the facility itself. One gubernatorial aspirant called a news conference in the doorway of the convention center to do so. But the bandwagon was taking them on a journey to nowhere. There was even an effort to change the enabling legislation as a prelude to firing Joyce. It failed.

In time, all the criticism faded away. The pot they had tried to stir had proved to be a pot of gold. Over the years, the convention center has generated billions in taxes and in benefit to our general economy. A ring of hotels has been built because of it.

Raymond Flynn had wanted for some time to be mayor of Boston. He had finally made it in 1984.

Prior to that election, there had been a major impediment to his goal: he had been elected to the House and the city council as a vigorous foe of forced busing, which meant the media would savage him should he run.

Flynn lived in the vortex of busing agony in South Boston. He knew what happened there. But I had expected his ambitions would cause him to revisit his judgment of the equities of that ordeal. In fact he did precisely that, but he did it softly, using two-edged words many of his neighbors at first did not understand.

He said he was opposed to violence in South Boston — as were all of us — and the media took this, *as he meant them to take it,* as condemnation of any protest by the victims. He said he was concerned about injustice to blacks — and his neighbors agreed. They thought he referred to two things they had publicly and repeatedly espoused: the right of black parents to send their children to any school, and the duty of the city to rescue blacks from the thugs and drug dealers terrorizing Roxbury's streets. That wasn't what he meant. And the pro-busers took him to mean, *as he meant them to do,* that he was beginning to support forced busing — and disown us.

He became the toast of the *Globe* after he talked on a plane to Washington with William O. Taylor, whose family published the paper. Joe Moakley phoned and told me about it: "I couldn't believe it. Taylor thinks Ray would be a great mayor. He kept going on and on about what a smart guy Flynn was — how Flynn was this and Flynn was that." We discussed it awhile, because Joe and I were more restrained in our assessment of Flynn's intellect.

Bill Taylor, with whom I have worked on many things for many years, has always struck me as too easily impressed by his own editorial writers. But he is a bright and sophisticated man, so I saw only three reasons why he should become fascinated by Flynn. One, Taylor had suddenly become stupid, which was absurd. Two, Flynn had suddenly become brilliant, which was more absurd. Three, Flynn was saying what Taylor believed and wanted to hear — bingo! How sweet to the ears of a True Believer is the sound of his own words echoing from a once-hostile source.

At all events, Flynn emerged as an enlightened citizen — proof that at least one of those our critics considered South Boston apes had climbed down from his tree and joined civilization.

Most of the media, as usual, followed the *Globe*'s lead. It was explained that, though once duped by the anti-busing crowd, Flynn had "grown in his job" as a public servant, implying he deserved the acceptance of a prodigal son.

He got it. He was elected.

When he lost the South Boston wards in his quest for reelection, he was asked why his neighbors voted against him. He said, "They don't understand I have to represent all the people."

We understood. We understood him well.

One of the ways he "represented all the people" was by leading a campaign to dump 750 tons of waste daily in my district. Backed by the Chamber of Commerce and similar exemplars of social conscience, Ray said it was the ideal spot for a desperately needed new incinerator.

Michael Goldman, formerly a mortician and now a political consultant with strong media ties, represented the firm that would build the waste disposal equipment. He made sure the plan — and Flynn — got laudatory exposure in the press. So overwhelming was the support that proponents considered the matter resolved.

There was one more or less formal technicality: the plan required enabling legislation. That brought a delegation to my office. I told them they would have to look elsewhere for support. I said I had read the study and supportive literature and was not at all persuaded we needed a new incinerator — at least not at the present time, and certainly not in our capital city. Boston's air was already poisoned by exhaust from automobiles; our traffic glut would be exacerbated by fleets of trucks serving an urban incinerator.

The delegation was surprised and unhappy to hear this, and Flynn, counseled no doubt by the flamboyant Goldman, scheduled a news conference on the statehouse steps.

It was the sort of thing Raymond relished. As mayor, his appetite for attention was insatiable. It was, I suppose, a benign sort of gluttony, but irritatingly predictable. When it snowed, he would climb on a plow and be photographed for the papers and taped for TV; when the media focused on some family tragedy, he would arrive with sirens howling, to be photographed in his shirtsleeves at a kitchen table bringing solace to the bereaved — while looking fixedly into the camera.

Press releases flowed from his office relentlessly. At one time or another, Flynn appeared on every talk show on radio, every news show on television. For many years he even came to my St. Patrick's Day breakfast, knowing courtesy required there be no hostile reception. When my staff would review the hundreds of photographs taken at those functions, it was astonishing to note how he had managed to move into most of them. In 1993, when the pope visited Denver, there was Raymond, shouldering security men aside to stand in the rain holding an umbrella over the pontiff's head. A television audience estimated at four billion saw him that day — undoubtedly the apogee of his attention-seeking career.

Our statehouse steps provided a more modest but still an ideal stage at the time of his news conference: colorful, even dramatic — and *safe*, because he knew I avoided media happenings.

But he was invading my turf.

He looked startled when he saw me coming down the steps to where he stood facing the assembled media.

"I've been looking for you for three days to discuss your incinerator," I said. "I didn't think I'd ever find you — until I saw all these cameras. Then I knew where you'd be."

Flynn didn't appreciate the laughter. His face reddened. Leaning into the microphone, he said, "Mr. President, with all due respect to you . . . until yesterday's paper I had no idea you were opposed to my incinerator plan."

"No, Mr. Mayor," I answered, "with all due respect to you, as soon as you got the green light from the most persuasive powers in the city . . . you thought no one would dare oppose it."

And so it went, with all its hackneyed forms of address, all its insincere formalistic expressions of mutual respect, until I felt satisfied Raymond would not soon stage another demonstration on the steps of the House where I lived.

The following day, Bruce Mohl wrote on page one of the *Globe:* "Mayor Flynn got bushwhacked yesterday at his own news conference . . ."

By this time, Goldman's client must have wondered whether its multimillion-dollar incinerator project was in danger of slipping away. There was a nervous demand that I propose a site.

I avoided responding for weeks, badgered by constant remind-
ers that I was delaying an *essential* project. Finally I said, "I think
a deep stone quarry, easily accessible by trucks, would be perfect.
There is such a place, an ideal location, at the junction of Routes
128 and 2 . . . in the town of Weston."

The reaction was ballistic.

Weston was our most affluent town, a citadel of the state's rich
and famous. Harold Hestnes, the president of the Boston Chamber of Commerce, a sponsor of the incinerator plan, was a resident.

Statements of dismay abounded. Editorial comments exploded
like the Fourth of July fireworks display when the Boston Pops
Orchestra plays at the Hatch Shell. My proposal was outrageous
. . . surely I was joking . . . no one seriously could consider such a
suggestion . . . In *Weston* — my God!

That was the end of the incinerator plan. Suddenly the project
was no longer considered essential.

It wasn't. It never had been.

But my Neighborhood was.

In May of 1987, Tom Finnerty sued Harold Brown for $426,000
in unpaid fees.

Brown filed a countersuit five months later. In his declaration,
Brown alleged that Finnerty had extorted $500,000 from him
and had promised to use influence — including mine — to help
Brown with the 75 State Street project.

It made me angry, but didn't surprise me. I knew that language in such suits often was grotesquely hyperbolic. Besides that,
Brown was a proven liar; certainly no one would credit anything
he said. In addition, I wondered whether he really had initiated
the accusation. The pleading reflected the hand of Harvey Silverglate, the lawyer who had said I might destroy Western civilization. He and his co-counsel Andrew Goode were a shifty pair: a
federal judge said they had involved "the U.S. attorney's office to
do their dirty work for them" in a plot to discredit a witness.

"I warned you Brown was a dangerous man," I told Tom.

"He's just a client who wants to welch on a fee — what's new?"

"He's a client accusing you of extortion."

"Oh, that," Finnerty said, laughing. "He's got Silverglate and Goode representing him. They'd accuse Mother Teresa of extortion. You know me — you know there's nothing to it."

"Of course I know it," I said. "But you're too good a lawyer to believe you're safe just because you're innocent."

"They can't produce evidence if there isn't any," Finnerty said. "They'll settle."

"Brown is a perjurer. I doubt he'll hesitate to lie about you."

"Bill, don't worry, I'll win. He'll lose."

I also became concerned about my former clients, the brothers Quirk. In the fall of 1988, rumors persisted that Robert and Bruce were being asked by a federal grand jury whether I had actually earned the fee they had paid me.

I had, of course. I had worked hard, and had been credited by opposing counsel with achieving the result. It had been an excellent settlement, and the Quirks had been delighted with it. But the rumored questions, if indeed they were being asked, irked me as they would any lawyer: my clients were entitled to confidentiality in their dealings with their counsel. The Quirks might be denied that because their attorney had a high political profile.

There was also a selfish concern. How might my future practice be affected? How might such intrusion discourage prospective clients from running the risk of a similar invasion of their privacy?

I had no intention of spreading rumors by contesting them, however, so I put it all out of my mind, a faculty I am blessed with — and to which I largely credit my excellent digestive system. I went ahead with plans Mary and I were making for a European vacation.

Then, a few days before we were to leave, I received a request to be interviewed for the *Globe*'s "Spotlight Report." The "reports," published intermittently, trafficked for the most part in rumor and suspicion. They were assembled by an amorphous team headed by Gerard O'Neill and Dick Lehr.

It was O'Neill who called me. He was concerned with whether

I had an interest in the St. Botolph Trust, the real estate trust from which Finnerty had drawn the money he lent to me.

I assured him I did not, and on a palpably inane impulse agreed to see him. What possessed me at that moment to ignore almost three decades of experience avoiding such people, I do not know. Perhaps it was — what does it matter what it was? It was dumb, and I did it.

So in came the Spotlight Team. O'Neill: an air of surly virtue; tall, fat, fortyish, soft-looking, shaggy; dressed like a mannequin at a flea market. Lehr: said to be a lawyer; dark, brooding; the charisma of a vacant lot.

My administrative assistant, Paul Mahoney, joined us. Lehr took notes. O'Neill did almost all the talking.

O'Neill seemed uncomfortable. He sweated and kept running his hand through his thick black hair. He never looked at me as he spoke.

The interview went along these lines:

"We have a lot of questions," O'Neill said, staring at the wall.

"Well, I don't have a lot of time. I'm getting ready to leave for Europe in a couple of days."

Fixed on some point a thousand yards away, O'Neill said, "We want to know about the Quirk matter. We want to know what you did to earn your fee."

"A lot," I said. "Anything else?"

"We want to know about the money you got from the St. Botolph Trust and your relationship with that trust."

"Anything else?"

O'Neill fired off dozens of questions. Had I received a loan from Finnerty? When? For how much? What did I do with the money? There were many more queries seeking precise details. It was clear O'Neill was trolling in what he hoped were deep waters, and all the while he looked at the rug, the door, the table. He looked into the faces of former Senate presidents whose photographs lined the walls of my office, but he never looked into mine.

When he appeared to have finished, I said, "You're asking

about things that happened years ago. I'll answer your questions, but I'll have to dig out some records."

"How long will that take?"

"I think Paul can have everything together by the time I get back from Europe — about twelve days from now."

"All right," O'Neill said. "We won't print anything until then."

He gave me a written list of questions. Then he asked the ceiling, "What did you know about the 1985 agreement under which Harold Brown paid Finnerty five hundred thousand dollars?"

His other questions had not concerned me, but the mention of Brown's name brought a chill. I was thankful I had acted so quickly to avoid even the most remote connection with that troubled man.

"I knew nothing about any agreement and I still don't," I said. "I did hear Brown had paid that fee to Finnerty."

When they had left, Paul said, "That was strange — the man never looked at you all that time."

Paul's words were fuel to a sense of premonitory unrest I already felt, the vague feeling of alarm one might experience at the mournful sound of a distant doleful bell. I said nothing about it . . .

The first stop on our vacation was Belgium. Mary and I were in our hotel room in Brussels when the phone rang and I heard Paul saying, "Well, it didn't take them long. They're breaking their word. O'Neill called and said they're publishing a story tomorrow."

"About what?"

"He wouldn't say."

We had the answer the following day — December 8, 1988 — when the *Globe* Spotlight Team printed a front-page story entitled "The Deal Behind a Skyscraper." The story began: "Senate President William M. Bulger has benefited from a trust bankrolled with money that a Boston real estate magnate claims was extorted from him in 1985 by Bulger's longtime associate in a downtown law practice." The Spotlighters went on to say that even if the transaction had in fact been a loan, I had broken the law by not reporting it to the state Ethics Commission.

Clearly the loan had not "benefited" me. The money briefly had lain in my account and then been returned. The transaction resulted in a net loss to me of the interest I had to pay. Further, it was untrue *any* law required me to report to the Ethics Commission a loan made and repaid in the same year. It was obvious that Lehr, in making such a mistake, was no more capable as a lawyer than he was as an investigator.

The story did not tell that Brown, whose suit against Finnerty was the basis for the entire piece, had already lied to a federal grand jury. It made passing reference — in the thirty-fifth paragraph — to his guilty plea on bribery charges, but that lapse was depicted as the act of one more or less harassed into wrongdoing.

I refused to return home, despite urgent recommendation by my staff that I do so. Mary and I went on to Vienna, to celestial music and sinfully rich pastries — while, back home, the band played on.

The *Globe* was hard at it, demanding I clarify my dealings with Finnerty. Paul called me in Vienna: "We've dug out the material to answer all their questions," he said. "Shall I show it to them?"

"Show them the door," I said.

I had seen the Spotlight Team in action many times before. Its technique was formalized. I knew what to expect:

The initial publication was typically a thunderous event with banners and drums, proclaiming a violation of some kind by a public figure who could be libeled with virtual impunity.

We had already *had* that.

Next would come pressure to persuade or coerce someone — *anyone* — to conduct an investigation. The *Globe*'s Spotlighters doted on investigations. Their purpose was to create an illusion of profound official concern, thereby giving a similitude of substance to their bombast. Should the end result show that the Spotlighters had laid a journalistic egg, which not infrequently was the case, it would be buried in silence, soon forgotten. But there was always the hope it might turn out to be a golden egg, hatching into a coveted award.

That's where the paper was now: looking for an investigator.

The *Globe*'s efforts to persuade federal authorities to become involved ended in embarrassment. To its evident chagrin, the paper discovered the FBI already had conducted and concluded a two-year investigation of Brown's allegations of extortion. Since that triggered no action against anyone, it was plain no evidence of culpability had been uncovered.

That didn't deter the paper. It switched gears smoothly and announced that James Shannon, the state attorney general, apparently impelled by the paper's amazing revelations, was investigating me.

Shannon promptly denied that. He admonished the paper for making a false report.

The *Globe* was unabashed. It didn't miss a stride. It now began insisting that Shannon *should* investigate, that he *must* investigate.

Other elements of the media weighed in, incensed because I would not respond to their questions. They wanted me interrogated by a grand jury. One publication that seemed singularly convinced I was guilty of *something* was the *Phoenix,* a newspaper that listed Harvey Silverglate on its masthead. Radio talk shows pounded away. Commercial TV news programs uncritically echoed the newspaper stories. Public television fulminated: Christopher Lydon, of Channel 2, who had once accused me of "thuggery" because I would not talk to him, interrupted his program frequently to make on-air demands that I telephone him. On occasion he had Alan Dershowitz, a ubiquitous Harvard professor of law and a man close to Silverglate, as a guest.

"Why isn't Bulger called before a grand jury?" Dershowitz would ask. "Is it just because he's a big shot?"

Later, Dershowitz called talk shows, saying, "Bulger's guilty, I know he's guilty." Of what, he never said.

Neither Lydon nor anyone else asked Dershowitz why, if he had knowledge of wrongdoing on my part, he did not share it with state or federal authorities.

I knew adverse publicity hurts anyone in public life, however false or unfair it may be — that is simply a fact of politics. I could hear in my imagination the inevitable refrain — one beer drinker to another at the local pub: "Well, you know, they say Bulger . . ." The propensity for harm in what "they" are alleged to have said is huge.

Bacon wrote that a sentence with the words "they say" is already half a lie. The poet Ella Wilcox wrote in 1883: "Have you heard of the terrible family 'They,' and the venomous things 'They' say?" There is an old Irish truism that one with a damaged reputation is already half hanged. I was damned if "they" were going to destroy my name, damned if "they" were going to half hang me.

I knew all the defamation was false in fact and implication, but as I had reminded Finnerty, innocence is not always enough. Still, the knowledge made me recall a conversation with my friend Seamus Heaney — a Nobelist who is almost certainly the greatest Irish poet since Yeats — in which I told him I had been required in school to memorize all 182 lines of "The Hound of Heaven." "Ah," he had said, "that's a very good banister to lean on, isn't it." Knowing I had done no wrong, while no guarantee of acquittal, was at least a very good banister to lean on.

All of this coalesced in a determination to affirm my innocence, and to do so convincingly. I saw no purpose in trying to do that through the prosecutorial media. My statement had to be made under circumstances that would vouch for its truthfulness; it had to be made under oath in a forum to whose disciplinary power I was subject, such as a court of law.

I was not party to the Brown-Finnerty litigation, but now Silverglate and Goode had conveniently opened a door: they were asking the court for access to my private financial records — an invasion of the confidentiality all my clients had a right to expect.

That gave me the opportunity I needed. In opposing access to my personal records, I could file an affidavit, a formal statement to the court, a complete denial under oath of any wrongdoing.

It would be the strongest challenge I could issue to the media. It would not be merely a denial advanced by some lawyer representing me. It would be one made by me under penalty of perjury. I would be responsible personally for everything I said. If it could be proved false, I would be guilty of a crime. I would be disbarred, probably fined, possibly imprisoned.

And so I sat down at the kitchen table and wrote my affidavit. In it I categorically denied any knowledge of Finnerty's deals with Brown, any interest in them, any involvement or interest in the work done for Brown by Finnerty, or any interest in any fees resulting from such work. I detailed my relationship with Finnerty and the particulars relating to the loan Finnerty had made to me. I swore that at the time of the loan I had not known the provenance of the funds, and that when I learned Brown was the remote source of them, I repaid the loan promptly. I swore Finnerty had never asked me for help "or to involve myself in any way whatsoever in connection with the 75 State Street project."

With reference to the request for access to my personal records, I wrote: ". . . what is being sought is not a search for truth but a license to prey on hard-won reputations without . . . substantial basis for doing so and with reckless disregard for consequences."

I said it all, and it felt good to say it.

In speaking to the court, I was saying to the media: There — pick up the gauntlet. If you can show I have lied to the court in *any* material particular, then you will be able to print my political obituary. You can burn me at the stake and light such a fire that it will be visible to the Pulitzer committee.

Fewer than three weeks after the allegations attributed to Brown first appeared in the *Globe,* the litigation between Brown and Finnerty was settled: Brown paid Finnerty $200,000!

Brown said he was pleased with the settlement. He said he had "a good deal." Odd behavior for a reputed victim of extortion.

My media foes hoped their jihad at least would cause my defeat in the election on January 4, 1989, for Senate president.

They worked at it: they threatened and cajoled my colleagues, they demanded I withdraw, they said I was under a cloud that made my election unthinkable.

But I was reelected.

When that was over — indeed, on the following day, January 5, 1989 — the *Globe* printed a correction to its charge that I had broken the law by failing to report Finnerty's loan. It was a two-sentence correction, demurely positioned below the Index inside the paper. It was headed "For the Record." Not exactly an attention grabber.

The *Globe* blamed its mistake on "incorrect information given to the Spotlight Team by the state Ethics Commission."

The explanation was as false as the original charge.

Andrew B. Crane, executive director of the Ethics Commission, issued a written statement. He noted that his office had informed the *Globe* on December 12 — *almost a month before the published correction* — that the report of unlawful conduct had been incorrect. "Why the *Globe* waited until January 5 to make the correction is not clear to me," Crane wrote, "but it is certainly not because we waited until now to correct the record."

Crane might not have known why the correction was held back until the day after my election — but I knew, and so did every member of the Senate.

Gerard O'Neill of the Spotlight Team admitted he had heard "some grumblings, some hearsay," about a possible error. However, he chose not to deal with what he considered "second-hand complaints." How the Ethics Commission could have been considered a "second-hand" source with respect to its own regulations was hard to fathom.

Kirk Scharfenberg, deputy managing editor of the *Globe,* was more honest: "We knew the first day there was a problem with the story. Finally we did what I think we could have done a month earlier." The *Globe*'s statehouse bureau chief, Bruce Mohl, said, "The question of accuracy was raised the night the story appeared, and yet it took a month to check it out. That's too long and it's not good."

The fact that the warnings of journalists such as Mohl and Scharfenberg were ignored by those higher up suggested to some the existence of an institutionalized antipathy toward me. I have no doubt that existed, along with a hunger for circulation, at whatever cost.

The media pursued Brown, pressing him to speak of me. Brown said he didn't know me, had no complaint to make of me and had intended to direct his complaints against others, never against me.

Tom Finnerty didn't know whether he was one of the "others" to whom Brown alluded, so he made an appearance on TV in which he called Brown a liar for having accused him of extortion. He challenged Brown to sue him for libel. Brown did not.

Still, the *Globe* kept after me like a wounded bull, trying to gore me day after day. I was said to be party to swindling a woman in a purchase of property . . . my Social Security number had been written on the original deposit slip when Finnerty put Brown's fee into the St. Botolph Trust . . . I had borrowed money from the Brown fee to buy stock in an electronics company . . . The stories shared a common defect: they were all false.

Next came a revelation that I had not been questioned by the FBI during its investigation of Brown's extortion charges. That at least was true. Of course, it was also true of Boston's Bernard Cardinal Law, of the city's leading rabbi, of the local head of the Episcopal Church and millions of others. They hadn't been questioned in the FBI investigation because there was no reason for doing so; there was no evidence against any of them, as there was none against me. But the implication of that story was that the FBI investigation had somehow been incomplete or superficial.

Shannon, who had resisted for many months, but who faced a difficult election, now gave in and asked federal authorities to reopen their investigation. He said he had been "whipsawed" into doing so. This was hailed in the media as a blow for justice.

Four days later, on January 29, interim U.S. Attorney Jeremiah T. O'Sullivan, who formerly had served as head of the New England Organized Crime Strike Force, responded: "One of my first priorities will be to review the case."

One of O'Sullivan's proudest accomplishments had been his prosecution of James A. Kelly, the former Senate Ways and Means Committee chairman, once seen as a likely successor to the Senate presidency. The media described O'Sullivan in glowing terms, implying that now there was a man at the helm who would *really* get things done, *really* deal with the rascals.

Apparently there was no end to the purgatorial ordeal. Once again I would be ambushed by reporters each time I emerged from my office or from the chamber. Walking a corridor of the statehouse was like running a gauntlet between ranks of hostile savages.

My silence was an irritant — I knew that. But certainly my affidavit had given all the answers anyone acting in good faith could want. I was not going to repeat them to accommodate the press.

"Why won't you give your side?" one woman reporter asked angrily. "Doesn't any of this bother you?"

Oh, it bothered me. Beneath my carapace of reserve, it bothered intensely. Only the culpable achieve true indifference to scurrilous innuendo, preferring it to its alternative: proof. The innocent, no matter how tough, bleed. And I was innocent. Still, I held my tongue. I smiled at her and kept walking.

There were times I felt drained, stalked by the black dog of melancholy. I remember one day in late December or early January when I left the statehouse, crossed Beacon Street, and walked without destination on the paths of Boston Common until I came to the refuge of an empty bench. I sat there for perhaps a quarter hour, surrounded by the plunder of winter: the streets with their seasonal garb of grime; the deciduous trees, stripped by the wind and looking appropriately forlorn. It was cold, and so seemed my world right then.

A young woman sat on a nearby bench eating a sandwich. Tourists, equally indifferent to the weather, strolled by with cameras hanging from their necks. Traffic crawled by on Beacon and

Tremont Streets. I thought: Don't any of these people walking our streets or the paths in our parks, any of these people in cars — any of these people, for God's sake, who are eating sandwiches amid the snow — don't any of them see what the media are doing in this city? Don't any of them care? I felt like a cramped swimmer watching people, unaware or indifferent people, going about their business on a nearby beach while hidden currents tried to pull him down into the dark fathoms — and all the while this blue, unpitying sky above, beautiful but empty as an idiot's smile, the paradigm of indifference.

The episode was brief, and of course pointless. These strangers were not aroused by my problems, and why should they be? They had their own, probably worse than mine. Nevertheless, the exercise was therapeutic. It was like a valve releasing steam. And after it came a spirit, a sublimity, an upwelling that sustained me. I rose from the bench with the inner tension gone and headed back to the statehouse with a lighter step, ready for whatever awaited.

My friends in the Neighborhood cared. I knew that. They stood solidly with me. They never wavered in their conviction that all would turn out well.

Someone, I forget who, handed me a penny and said, "Here, Bill, I found this on G Street. Put it in your pocket and see if it brings you some luck."

"Ignore them," John Reardon advised. "They're not fooling anybody with their lies. You're still our hero."

John had been a friend from time out of mind, and I appreciated his support. But I did not want anyone in or out of politics to become associated with me in this struggle, lest he or she somehow be hurt. I knew the pertinacity of the forces arrayed against me, the lengths to which they would go in their anger.

"Be careful of heroes," I told him. "They can break your heart."

I put the lucky penny in my pocket and hoped for the best.

*

In the midst of all this, I was awakened at three-fifteen one morning by a phone call from Finbar Foley, a client from many years ago. It was precisely what I did not need at that troubled time.

Finbar was a bookie, but disliked the description. "A lawyer," he once told me, "don't like being called a shyster. A doctor don't like being called a sawbones. I don't like being called a bookie. I'm into numbers, so I'm a numerologist."

As soon as I recognized the voice I said, "Finbar, it's after three o'clock."

"Look, Bill, I'm your client, the old numerologist —"

"You haven't been a client of mine for ten years."

"Counsel, I'm up here in this room at the fancy Sheraton Hotel with a young lady who is — well, she's really my niece, you know — and this guy comes in and says he's the house detective —"

"Honestly, Foley, I don't want any of this right now."

"Well, I told this guy I was calling my lawyer to tell him to sue the hotel, which is what I'm telling you to do," he said, his voice rising, obviously for the benefit of the detective. "I want you to sue this lousy detective, too," he added.

"Why don't you pay your bill and get out?" I asked, closing my eyes, groping for serenity, thinking how wonderful it would be to go back to sleep.

"I've already spent a pile here," he said, again raising his voice. "But I won't give them another cent, because this guy — you never saw such a fat slob in your life — this guy is insulting me. He says my credit card is phony."

"Is it really *your* credit card?"

Now the voice lowered, a just-between-us sort of voice: "Well, it's in my wallet, and possession is —"

"How much do you owe?"

The voice sank to a whisper: "About eighteen hundred."

"I can't deal with this on a telephone. When you finally get out of there, come to see me. Maybe I'll listen to your story then."

"That's one *hell* of an idea," Finbar said.

Silence — then an incredible racket: things smashing, a woman screaming, a deep voice shouting, "Come back here, you sonofa-bitch!"

I hung up and went back to bed.

A few days later, I was walking on Broadway when Finbar ran across the street and blocked my way. "Bill, that was the smartest advice I ever got."

"Stop right there, Finbar," I said. "My only advice to you was to talk with me when you got out of the hotel."

"Well, yeah, but that gave me an idea, see, so —"

I heard no more. I was walking away rapidly. I didn't want to know what his idea had been or whether the commotion I had heard on the phone had been the sound of Finbar fleeing.

I kept walking until I was well away from him. Then I took the lucky penny from my pocket and threw it away.

On February 9 there was a report the FBI was questioning people in its newly reopened investigation of 75 State Street — and me.

The *Boston Herald* reported that Mayor Ray Flynn was telling friends, "If that's what you get for being smart, I'm glad I'm stupid."

There is a German word I can't pronounce, *schadenfreude*, which describes the penchant for rejoicing over another's misery. There is no precise English equivalent, but there should be: the proclivity, as Flynn's words indicated, is universal.

I told my lawyer, Robert Popeo, that I thought I should take the same course I had followed with my affidavit: if the FBI had questions for me, I would be available to answer them under oath.

One recollection I have is of Popeo sitting in his office, urging the federal people on the telephone to obey the law. "The press is obviously hostile to Bulger," he said. "If word leaks out that you are interviewing him, they'll make it sound like an indictment. Bulger is seeing you voluntarily, and the law requires you to keep the matter confidential until the investigation is completed."

Popeo told me the agents had promised they would do so.

We met with the FBI at Popeo's office. I was sworn and then asked, "When did you first meet Harold Brown?"

"I've never met him."

"Have you talked with him by phone?"

"No. And I've never communicated with him by mail or through an intermediary or in any other way, directly or indirectly."

"Were you ever asked to do anything to help Brown?"

"Never. I was never asked to help, I never tried to help. In fact, I knew nothing of his specific problems with 75 State Street. Finnerty has assured me that my name was never mentioned to or by Brown."

"Do you believe that?"

"I do. And Finnerty has repeated it under oath."

I went on to reprise the substance of my affidavit with respect to the Finnerty loan and my repayment. The agents made copious notes. Before they left, Popeo reminded them of the promise not to leak the fact that I had been interviewed.

The next morning, *Globe* reporter Brian Mooney called, wanting to ask questions about the FBI interview!

It is ironic that I emerged from the FBI interview unscathed but that one John Morris, an FBI agent, was later suspended, following an internal investigation, for revealing the meeting to the *Globe*. I had broken no law, but he had.

The media were correct in depicting O'Sullivan, the federal attorney, as a dedicated and efficient dragon slayer. What they did not take into account was that he was also honest:

At the end of March 1989, the *Herald* — no friend of mine, but delighted to see its rival rebuffed — ran a huge front-page headline: FEDS CLEAR BULGER. The *Globe*, on page seventeen, had printed a brief unsigned item headed "Report Expected to Clear Bulger."

Federal authorities rarely publish the results of investigations that find no wrongdoing, but they deemed this a proper time to do so. O'Sullivan issued a statement in which he said, "No witness has even alleged that Senator Bulger was criminally involved in this matter . . . and any inferences that he was so involved are not supported by the weight of the evidence."

At a news conference, O'Sullivan was asked whether his finding of my innocence was a close call. "It was not a close call," he said. "It was a clear call."

In fewer than four months — from December 8, 1988, to April 2, 1989 — the *Globe,* under nineteen different bylines, had printed sixty-nine articles about 75 State Street, most of them on page one. It had also published six editorials, two columns on its op-ed page and five cartoons. In mid-March it published the results of a poll it said showed that "72 percent of respondents who were aware of 75 State Street thought that Bulger had used his position for personal gain."

As Richard Brookhiser would remark later in *The New Yorker:* "For the *Globe* to do a poll on the public's perception of Bulger in the wake of 75 State Street was a little like assigning an arsonist to cover a fire."

Silverglate and Goode did not share my joy at seeing it all end.

They did not have to worry — not yet, anyway. It hadn't ended.

Meanwhile, life had to go on.

A district court judgeship came open in 1990, and Paul Mahoney, my administrative assistant, was appointed subject to approval by the Executive Council, as the law of Massachusetts requires.

I appeared before the council to testify in Paul's support. Alan Dershowitz and Harvey Silverglate were there to oppose. The two men undoubtedly have their good points. None springs to mind immediately, but they must have some. They may hold doors open for the elderly. They may put their litter in proper receptacles. Perhaps they feed birds in the park. But I do not warm to either.

Someone — not Mahoney and certainly not I — had alerted the media to witness the Dershowitz-Silverglate attack. The room was glutted with cameras.

Since I was a proponent of Mahoney's appointment, I spoke first, and began by reciting points in his favor. But there was no doubt in my mind that Mahoney — who besides being an excellent lawyer was a gentle and most compassionate man of strong character and integrity — was about to be savaged. That had to be addressed.

I had never responded to anything Dershowitz had said about me, and I suspect he thought I shared the timidity he inspired in many by his pitiless tongue and bullying manner. But where I came from, confrontation was a popular sport. I looked forward to it.

Knowing Paul's character allowed me to say with assurance that neither Dershowitz nor Silverglate would offer a single fact militating against approval of Mahoney. I said no such fact existed, only vicious, unfounded smears. Looking at Dershowitz and Silverglate, I said, "These men have no grievance against Paul Mahoney. All you will hear from them really is their antipathy toward me. With that in mind, consider their credibility, for they are crafty men, vindictive men, manipulative men, true connivers."

Christopher Iannella, the chairman, was so shocked by my preemptive strike he tried to silence me. "Now let's be calm," he said. "Just talk about Mr. Mahoney."

I was calm, but I had no intention of *acting* as though I were. I quoted Edmund Burke's admonition that there comes a time when forbearance ceases to be a virtue. "We've reached that time with this pair," I said.

"These two are *murderers*," I told the council, "murderers of reputations. Too many have put up with them for too long."

I said more. A lot more. As I approached my conclusion, I pointed at the pair and said, "Look at them. Just look at them!"

That brought an awful stillness to the room. Later I was told that, for some reason, Dershowitz and Silverglate were particularly incensed by that gesture and those words.

Dershowitz seemed uncharacteristically contained. He looked startled, even shocked. The familiar slashing courtroom manner was not in evidence — pomposity, yes, but no sign of a will to do combat.

As I had anticipated, he offered no fact damaging to Mahoney. What he did in substance was to ask the council to see whether *it* could discover some such fact. He urged the members to investigate rumors — that he alone alleged existed — to learn whether something might be found to substantiate his gossip.

It amounted to little more than an imperious demand for delay.

They made quite a pair, Alan and Harvey: Silverglate, looking like one cast by nature to play Iago, busily whispering to Dershowitz; Dershowitz, with his fright wig of hair and his petulant self-righteousness, telling the council what he wanted done — as though he were assigning homework to his students. And poor Paul, staring at them in astonishment, wondering what he might have done to arouse them so.

What he had done, of course, was become my administrative assistant. That, I have no doubt, was the answer, simple and entire.

The council approved the appointment. That meant Paul Mahoney received what he deserved. Dershowitz and Silverglate had received what they deserved.

The whole thing made me feel deservedly happy.

Scott Harshbarger, seeking the Democratic nomination for attorney general, attacked his foe, the incumbent James Shannon, for having referred to federal authorities the investigation of 75 State Street. If elected, Harshbarger said, he would reopen the case.

Little in politics astonishes me, but that did. Then I remembered Harshbarger had hired Michael Goldman as his political consultant.

Goldman had approached me during the height of the 75 State Street affair, suggesting I would be wise to retain him to "handle the media" for me. He spoke of his remarkable contacts in the press.

I wanted no backdoor dealings with the media. I did not want a consultant I suspected would be shopping our relationship to win more clients. I did not want *him* — and I said so. It was plain the rebuff did not sit well.

Goldman was not accustomed to rejection. He had achieved

celebrity status in 1985 as a member of a cabal that ousted Thomas McGee as Speaker of the House and replaced him with George Keverian. A feisty little man, McGee had been an effective Speaker; Keverian, who was indecisive, unreliable, slothful and terrorized by the media, was a disaster. The only winner had been Goldman, whose clients and prospective clients believed he had achieved great influence in the House.

Now, if an investigation by Goldman's client Harshbarger could help unseat the president of the Senate, well . . .

So began yet another chapter in my personal horror story. And it was a long chapter. It was January of 1992 before Harshbarger concluded his investigation by finding me innocent of any wrongdoing.

When that happened, I thought again of the need for endurance in politics. So often, if one can just stick it out, all the hurtful lies, however attested to by powerful men, however cozened by the media, will be gnawed away by the tooth of time, leaving the bones of truth laid bare . . . So often, it just takes endurance.

I was so exhilarated, that day in January, that I walked all the way home from the statehouse to burn the adrenaline away. On the way, I stopped on the bridge and stood there, even after a soft shower wept in from the harbor, enjoying the wetness on my face. I was so happy I felt I could stay there until the night itself was tired. Below me the water of Fort Point Channel, reflecting the moon like a sullied looking glass, sludged its way toward the sea. It made me think of the pollution I had swum through — finally.

At last, at long last, it was over.

F RANK BELLOTTI was certain to be nominated for governor. He had the votes; everyone knew that. The issue was
whether the president of Boston University, John Silber,
could run against him in the primary. To do that, Silber had to get
his name on the ballot. And to do *that,* he had to win fifteen
percent of the votes at the state's 1990 Democratic convention.
The convention took place in the Springfield Civic Center on two
hot days in June — hot in temperature, hot in political passions.

Bellotti's forces were determined to prevent Silber from running. They spent weeks before the convention attempting to do
so. They were helped by the group that would dominate the convention, the Massachusetts Teachers Association, the state's most
politically active organization and — where contributions for com-
pliant candidates were concerned — a bountiful cornucopia.

Silber stood for things the union feared: testing for the compe-
tency of teachers, testing for the progress of their students. He
promised that if he became governor, the best interests of students
would have priority over those of the union. Worse than that, he
meant it.

Many teachers privately supported him; their union heads did
not: they wanted Bellotti, but they wanted most of all to stop
Silber and lobbied fiercely to keep him off the ballot.

Silber discussed his ambitions with me, and I encouraged him. I thought it wrong that a man with such talent should be denied because he was an independent thinker and a political outsider. Tip O'Neill, the former Speaker of the national House, agreed with me, but did not want to become publicly involved. Nor did I; I anticipated a fierce contest for my Senate seat in the general election and needed no distraction. In addition, Silber had been assured by his organization he had all the convention votes he needed.

Robert "Skinner" Donahue, a Boston political operative, was in charge of the Silber effort. He came to see me soon after I arrived at the convention.

"How are you doing, Skinner?" I asked.

"Well, we have a lot of commitments."

"May I see the list?"

"List? I don't have a list."

"Then you don't have any votes," I told him.

Donahue looked annoyed. Since I had encouraged Silber, I began to feel a growing sense of responsibility.

"Well, let's get on the phone and put a list together," I said. "I assume you have a rundown on where all the delegates are staying."

"I haven't got to that yet."

That's how it was, and only hours to go before the final vote.

Skinner left, and my room in the Sheraton Hotel in downtown Springfield became from that moment the unofficial headquarters for Silber's delegate campaign.

I asked an aide, Jim Julian, to get a list of delegates from the Democratic State Committee. The committee had a strong alliance with the Bellotti camp and refused him. But I had a few friends too, so we quickly and quietly obtained a copy of the list.

The first problem was to find where we could reach anyone. We called hotels blindly, asking for members. We called the homes of delegates, asking whether the family knew how we might make contact. I sent aides cruising bars and restaurants. Slowly, things began to take shape. As soon as we found the whereabouts of a potentially friendly delegate, I tracked him or her down. I spent the night on the phone, rousting sleepy targets out of bed until dawn had come and gone and bright sunshine streamed in my windows.

We kept picking up commitments. There were even some Bellotti delegates who could not vote for our man but who promised to talk privately with friends who might. By breakfast time, I felt we were edging close to the fifteen percent we needed.

But one who is close to winning is also close to losing, so we still had a lot to do . . . and so little time.

Help came from an unexpected source that final morning, a steamy Saturday. The police union, involved in an ongoing labor dispute with Springfield Mayor Mary Hurley, suddenly mounted a picket line around the Civic Center. That gave us more time to work.

Many of the delegates were members of a union and would not cross the line. As the June heat increased and convention organizers pondered how to respond to the picket, some delegates went home; some who defied the line and crossed were manhandled by police; at least one was punched. But thousands of sweltering delegates paced around under the furnace of the sun outside the building, where we could talk with them.

Representatives of the candidates met to decide what to do. I attended, listening to the suggestions and waiting for Skinner Donahue to speak up for Silber. When I heard nothing useful coming from him, I said almost any resolution would be all right with me as long as Silber was given a place on the ballot.

"I'm the only one who can speak for John Silber," Donahue protested. "The Senate president can't speak for him."

No one paid much attention to that, and the discussion went on. It was said that Ron Kaufman, an adviser to President Bush, had been seen near the Civic Center.

"He's the one behind this picket line," one woman said. "The police backed Bush last election, and Kaufman went and rounded up friends in the union to embarrass us. He does stuff like this all the time."

I don't know whether Kaufman rounded up the picket line. I do know we rounded up many votes while it lasted.

Late that morning there was a breakthrough: the police union agreed to classify the picket line as "informational." This allowed union delegates to cross, and the convention began. It was called to order at 12:25 P.M., three and a half hours late. We had made progress during the hiatus, but still not enough.

It was hotter inside than out, because the air-conditioning system had collapsed. The temperature on the floor boiled above 100 degrees. I worked in my shirtsleeves, urging friendly delegates to circulate. "Don't sit down," I told them. "Keep going around the floor looking for people you know. Get every vote you can. We're still short."

It was hard going, trying to float through that sea of Bellotti supporters, but I enjoyed it more with each passing moment.

Peter Berlandi, a fundraiser and adviser to Bellotti, watched us closely. Delegates who were also members of the teachers' union scurried about in our wake, keeping tabs. An aide to Mark Roosevelt, Bellotti's campaign manager, followed me into the delegation from Roxbury, an all-black delegation. He was visibly disturbed when he saw me winning pledges from old friends there.

Bellotti had run ads on TV excoriating me: "Billy Bulger" was to blame for this, "Billy Bulger" was to blame for that. He made it clear this "Billy Bulger" was a particularly undesirable type. He and his staff began making harsh comments to reporters. Referring to me and my associates, Bellotti said, "Principle is not the strong suit among that group." Roosevelt called us members of a "hall of shame." He said Silber was being assisted by "every near-indicted" politician in the commonwealth. Berlandi said Silber and I were "corrupt" forces at the convention.

After the nominating speeches, the balloting for governor began. I was not confident there were a sufficient number of votes for Silber. I knew it was very tight. I listened closely and tried to keep the count in my head.

Radio booths were set up behind our delegation. Some of Boston's most depraved talkmasters were among those stationed there. They attempted to follow the tally also, and when the vote was complete we could hear them proclaiming that Silber had lost — and attributing his failure to his association with me. They were obviously delighted, loudly triumphant.

I climbed on a chair and looked at the disconsolate faces of the pro-Silber delegates who had heard the mordant crowing and acid comments from the radio booths. I said, "It was a near thing, but I assure you, Silber made it."

Soon thereafter, the results were announced: Silber had won, with a buffer of only about twenty votes. He was on the ballot!

Later, the *Globe* called Silber's achievement "a minor miracle."

A second vote for governor would be needed so Bellotti could get the percentage required for nomination. That did not affect our candidate, however, who left and went home.

While we were waiting for the second ballot, Bellotti approached me from behind and embraced me. I pushed him aside. He cast a nervous glance at the reporters who had trailed him, knowing they had seen the rebuff.

Roosevelt blocked the reporters and raised his voice to prevent them from hearing what was being said. Paul Mahoney stood with me.

"Bill — " Bellotti said.

"Bill? What happened to 'Billy Bulger,' the bad guy?"

"Hey," he said, "we come from the same school. This time I need your help — I'm short about two hundred votes."

"You want help from us insiders?"

"Come on," he said. "We've always been pals. You know me."

I knew this was his idea of deep manipulation. All I said was "Yes, you're right. I know you."

Bellotti was uncomfortable. He kept glancing at the TV cameras grinding away on us. Finally he turned and walked off.

In the days following the convention, Roosevelt moderated his statement that Silber was backed by near-indicted politicians: "I was not referring to Senate President Bulger when I said that," Roosevelt insisted. "I would never, ever question the Senate president's integrity."

Bellotti promptly downgraded Roosevelt. News of his "reassignment" was leaked and he was publicly humiliated.

I have heard many rationales for Roosevelt's abasement, and I don't know which, if any of them, is true. The reason could not have been that he did not work hard and loyally for Bellotti — and effectively enough to win the gubernatorial nomination for the man who cast him aside.

One of Bellotti's fatal weaknesses, I believe, is an abiding, and perhaps unconscious, distrust of others. It is a flaw easily developed in politics, but it is a recipe for losing.

I have tried deliberately to avoid that pitfall ever since a day long ago when I inadvertently cost Bernie Levitan $200 because I instinctively distrusted him.

Bernie was a chronic user of other people's money. In his salad days, he brazenly listed his occupation as paperhanger — street argot for one who passes bad checks.

Everyone seemed delighted to accept his drafts, which flew through the business community like confetti borne on an ill wind. This was astonishing, since Bernie — furtive, fox-faced and scruffy — looked unreliable. He was infectiously cheerful, though, and he was possessed of an air of helplessness that gave him a certain winsome charm. You might not trust Bernie, but somehow you liked him. Possibly he touched a subliminal sense of charity in his victims because he always looked as though he really needed the money.

Withal, he was a crashing failure in his line of work. Soon or late, each transaction led him to a court, where he would retain me to represent him. We fared very well, until that day in Middlesex Superior Court when we faced a most perceptive judge.

For reasons too obvious to labor, lawyers routinely require clients in criminal cases to pay fees in advance. Bernie offered me a check, and I said, "Perhaps we should deal in cash."

He left the court and was back in minutes with the money.

"Was that check you cashed good?" I asked nervously.

"Absolutely," he said. "Bill, I've learned my lesson."

He then went on to tell me that his life had been unhappy. That he had nothing to show for it. That he might do *some* wrong things in the future — don't we all, Bill? — but would never, ever utter another worthless check. He impressed me; I believed him.

I urged the judge to look kindly upon Bernie. He had never been accused of a violent crime. Though he had an irritating weakness for passing out what one might call IOUs in the form of checks, he had never forged a name and had always made restitution. The latter grace, admittedly, had been strongly encouraged by the various judges before whom he had appeared, but it was nevertheless true. And now, I assured the court, Mr. Levitan had firmly resolved to abandon the habits of his troubled past and never to write another worthless check. "And I believe he means it," I added with entire sincerity.

Bernie and I sat there for what seemed a long time while the judge thought things over. Then he assessed $200 in court costs.

After the session was over, I told the judge, whom I knew well, "I'm glad you continued the matter — but why the court costs?"

"Well, Bill," he said, "I was moved by your assurances that your client had reformed. You sounded very convinced."

"I really was."

"But Bill," he said, "when I learned *you* had just refused your client's check a few minutes earlier, I had to wonder."

I hadn't thought about it. Refusing Bernie Levitan's check was just something I had done automatically because of an instinctive mistrust, which had cost Bernie $200.

Of course, he couldn't pay the court, but I returned the fee he had paid me. I thought what I had learned was worth more anyway.

Prior to the convention campaign, my relationship with Bellotti had never been warm, but at least it had been affable. Had he left it that way, he would not have had an opponent as intense as I became in the primary fight on behalf of Silber.

Now I felt I could not ignore the things that had been said

about me by this man, a member of my own party. He might go on to win, but I was going to do what I could to prevent it.

Bellotti, seeing my commitment, resorted to his convention tactics: demonizing me. In his debates with Silber, after depicting me as an unprincipled tyrant, he would look at John and say, "As governor, you will only do what Billy Bulger wants."

That was amusing to Silber, who was constitutionally unable to accept dictation from anyone. Nevertheless, he felt an obligation to rebut some of the ugly personal things Bellotti said about me.

"Talk about the issues," I would urge him. "Bellotti can't do that; he isn't up to it. Don't worry about me, I can take care of myself."

The Silber-Bellotti debates were the highlight of the primary campaign, and the academician — quick, tough, informed and highly articulate — in my opinion destroyed his opponent. He made Bellotti look unfit for the office he sought.

Almost as important as the debates was the activity on the sidewalks outside. The TV evening news would cover that action, and each candidate wanted the more visible demonstration of popularity, for it is axiomatic in politics that the perception of support can translate into actual support.

Most of Silber's field organization came from my friends in South Boston and Savin Hill. Throughout the primary they provided hundreds of sign holders at South Station, North Station, Copley Square, and many other high-traffic areas. They made up most of the pro-Silber presence outside the debates.

Bellotti was friendly with the leadership of several unions. He bused hundreds from those organizations for the activities on the streets. Some of the people were tough indeed, and they were brought in to discourage others from demonstrating.

It worked for him — but only once. When we saw what was happening, we countered with volunteers from South Boston — members of the boilermakers' union, stevedores and other very sincere people. That brought an instant end to any notion of intimidating us.

I don't think Silber was even aware of much of the politicking that went on. He was genuinely preoccupied with addressing issues.

Though opposed locally by the *Globe,* Silber attracted national support. The syndicated columnist George Will called him "the nation's most interesting candidate in 1990."

Silber won the primary handily. He would now oppose the Republican nominee, William Floyd Weld, in the general election.

"We're going to have a time tonight," Marty O'Brien, one of my assistants, said.

In South Boston there is a time for almost every occasion. It is not a time in the Ecclesiastical sense — a time to live, a time to die, and so on — it refers to an event, a gathering. A time will be held to celebrate a wedding, the birth of a baby, a new home, even a new job. A time will be held to raise money for one who loses a job, for those who are ill or are injured, for families burned out of their homes. In this case, it was to be a time held at the Cornerstone Pub to celebrate Silber's victory, an event for which many of my neighbors felt they might claim a share of credit.

I was free at last to address my own concerns:

My opponent in the general election was a fire-eater named John DeJong from Boston's Back Bay — and it looked like a good year for Republicans. I had won my primary contest by a margin of almost two to one over Stephen Michael Palmer. DeJong was a far greater challenge. I had a fight on my hands.

Now, being elected to office is, of course, simple.

It is not easy, but it *is* simple. People vote their interests, economic, social and philosophical. The candidate whose election appears most likely to further such interests wins. Financing and a good organization help get that message across.

Anyone can readily see how simple all that is. But not always easy, especially against a newcomer to politics who is able to promise as many things as his or her conscience will allow — which often is a wonderfully extensive ambit. An incumbent, on the other hand, has amassed a record, a yardstick if you will, by which his future performance may be, and is, rightly or wrongly, measured.

That is the respect that often makes calamity of long political life. However many you have pleased, your every act has displeased *somebody* — often a great many somebodies. And since anger is a sharper spur to action than satiety, the disappointed voter hurries to the polls while the contented citizen may stay at home. Thus the longer you are in office, the more difficult it is likely to be to convince the electorate to prefer you to a newcomer.

The media, aware of a general surliness among voters, a will to express discontent with the sagging economy mostly, sensed an opportunity to be rid — *finally!* — of the Bulger nuisance.

Both the *Globe* and the *Herald* strongly endorsed my rival, as did many electronic outlets. Most of the accompanying polemics were, in my opinion, fair, however misguided. Editorial writers and TV commentators called for my defeat as a step toward "rejuvenating" our political process. They called for younger, more vigorous leaders. They suggested that the winds of change alone would bring relief.

That was the message from the high ground. From the gutter, some radio talkmasters sleazed the airwaves with their usual crude and epithetic biliousness. All of which made for an intense campaign.

DeJong, an articulate veterinarian, made the most of it and campaigned frenetically. He appeared to hold me responsible for many of the woes of mankind, including the recession afflicting our state and the rest of the nation that year. One radio station held a fundraising effort for DeJong on Boston Common, a unique demonstration of purpose even for Massachusetts politics.

It was difficult to fight back against a man with no political record. I could hardly fault him for worming distressed house pets or otherwise ministering to the ailments of suffering animals, all commendable pursuits. The best I could do was say that even though the economy is going to the dogs, we shouldn't call a veterinarian to fix it.

Not an argument pregnant with meaning, but some found it amusing. I think it was Willie Brown, the maven of California politics, who told me, "When you can't make them cheer, make them laugh. At least you get their attention." It was good advice.

My district extends to Beacon Street, with its proper Yankee Bostonians; to the eastern extremity of Beacon Hill, considered a bastion of liberalism; to the South End, a trendy and unpredictable area abounding in artists and residents of many races. There was speculation I would find it hard going in those areas.

The critical core of my district is, of course, South Boston. In the ethos of my old Neighborhood, fighters are admired, bullies despised; and the community had decided I was the victim of a gang attack, which boded well for me. This was never more evident than on the Sunday before the election when I attended a huge gathering of veterans at Gate of Heaven hall, an adjunct to South Boston's cathedral.

Monsignor John McNamara, pastor of my church, St. Brigid's, rose to speak. He had been head of chaplains in the U.S. Army, had served in Vietnam, and if he hadn't worn a cassock might have been a very hard-nosed citizen.

He surprised me when he began discussing politics. He noted that the cardinal had instructed the clergy to refrain from involvement in political matters. Then he added, "I am, of course, obedient to Cardinal Law's order. But I can, and do, urge all of you to vote on Tuesday. Vote *your* way. Make up *your* mind. Don't let *anyone* tell you how to vote." There was a significant pause. Then he said, "All *I* hope is that those ballot boxes will be *BULG*-ing!"

The audience rose and cheered, presaging the bulging vote that came out in the Neighborhood that Tuesday.

One young woman who supported my opponent attempted to vote for a second time at — of all places — the L Street polling center. She was challenged. When it was found she was using a fraudulent name, she was arrested. The district attorney called me and asked whether I wanted to press charges against her.

"Good heavens, no," I said. "After the things that she read about me in the papers, she undoubtedly thought she was doing her civic duty."

Her vote would have made no difference. I won by a margin of more than two to one and carried every ward but the one where DeJong lived.

In the general election, the tickets were headed by John Silber and the Republican candidate for governor, William Weld.

The timing of Weld's announcement had been unfortunate. It came on a day when the papers were full of the surrender to U.S. authorities of General Manuel Noriega of Panama and the suicidal plunge from the Tobin Bridge of a suspect in a much publicized Boston murder. But elections aren't won by announcements.

Frank Bellotti behaved like — well, like Bellotti. He did not support Silber. It was clear to me that, just as he had undone Chub Peabody in 1964, he now sought to undo his party's nominee in 1990. He did not publicly aid Weld, but members of his organization did. Bellotti's chief fundraiser, Peter Berlandi, openly defected to the Republican camp and raised millions of dollars for Weld, an independently wealthy man.

In his first and only other attempt to win political office, Weld had run against Bellotti in the 1978 race for attorney general. It pitted a political amateur against a seasoned professional, and Weld carried only 2 of 351 cities and towns. Weld described that daunting experience as "a lot of fun," and went on to serve as a U.S. attorney in Boston and in the Justice Department in Washington. Now Weld and his fellow Republicans picked up the Bellotti tactic of hammering me. It was their campaign theme.

It came naturally to Weld. He seemed to regard all legislators as corrupt and arrogant. The *Globe* columnist Mike Barnicle joked that when Weld became U.S. attorney, his first order was to "arrest everyone in city hall who has ever had a nickname."

Like so many fictions, it spoke a kind of truth.

If nicknames were regarded by Weld as a badge of wickedness, half of South Boston would be suspect: we had The Good Robb, Joe Wetwash, Blockhead O'Rourke, Handles Houlihan, thousands more. There was Roaming Crowley, who was given his nickname by nuns at parochial school because of his penchant for wandering off. By the time he achieved manhood and went to work at Cassidy's funeral home, lazy tongues had dulled the suffix and he was known for the rest of his life as Roman Crowley. For thirty years I never knew him by any other name.

I recalled the time a letter from home reached me at Fort Dix, New Jersey, to inform me that Spider Kelly was stationed there. He was a long-time friend and the leading pass receiver on our high school football team. I went to the post locator office and tried to find his unit.

"We've got thirty-six Kellys," a bored clerk told me. "What's his first name?"

"Spider," I said. "Well, that's his nickname."

"We're a little more formal here. What's his real name?"

"I never heard him called anything but Spider."

"How long have you known him?"

"Fifteen years."

"And you don't know his first name!"

I walked back to my barracks thinking about all those I had known only by a nickname. It was an anomaly of life in the Neighborhood that, close as we were, we often did not know the given name of a friend because we never used it or heard it. Perhaps it is the same in other tightly knit areas.

Weld himself came from a social stratum abounding in such sobriquets as Binky, Beany, Tootsie and Pebbles, but apparently he perceived a hierarchy of elegance in such things. Notwithstanding all that, he was a Tartar as a campaigner.

One Weld television advertisement featured a succession of pictures: a picture of a suitcase filled with cash, a picture of convicted Mafia mobster Gennaro Angiulo and, for a finale, a picture of me. A faceless voice in the background declaimed, "As U.S. attorney, he convicted banks for money laundering, mob racketeers, corrupt public officials . . . Wherever Bill Weld has gone, he has brought change. Real change."

As for Weld himself, he went from podium to podium insisting that state politics were "rotten to the core" and that I personified all that was wrong with legislators in general. He explained that the "old way of doing things" must go, but they never would "as long as Billy Bulger holds on to the reins of power."

On an occasion when an indictment was returned naming fifty-one persons, Weld called a news conference at the Parker House. He said the accused were *believed* to be associated with my brother, James. This, he said, compelled him to speak out about me and to ask me not to seek reelection as Senate president.

It seemed to me he had been speaking out about me on a fairly regular basis. I doubted the accused, even if found guilty of some crime, were associated in any culpable sense with my brother — and, as it developed, they were not. That aside, I failed to see how the conduct, whatever it might be, of fifty-one persons I did not know could render me unfit for office.

According to the *Globe* report of that same day, "Weld also appeared to politically link Bulger and his brother James . . ." James was indeed linked with me as my brother, and as my brother I loved him. But he was never, nor wanted to be, involved in my political life; nor did I wish him to be, because he knew nothing of politics, and cared less.

Later, Weld said Senate inaction on term limits "illustrates, if nothing else, and a lot does, that Senator Bulger is part of the problem, not part of the solution." This was, I believe, the only time I commented on anything he said. I noted that Pennsylvania originally had written legislative term limits into its constitution — then had dropped that provision when it became clear it was eliminating the state's most effective public servants.

But the Weld campaign was into fiction, not history.

There was no sign that I could see that the Republicans were making gains by abusing me. In fact, I thought its heavy-handed absurdities might be counterproductive. And I thought Silber had the better of Weld because of his ability in debate. But some media — conspicuously the *Globe,* which had endorsed Weld — depicted Silber's independence as irresponsibility, and his intensity as egotism. They frightened some people, undoubtedly. The result was that Silber was at the same time fighting Weld, the *Globe* and all of those lesser media outlets which relied upon that paper for their guidance.

I thought the election as close to a tie as any I had ever seen. The outcome was in doubt to the end. But just as that end arrived, Silber was interviewed by Natalie Jacobson of Channel 5. The event was a disaster for Silber.

It is said of some that they will not tolerate a fool gladly, but Silber won't tolerate one at all. Natalie Jacobson is certainly no fool, indeed she is a courteous and competent journalist. She asked a question and John misconstrued it. He thought it foolish, and he answered with acerbity.

The general reaction of those who watched was that Silber had been rude. There was much talk about the incident. I think it hurt Silber badly, especially among women voters. It may have made the difference in the campaign. Many think it did.

At all events, on election day Silber was narrowly — very narrowly — defeated. Weld, who had lost by the biggest margin in Massachusetts history when he ran against Bellotti in 1978, had now defeated Silber in the closest gubernatorial election of the century.

Knowing Weld as I now do, he must have been amused by the irony of being sworn into office by me.

In 1994, when Mark Roosevelt won the Democratic nomination for governor, Bellotti advantaged Weld by deserting his own party and his former campaign chairman. He accused Roosevelt — who had been critical of Berlandi's desertion — of being anti-Italian.

Roosevelt said that Bellotti privately had explained his fealty to Berlandi and his hostility to Roosevelt by saying, "Business is business."

Weld, as everyone knew he would, won reelection easily. The political apostasy of Bellotti contributed little to a victory that was certain, but it fortified a belief that he was devoid of party loyalty.

Dante wrote of the ninth circle, the innermost circle of hell, as that place reserved for those who betray. As our expectations of human conduct diminish with the passing years, our sense of outrage cools to mere sadness. The thing about sadness is we all learn to deal with it. And we get better at it as we go along.

Weld certainly was not the only Republican victor in 1990. The elections were a disaster for Democrats. My party was ravaged: Republicans captured all the major administrative offices, and they made significant gains in the House. In the Senate, six Republicans beat Democratic incumbents, and three won open seats — a total of nine freshman senators on the other side of the aisle. They joined the seven GOP incumbents to form what many heralded as the vanguard of the Weld revolution. A shift of only five thousand votes statewide could have given Republicans control of the Senate.

As it was, there were only twenty-four Democrats left in our chamber, while Republicans had doubled, to a total of sixteen. For the first time since 1959, Senate Republicans, if they stood together, could sustain a gubernatorial veto over the thinned Democratic majority.

The tottering economy had been a factor. Some said the results reflected an eruption of anti-incumbent fervor — a public will to turn the rascals out. But the prevailing view was that it had been a crushing personal defeat for me: I had been the principal target of Republicans in all of the contests, and they had won so many of them. Alexander Tennant, executive director of the state Republican Party, proclaimed, "Bulger is five votes away from being removed as Senate president."

That time, at least, Tennant told the truth — not an ingrained habit.

David Locke, the Senate minority leader, could not contain his enthusiasm. He spoke of "the biggest facelift on Beacon Hill in memory."

Locke and I were old adversaries, first in the House and now in the Senate. Our debates were often fierce, but without venom. I recall once when I was speaking of problems in Boston, Locke — who came from the affluent suburb of Wellesley — repeatedly interrupted.

"We are discussing urban problems," I told him. "Complex matters of great import. If I have a question about agriculture or other rural concerns, I will welcome your advice."

The following day he interrupted proceedings to present me with a basket of tomatoes from his garden. "At least," he said, "these make it evident we know how to deal with our rural concerns, which is more than I can say for Boston."

But now he wasn't bringing me gifts of tomatoes. Had he brought any to the chamber, he might have been tempted to throw them, given the way he was describing my lot: "He's like General Custer at Little Bighorn looking at the bodies of his comrades. Yes, *he* has survived, but he's lost his vise-like grip over the Senate."

To survive "like Custer" was a simile offering small comfort.

"You've lost your clout, Bill," he told me privately. Then he smiled happily. "Sorry about that."

He didn't look sorry.

So on and on it went, the interminable crowing and scolding, the florid declamations of the dawning golden age of Republicanism. I was appalled at the naiveté of some first-termers who seemed locked in a dream of political sagacity within a dream of political change. In fact, they were completely unaware of the realities of government. Most tedious of all were the rambling lectures, well intentioned but abrasive, by those who wanted to share with us their startling discoveries of the obvious: "Massachusetts faces a severe economic challenge!" Or, "If we spend more than we take in, there will be a deficit!"

One afternoon I sat behind the lectern, benumbed and waiting out the tidal flow of such oratory as the session dragged toward twilight. My attention turned to the architecture of our three-story chamber, its colonial colors of blue, white and gold, its columns, its ceiling, its —

Suddenly my reverie was halted. I saw a man climbing from the visitors' gallery to a narrow ledge that circled the chamber some thirty feet above our heads. He was a tall, dark man with angular features and close-cropped hair, and he walked on the ledge with the casual agility of a mountain goat.

Total silence descended on the Senate. Every face was turned upward, every eye on him. We did not know, we could not know, whether we were looking at one bent on flamboyant suicide, an assassin or some poor soul out of his wits.

Finally he reached a recess, a sort of niche designed, I suppose, to hold a statue. He climbed into it and looked down on us. "I'm tired of listening to all this," he said in a reverberating bass voice. "Every election, you promise us you will come here and do something important. But all you do is talk to each other and say nothing." He seemed calm, but quite annoyed with us. "Why," he asked, "don't you start passing some good laws? All you are doing is loitering . . ."

By this time, the capitol police were moving toward the visitors' gallery. I signaled to them to stop. While the man in the niche continued to berate us, a police captain came to the rostrum.

"Mr. President," the captain protested, "we should get him."

"You might cause him to fall."

"Well, that's true — "

"Besides," I told him, "what he's saying makes more sense than anything else I've heard this afternoon. Leave him alone."

Eventually the man finished what he had to say and returned on the same treacherous ledge to the gallery. The police led him off.

I assume they cautioned him and sent him on his way, because I heard no more of it. But I recall it as a blessed interlude of relief.

9

IN 1991 my brother James became a millionaire. Of course many men and women became millionaires in the fast lanes of our economy at that time, but James, being James, had to do it in bizarre fashion.

I had taken a group of my own children and their friends to ride the rapids of the Colorado River, a vacation that Mary flatly refused to share. Our group included my long-time friend Barry Gottehrer and his son Kevin.

We had been rafting for a week when I called Mary from a hotel pay phone to confirm that our family was still intact.

"What do you think Uncle Jim has done?" she asked.

"Gone to Tibet to become a monk?"

"No, he's won the Massachusetts lottery," Mary said.

"Well," I said, "I suppose that figures."

Mary explained that Jim had been one of a group that had purchased a lottery ticket together, and that his share amounted to a million and a half dollars, to be paid in installments.

The ticket had been bought jointly by Mike Linskey and his brother Paddy, Kevin Weeks and Jim. Half the purchase price had been paid by Mike, who was thus entitled to half the proceeds of the $14.3 million prize. The remaining half was divided equally among Paddy, Jim and Kevin. My brother's share amounted to about $1.6 million — $80,000 a year for twenty years.

"There's been a lot of publicity," Mary went on. "People all over the world want him to invest or donate money. Some letters from abroad are just addressed 'James Bulger, USA' and they're being delivered to him."

I was of course happy for Jim. At the same time, I anticipated there would be speculation, as indeed there was, that he had somehow contrived to cheat. The new Republican state treasurer, Joe Malone, who was required to return state funds he took for meetings he had not attended, rolled his eyes ceilingward and said, "I could not be more embarrassed if my mother had won." He expressed chagrin that he could not deny Jim his winnings.

More significant than the speculation or Malone's tawdry posturing was the likelihood that the more attention my brother received, the more attractive he would become as a target for media-prodded law-enforcement authorities.

My apprehension proved well grounded.

At the time of this writing, Jim has been characterized a fugitive from justice since early January of 1995. Regrettably, he has placed himself in a position where anything goes — planted press stories, absurd rumors, wild exaggerations, the lot.

It is understandable that anyone who is accused based on purchased testimony would be fearful of such an accusation.

For good reason, the Model Code of Professional Responsibility of the American Bar Association states: "A lawyer shall not pay, offer to pay, or acquiesce in the payment of compensation to a witness contingent upon the content of his testimony or the outcome of the case." The ABA Model Code of Ethical Consideration states: "Witnesses should always testify truthfully and should be free from any financial inducements that might tempt them to do otherwise. A lawyer should not pay or agree to pay a non-expert witness an amount in excess of reimbursement for expenses and financial loss incident to his being a witness."

Unfortunately, prosecutors seem now to have secured an exception from the rules and laws that disallow the purchasing of testimony.

The bar against purchasing testimony obviously is meaningless if limited to payments of cash. If it does not condemn the payment of *anything* of value, a lawyer is free to buy testimony by giving a prospective witness anything other than money.

It has been known for many years that a "get out of jail" card has been available to anyone who would give testimony against my brother. As long as this behavior is countenanced, prosecutors may and do buy testimony, with all the dangers attendant to such purchases.

In the well-publicized case against my brother, *all* of the evidence has been purchased. Inducements more precious than money — release from prison, the waiver of criminal charges — have been offered time and time again. Some of those who insisted they had nothing to offer at the beginning of their incarceration have had second thoughts and suddenly "remembered" things they could barter for advantages. Without such purchased testimony there would be no accusations.

In the gaudy circus of the O. J. Simpson murder trial, a witness swore she had taped an interview with Los Angeles police officer Mark Fuhrman in which he had recounted fabricating evidence against someone he considered a criminal. Whether the alleged incidents actually occurred or not, recounting them bespeaks approbation of such conduct. The Mark Fuhrmans in our society may be few, but when police and prosecutors become determined to prove someone guilty of something at all costs, the Fuhrman spirit lives.

Buoyed by the huge Republican gains in the 1990 state elections, Governor Weld moved to assemble an effective administrative team for the future. He chose Mary Padula, a five-time senator, to be secretary of communities and development. It was an excellent appointment — Mary was bright and able. It was also a safe choice: her district had been solidly Republican for two decades.

An astute politician, Padula delayed resigning her Senate seat for two months to allow Paul Fontaine, a popular Fitchburg city councilor, sufficient time to qualify for the primary.

"Fontaine has a French father and an Italian mother," Padula said. "That's important in my area. He's proved he's a big vote getter. He's a registered Republican. We can't lose."

Fontaine's opponent would be Representative Robert Antonioni, a youthful and — compared with Fontaine — woefully inexperienced aspirant from Leominster. Bob was a capable legislator but conspicuously unfunded and almost totally unorganized, a Democratic challenger in a Republican citadel.

I called Senators Boverini and Bertonazzi into my office, along with two of my assistants, Jim Julian and Marty O'Brien. "The subject," I said, "is the special election."

"You mean to replace Mary?" Marty asked. "What's to talk about? If the Republicans can't win *that,* they can't win much."

"That's why we have to talk about it," I said. "It's because they're so sure they can't lose that we have to make sure they do."

I reviewed what they already knew — the stunning Republican gains in the last election, the tenuous nature of our majority, the fact that we could no longer override a veto if the people on the other side of the aisle stood together. "And I've had enough of the interminable crowing about it," I said. "This is where the road back starts. Right here. Right now."

"With . . . what's his name?" Marty asked, trying to remember.

"Antonioni," Jim said.

"Yes, with Antonioni," I said.

I told Jim and Marty that I was convinced all the elections of 1992 would be affected by what happened in this special senatorial contest between Fontaine and Antonioni. "We have to help Antonioni. And he has to win."

Everyone pitched in with a will, though more than a few wondered whether we were trying to make two and two equal five. I worked as though I were running in Fitchburg myself.

Fontaine was well funded, so we struggled to level that field. He had the organization, too, so a battalion of volunteers went to help Bob — men and women expert at political skills. They took the heretofore unseen techniques of big-city campaigning to Antonioni's district.

South Boston responded with that boiling over of spirit, that tribal ebullition if you will, that a political challenge evokes in my Neighborhood. There was no end of volunteers: even women in our Old Harbor project, many of them campaign veterans, contributed. They wrote letters extolling Bob's qualities to almost everyone in the telephone directories of Antonioni's district.

The Republicans recognized the importance of the election. Governor Weld campaigned for Fontaine, as did Lieutenant Governor Paul Cellucci, Treasurer Joe Malone and many others. President George Bush sent his labor secretary, Lynn Martin, to endorse Fontaine.

Following the Republican Party playbook of 1990, Fontaine ran a wholly negative campaign. "Don't give Bulger another Democratic senator," he urged.

The *Worcester Telegram* warned that Antonioni would be my captive because I was helping him. Other papers echoed that theme. "Given all the importance that Beacon Hill power brokers are attaching to Tuesday's special state Senate race," the *Globe* said, "the names on the ballot might as well be those of Weld and Bulger."

"We *want* the race to be a referendum on Weld," Republican State Committee Chairman Leon Lombardi said.

When Padula resigned her seat, the Senate scheduled the special election for the same day as the Massachusetts presidential primary, when Democrats would be out in force.

The Republicans, who wanted the elections a month apart, were outraged. They accused me of political machinations. A group of them staged a perplexing protest by dumping a shoebox full of tea into the Nashua River. Even the media seemed bemused by that.

Straight-faced, I said, "The environmentally incorrect antic of polluting the waters of the Nashua River shocks me. The riparian ravages may be severe." For good measure, I added, "I am further upset that the party of fiscal responsibility wants to spend an additional $40,000 to have the special Senate election take place on a separate day. We cannot countenance these excesses."

Antonioni came to my office and said he thought he now had a chance to win. I told him that wasn't enough — he had to be sure.

"What do the people in your district talk about most?"

"Hockey," he said, laughing. "I'm joking, but — "

"That's no joke," I said. "If they talk mostly about hockey, and if they associate you with hockey, they'll talk a lot about you."

"Why would they associate me with hockey?"

I asked him whether it would help if Bobby Orr, the great former defenseman of the Boston Bruins, endorsed him.

"Bobby Orr!" he said reverentially. "My God!"

And so I asked Orr, a good friend, to appear with Antonioni.

"I've stayed away from politics," Orr said.

"I know. But this is an exception. The state where you live needs this young man in the Senate. You can put him there. Think of it as a public service."

Orr did as I asked. It is not possible to measure precisely the impact of such things, but Antonioni beat Fontaine by 188 votes.

Most Republicans blamed me and the scheduling of the election for Fontaine's defeat. But Weld was his usual candid self. Asked if Antonioni's victory could be a harbinger of other seats going Democratic, he said, "Could be . . . We really thought we'd win that seat."

If Republicans were surprised by Fontaine's defeat, a much greater jolt was in store for them in the fall elections. Fontaine lost in a rematch to Antonioni, this time by a huge twelve percentage points. One Republican freshman senator, Nancy Achin Sullivan, did not run, and her seat was won by a Democrat. In addition, five Republicans lost their reelection bids, including David Locke, who had served in the legislature for thirty-four years and was the leader of the new Republican bloc in the Senate. Locke was handily defeated by Democrat Cheryl Jacques, who was born two years after Locke was first elected to the House.

Ironically, Locke attributed his defeat to the same blind frustration with government that I believe resulted in the ouster of his

Democratic colleagues just two years earlier. "The voters summarily rejected the Republicans," he said. "It was a mood of discontent, frustration, a throw-the-rascals-out syndrome. Plus, it was 'the year of the woman.'"

In a column by David Nyhan in the *Globe,* Locke was quoted: "To some, everybody in public office is a hack. If you hear that long enough, as the public does, it begins to sink in. What they read has the ring of authenticity . . . There's a feeling those in public office are by and large in there for personal gain, to feather their nest. I think that's a false image. The majority of public servants are hardworking, very committed; many are extremely talented as well."

I was used to Locke, abrasive but honest, and I would miss him, in a perverse way. But I was delighted with Cheryl Jacques, a woman of great talent and integrity, with courage to spare.

With the number of Republicans back down to nine, Democrats were once again in a comfortable position to set their agenda. In 1992 we had reversed the Republican victories of 1990.

Or so it seemed — but in politics, nothing is writ. While we were winning those state offices, Democratic congressmen in Massachusetts and across the nation were suffering their first defeats. It was an ominous portent of the 1994 congressional elections.

The great political turnaround of 1992 in our commonwealth caused much celebrating in Democratic South Boston.

The pubs did a land-office business — and we have a lot of them. For within our area are perhaps twenty subneighborhoods, and each has its own pub, sometimes two. They tend to be small and generally would not appeal to one seeking a postprandial snifter of Remy Martin, but the clientele are faithful, usually well behaved, and include some colorful sorts:

Foghorn Finley was a stentorian type given to startling outbursts of Gaelic verse at Connolly's. Eyebrows Hardy, John McCormack's law partner, on the other hand, was a man who almost never spoke, but who was reputed to be a deep thinker.

Eyebrows, who commanded much respect after his appointment as state director of Social Security, was a fixture at Sullivan's Pub.

There was a failed artist called the Major, a patron of many barrooms, who worked in Boston's theatrical district at a store that rented costumes — which he borrowed frequently. The Major would arrive at various pubs dressed as a postman, a marine, a Royal Canadian Mountie or a Turkish bey, but most often as a U.S. Army officer, which led to his nickname.

Major's particular friend was a large white mongrel with the brown velvet eyes of a Jersey cow that accompanied him on his rounds. He had named the creature Dog, which struck everyone as astonishingly unimaginative for one who painted in oils.

Man and beast were oddly similar. Major wore an ugly wig and a hard look, but when he spoke he seemed amiable. Dog, who lay at his feet in the bar most of the time, occasionally rose, looked about and snarled, showing his teeth, although there seemed no malice in it. Only strangers were alarmed by the outbursts. To the regulars, Major and Dog were just part of the decor.

There was Freddie St. Germain, a teacher at South Boston High, a manikin of a man with a tiny waxed mustache who claimed a vague descent from royalty. He was known by the improbable nickname Speedy; only the regulars knew its origin. St. Germaine's sin was, to be harshly blunt, drunkenness, a sin that is its own punishment — as Freddie discovered.

At a time when elections were less closely monitored, he voted for Mike Ward, a candidate for the school committee, and then repaired to Fitzie's Casino where, after several Bushmills, he decided to vote again.

He went to the Parkman School, in the lower end of South Boston, and announced himself to the warden keeping the list. "I'm Joseph Chase of Fourteen Bolton Street," Freddie said.

"Deceased," the warden said.

Freddie, his hearing dulled by his visit to Fitzie's, said, "No — the name is Chase."

The warden, a no-nonsense woman, turned to the police officer on duty and said, "Arrest this man."

266 🔖 William M. Bulger

Fortunately for Freddie, the officer was a friend, Pug O'Reilly, who took St. Germaine to one side and advised him, "Run for your life!"

Freddie did, surprising everyone with his agility — and earning the nickname he never lost.

There was John B. Wenzler, a state representative who owned a barroom. His political foes said he had been a spy for the Germans in World War II. Wenzler would unnerve newcomers to his bar by abruptly volunteering to them the gratuitous assurance that he was not and never had been a German spy.

He didn't restrict this odd behavior to his pub. He once appeared at the statehouse in a bathing suit to protest the lengthy session. "We should all be at the beach," he kept shouting.

One incident involved an FBI agent, an attractive woman who sat at the bar in Amrhein's Restaurant in South Boston. She happened to be beside Johno Coleman, an old friend of mine, whom of course she didn't know — just as he didn't know she was an undercover operative. He told me what happened:

"Who comes along and strikes up a conversation with this woman but Skinny Shannahan," Johno said. "He was cruising like always, and she certainly looked friendly."

I did not know Skinny, but I had heard much about him. He was a notorious womanizer. It was said he had been dazzled in his youth by the motion picture *Gone with the Wind* and had tried to adopt the persona Clark Gable had given the character Rhett Butler — dashing, debonair, devil-may-care. Actually, I was told, Skinny had done a pretty fair job of it, if you weren't too picky about a regional accent and a certain casualness with grammar.

Smiling, charming, full of information — and usually drenched in enough musky after-shave lotion to inflame all the bulls within a ten-mile radius — Skinny aspired to fame as the Don Juan of Boston. He was completely serious about it. With Gable dead, he hoped George Hamilton would play him in the movies. I was not surprised to hear he had unleashed his fabled talents on an attractive and unescorted woman sitting at a bar.

"She's asking him questions about everything and — you know Skinny — he's got all the answers," Johno said.

That was not surprising either. Who can imagine a Rhett Butler responding to a query with, "Frankly, my dear, I don't know a damn thing about that."

"So she asks him can she get an apartment, a *cheap* apartment, in South Boston," Johno went on, "and Skinny says it's no problem. He'll put her in touch with the right people.

"Then she wants to know is there any jobs open. Skinny says there's plenty, if you know how to get 'em. So she asks how do you get 'em. Skinny says, 'Why, my dear, you pay for 'em.'"

"Why are you telling me about this?" I ask.

"The woman asks him how much a job costs," Johno went on, ignoring my question. "Skinny says, well, that depends. He says if you want a job on the T" — the MBTA rapid transit line — "it's a thousand dollars. So she says that's a lot, but she could pay it if the job's good. Then she wants to know who she has to pay it to."

"And Skinny gave her his own name and address, I assume."

"No, Bill, he's not looking for money, he's hitting on her. He's making a big impression, see? So he says she'd have to pay it to *you*."

It all went into her report, into the FBI files. I was never asked about the incident, nor did anyone try to test its veracity. But it *was* leaked, as usual, identified only as "information." The allegation then appeared in the tawdrier tabloid columns, as though its source made it true.

Nature was kind to Weld. He is a tall, lean man with red hair, an affable expression and a long, open face — a vintage Yankee, but happily free of the clenched jaw of the very rich, which he is. He is very bright and witty, a crypto-intellectual. And he has never made the mistake of trying to survive in politics on the basis of his trust funds.

In the beginning, he seemed incredibly innocent. He allowed himself to be influenced by advisers who made him appear to be a man so suffused with his own rectitude that he saw only evil in those he considered foes. But he is fundamentally independent, and it was not long before he began to modify that image to a considerable extent.

Many with Weld's affluence enter office believing they are tenured because voters will conclude they need nothing and thus can be trusted. That is a short-lived delusion. Most voters are not rich, and can hardly be expected to agree that only the wealthy are honest.

In fact, voters are quick to perceive that a candidate who does not need money may well be impoverished in other respects: in intelligence, creativity, compassion. This explains the legion of wealthy politicians who have been abruptly retired from public life.

During the period between the election in November 1990 and the beginning of our session in January 1991, the media pondered: how would Weld fare with a Democratic majority — however thinned — in both houses? How could he work with a Senate president he had vilified?

There were several reasons why he would have no problem with me. To begin, the state faced critical problems, particularly in its economy. Most of what bedeviled us was part of a national recession, a phenomenon that had brought a sense almost of despair to the land.

"Relax, Bill," a young senator advised me. "Anybody with a brain in his head knows we're not to blame for the recession here."

"Anybody with a brain in his head knows we *will* be to blame if we don't dig Massachusetts out of it," I assured him.

Obviously, the economy was more important than any political differences, more important than ruffled feelings. I made several public statements to the effect that we had to find areas of agreement and work together. That theme was echoed and joined in by Speaker Charles Flaherty in the House.

Personal animosity would not interfere: I had worked with many in government whom I disliked. Further, I had met Weld several times and thought he was personally a decent sort.

In his campaign he had struck at me with blatant falsehoods; but while Bellotti, who had said the same things, knew them to be untrue, I thought the politically ingenuous Weld actually believed them — that he had been convinced by others that Democratic legislators were an evil bunch, and that I was their paradigm. In short, I thought him to be honest, however misinformed, and felt experience would gentle his perceptions.

We had to reduce spending, and we worked with Weld on that. Some objected:

"I know we have to cut," Senator Berry told me, "but some parts of that budget will hurt me in my district."

"Everybody knows we have to cut," I said, "but nobody wants his or her district to feel it. This is a fair and necessary budget."

"Bulger and Weld," he said disdainfully.

Well, I liked the billing, anyway.

Massachusetts had a near junk-bond status in 1990, and we met with the bond-rating people from New York. It was the first time they had been able to meet with the governor, the Senate president and the speaker at the same time: they said they were impressed.

That was the beginning of the road back for our bonds.

Weld said he liked dealing directly with Flaherty and me, so we began regular meetings in our various offices, rotating among them each week. Members of Weld's staff, particularly John Moffit, warned him the plan was unwise, that he would be misused or in some way co-opted. He ignored them. While we of course communicate frequently when matters arise, the practice of holding a scheduled weekly meeting has continued to the time of this writing, some five years later.

As it developed, Weld and I shared many views. We both felt deeply concerned with the failings of our public education system. For years I had been trying to establish school choice — the right of parents to choose the schools their children would attend. Weld said he supported me in that undertaking, and he has done so. He also agreed with the creation of charter schools — public schools independent of the union rules and bureaucratic strictures that were making improvement virtually impossible in many schools.

Weld and I also had differences, and he preserved his political opposition to me in many ways. For example, he chose John DeJong, who had run against me, as chairman of the Boston Finance Commission, which monitors the financial operations of the city. He vetoed some measures I had supported.

While I backed many of Weld's economic proposals, I opposed others, such as his plan to deny aid-to-dependent-children funds to mothers who did not find work within a specified period. The program was being misused, no doubt about that. It was probably also true that some of the women considered AFDC a way of life. Denying support to them, however, meant denying support to some 400,000 children who were guilty of nothing. There had to be a better way of controlling the funds. I spoke in the Senate against it.

"We have no obligation to preserve programs in their original form," I told one of Weld's aides. "We have the right to change them. We do have an obligation to care for the helpless — and that we cannot change."

"You can't save AFDC," he said. "That bird just won't fly."

I thought it a particularly sad metaphor. When you kill a bird, you kill its song — and in this case that song was the underlying compassion for children that was the genesis of AFDC, however ineptly it had been written into law. Even if all the mothers on AFDC were malefactors, which was a ridiculous notion, it would be criminal to punish their children because of it. As of this writing, the dispute continues.

Although each of us remained loyal to his party and to his party's philosophy, and thus differed often, ours was a symbiotic working relationship almost from the start. And it became more trusting and relaxed as we came to know each other better.

There was a degree of trading. At times when Weld lacked the votes for something he wanted, I would present his views to senators or even in a caucus. Occasionally that was helpful to him.

There were times I wanted something. I recall one day when we were in my office and Weld was about to leave.

"How about the Metropolitan District Commission?" I asked. "People in your office are still pushing a plan to eliminate it."

He stopped in the doorway. "What about it?"

"Well, the MDC does valuable work. You know I want it left alone."

"You forget," he said, "that I am the governor."

"Never mind that stuff," I said. "*We're* the governor."

We both enjoyed a laugh, and then he returned to my desk, leaned toward me and said, "That plan that bothers you — we'll strangle it in its crib."

We worked together in many ways, and much good was done.

Weld came to my St. Patrick's Day breakfasts and repeatedly stole the show. When I said his Yankee heritage dated to the arrival of his ancestors on the *Mayflower,* he said, "Not really. We sent members of our domestic staff on that vessel to get the cottage ready."

At the 1993 breakfast he said, "A number of people in my office said I shouldn't be here this morning. Many of them wonder how I feel about William Michael Bulger. I do not shun controversy. I will state my position.

"My position is that if, when you say Billy Bulger, you mean the sultan of South Boston, the suzerain of the statehouse, the tyrant who terrorizes the goo-goos and suckles the suspect, the Napoleonic oppressor whose fast gavel denies every citizen a vote on term limits and basic rights;

"if, by Billy Bulger, you mean the evil hand behind the hateful Hynes [convention center], the would-be kingmaker to Democratic pooh-bahs, the back-room puppet master, the power broker of patronage at Mr. Bulger's Transit Authority;

"if you mean the very man who thwarts everything that is good and right and pure about Massachusetts, then certainly I am against him.

"But if, when you say Billy Bulger, you mean the learned leader of his esteemed chamber, the sage whose single words steer his colleagues back from the wayward path, the saint of East Third Street, the pious husband of Mary, the loving father of the Bulger brood;

"if you mean the champion of the workingman and the guardian of the widowed, the trustee and protector of Massachusetts General [Hospital] and the patron of the public library, the man who would open the beaches of this beautiful state for all to enjoy, yea, the brave Latin scholar and philosopher who resists the evils of television and the *Boston Globe;*

"if you mean the public servant who wants nothing more or other than to succor men and women as they toil on the graveyard shift to give their little children a humble home and a solid schooling, then certainly I am for him.

"This is my stand. I will not retreat from it."

Commentators are forever assuring the public that I am at war with the media. I have had battles, and most certainly an occasional war, with the press. But each had its beginning and, as far as I am concerned, its end. There is no general, ongoing hostility on my part.

There *are* reporters like the one who told my administrative assistant, "If Bulger cooperates with me, he'll like what I write. If he doesn't, he won't like it at all. Tell him he can count on that."

Some were more subtle, but the message was the same.

Such people belong to a discrete criminal class of reporters. They attempt to bribe and blackmail men and women in public life. They coerce some to violate oaths of office. They are very few in number when compared with the universe of journalists, just as rapists are few when compared with society as a whole. We have laws to deal with the latter, but the rogue journalist has a license under the present law of libel to hunt his prey with virtual impunity.

The capacity of such miscreants to wound or even destroy the noncompliant with dark innuendo or scandalous allegations is ever present. Even with their frightened sources, the threat is always there. It is a sword — in a scabbard, yes, but instantly available at the first sign of independence.

No peace is possible for me with such individuals; but that's what they are, individuals. I have no animosity toward the media in a generic sense. I am satisfied most journalists genuinely aspire to public service, however much I disagree, as so often I do, with their attempts to perform it. I have come to admire a great number of them. I have no doubt they are morally superior to many of their editors — some of whom, I suspect, harbor secret rhapsodic dreams of the marketability of World War III.

I have no quarrel with journalists who fault me, as so often they do, for denying interviews, ignoring questions, refusing to be accountable to the press. What they say is true. Wise or unwise, it is the path I have chosen. I do not commend my style to others; it is a matter of choice. But I am still here.

My position devolved from careful deliberation:

To begin, I knew the media were of necessity in the business of making profits to compete and stay alive, that their "guardianship of the public interest" must be outdistanced by commercial imperatives.

I felt accountable to the public, not to a private industry.

The economic compulsion of the media in turn compels reporters to have a vested interest in defamation: neutral news is no news; scandal sells. It is defamation that provides the shortcut to high status and pay raises. That is why journalistic queries routinely seek conjecture that can injure the innocent.

I see no purpose in cooperating with *that* enterprise other than to sell papers and improve ratings, neither of which is my concern.

Equally irksome to me are editorialists who are persuaded of their own infallibility. They seek unthinking support for their views. When denied, they tend to be petulant scolds, and are best avoided.

Every state has a leading newspaper, a counterpart to Boston's *Globe,* which I have mentioned frequently, rarely with approbation. Some of these publications are great institutions, others are not. The *Globe* is indeed great with respect to its journalistic dominance and the quality of many of its reporters and columnists, but it has missed greatness in the past because of episodes of selective reporting and even outright duplicity harmful to many.

In the early nineties, the *Globe* appointed a new editor, Matthew V. Storin, and for the first time in my experience that paper began printing without restraint or distortion views of those with whom it disagreed. For example, to my astonishment, a speech of mine — expressive of opinions that must have distressed *Globe* editorial writers — was printed in its entirety without comment.

I do not know Storin, with whom I have spoken only twice, I believe; but the apparent effect of his stewardship would indicate two things: first, that it was not Bill Taylor, the publisher, who was behind the mendacious character of much prior reportage in the *Globe,* else Storin would never have been chosen or allowed to continue; second, that the paper may now and henceforth reflect as an institution the integrity that heretofore was shown only by some of its individual employees, a consummation devoutly to be wished.

I do not suggest that the social or political views of the paper have changed at all. They have not, so far as I can see: surely I remain a constant target of its wrath and disapproval. I have never objected to that, only to the prior institutionalized effort to fortify positions with false defamation craftily contrived.

Journalists were forever telling me of their ethical obligation to maintain an adversarial relationship with those of us in politics. They had to be vigilant to see whether our acts were in the public interest.

We in elective office, I responded, likewise should maintain a similar relationship with reporters. We should be vigilant to see whether the questions they asked were asked in the public interest — or to benefit their own business interests.

I had no problem with the position of journalists, but I found them outraged by my assertion of its reciprocal.

Each time a press query was addressed to me I asked myself:

"*Cui bono?* For whose benefit?" The answer that came to me often, so very often, was "Not for the public good, but for the benefit of the media." So — just as often — I thought silence the better course.

Boston is not a comfortable venue for thoughts such as that.

Newspapers in our capital city swamp officeholders in angry floods of ink, making our passage perilous. To port is the *Globe,* the Scylla of relentless liberalism. To starboard is the *Herald,* the tabloid Charybdis of right-leaning and often inscrutable malevolence. Both papers believe they know precisely what the rest of us should think and do, and evaluate our worth by the extent to which we parrot their words and support their campaigns.

The storm that shocks and consternates our public life is roiled by gales of simplistic TV sound bites and the squalid epithets and innuendoes of radio talkmasters. Some of the latter strike me as cases of evolutionary retrogression. And through it all comes the song of the enchantress: "*Cooperate. Do as you are told. Stop thinking for yourself. And if you do those things, the storm will end, the waves will calm, the sun will shine through — and you will be dubbed a statesman!*"

A few in political life, a sad but tragic few, have made that bargain. They have "cooperated," not because they believed in what they were doing, but because they believed what they were doing was the clever way to play the game, the way to buy peace.

I find more grief in that fact than ever I could feel from the wildest winds of the political sea. It is a shabby business, and in the end the game is one that only losers play.

From the beginning, I heard that siren voice. I understood it. And surely I had no perverse wish to be disapproved.

Still, a confluence of motivations — some creditable, some not — made me confrontational: I would not barter myself for friendship or acclaim, which was all to the good. Yet at the same time I was conspicuously to blame for my strained relationship with the press. Often I exacerbated matters by being brusque or even cutting when I deemed a query to be overreaching or an editorial view misguided. It was a self-righteous manner that did me no credit. I hope it is gone.

Some apparent instances of strife did not involve differences with the press at all but with persons who sought a benefit — and used the media in an effort to coerce me to accommodate them.

There are countless examples. Perhaps one will do:

Johnny Powers, my would-be nemesis in prior years, had left the Senate in 1964 after persuading Governor Peabody to appoint him clerk of the Supreme Judicial Court.

Now he wanted a pay raise, which required legislative approval.

He had become something of a character, writing letters of gratuitous advice to officials who did not know him, and growing a forest of greenery in an open space outside his courthouse office.

When he began lobbying for a pay raise, he resented the fact that I did not hurry the matter along. We were dealing with many thousands of other bills at the time, some of which were, in my opinion, more pressing than Johnny's salary.

Powers was impatient. He told the press I was delaying action. He said I wanted to frustrate him. He was asked why I would do that.

"Because of his brother Whitey," Powers explained.

He said he had been horrified to discover I had arranged for my brother James to have work at the court.

"So I fired Whitey," he said. "I had to. I considered such an employee to be a threat to the security of this court."

Powers explained that he was paying the price for doing so.

He wasn't talking about his horticultural efforts now. This was news! The media saw him as a latter-day Horatio on the bridge, Saint George slaying the dragon. All the past speculation about Jim's alleged criminality and status as a powerful gang boss was unearthed from reference libraries and republished to explain Powers's concern for the safety of the court.

It was true I had been instrumental in getting my brother a job as a helper in the custodian's department at the courthouse. I wanted to see him start somewhere in regular employment.

Jim tried, I really believe he did, but he was too restless for a routine eight-hour-a-day job. "I can't stand it, Bill," he told me. "I'm bored sick." A short time later he quit.

Powers did not fire him. No one did. It was a matter of record that he had quit — and Powers knew it. He was merely looking for a cattle prod to move me to action.

His pay raise had not been held back by me, but now it was. I told my fellow members, "I don't want this man or the media or the public to think he can intimidate me."

No one was asked to vote against the bill, but I kept it from coming to the floor, and no member objected.

Powers complained bitterly to the media. The press complained bitterly about me. I paid no attention to either. Time went by and the bill went nowhere. That is where it would have remained if Judge Joseph Nolan of the Supreme Judicial Court had not called me. The judge was a man I respected greatly, and a close friend.

"All Powers thinks about is his pay increase," he said. "It would be a blessing to the court if he could get that behind him and think about his job."

"He'll think I'm caving in to him."

"Bill, do you really care what Powers thinks?"

So I gritted my teeth and the pay raise went through.

Johnny Powers, still angry at the world, has retired to Cape Cod. But the incident, as so many like it, is often cited as an example of my chronic warfare with the media.

I have never faulted the press for publishing what it believes is news, as it did in the Powers incident. There it was a victim, just as I was. It was used — used as a weapon or, perhaps more accurately, as a stage upon which Powers could play his melodrama. One hardly blames a stage for the play that appears on it, nor did I. I felt antipathy only for the man who contrived and directed the production.

Admittedly, I have been guilty of baiting the media. One incident involved my younger brother, Jack. The two of us were always quite close. We still meet for walks around Castle Island. He is as reserved as James is rebellious.

Jack had worked as an assistant clerk in the juvenile court for years, and when the senior clerkship came open, I asked that he be considered. He was appointed by the governor. A brief squall erupted in the media, which seemed appalled that "politics" had been a factor in the appointment.

The allegation was certainly true, but the attempt to give it a pejorative cast struck me as absurd. When anyone in public office makes a recommendation, it is per se a political action. When anyone in public office makes an appointment, it too is, by definition, a political action. The only time such acts are reprehensible is when they involve shoddy politics, a wrongful or improper arrangement to accomplish a decision. The press had no basis to object on such grounds, so it deplored the appointment because of what it called my arrogant display of power.

None of it mattered, really. It was a windmill, and not worth charging. The appointment was sound; the criticism fast dying.

But I wouldn't let it go.

I went to the next meeting of the governor's council. I reminded the members I had appeared at many prior sessions to recommend the confirmation of judges and other personnel for our courts. "However," I told them, "I am here to make a statement."

That caught the attention of the reporters in attendance. I waited for silence so they would not miss a word. Then I said, "Never have I seen a person so qualified, a person so deserving, a person so capable in every material respect, a person so clearly without peer as the candidate in whose behalf I speak today: probably the most brilliant choice ever to come before this council — *my brother!*"

He was confirmed, and the next day the press blustered about it, which brought joy to my heart.

In time I will learn the futility and shallowness of such frolics. I suppose I will. In time, perhaps. Well, it's possible . . .

However imaginary my bellicose attitude toward the press may be — and it is pure fiction as far as I am concerned — it has become accepted as fact. The notion was born in the earliest days of my tenure as a presiding officer in the legislature. It has endured in the minds of many throughout my career.

It may be with me to the end.

It probably will, because I remain convinced that the most stupid statement a politician can make to the media is "Now, ladies and gentlemen, let me explain my position . . ."

Few men are worth their women, or are nearly as smart. Surely that is true of me.

Our early years had been so hard on Mary: small children, a house to care for, an inadequate budget, a husband so often tied up in the legislature or in court. It was not surprising that at times she became annoyed.

I remember one evening — very late one evening — after attending a banquet for somebody or something, I walked into our house and Mary walked out. She passed me without a word and went to sit on a bench across the street.

Knowing what was wrong, and knowing Mary, I thought it best to say nothing. So I watched her through a window until, after a quarter hour or so, she left the bench and returned to the house.

"I'm sorry I'm away so much, Mary," I told her. "I truly am."

"I know you are," she said. "That's why I can stand it."

"I thought you'd cleaned the house, given the children their dinner, and then run off and left me," I said, trying to make light of it.

Mary, who enjoys baking but hates cooking, said, "If I ever run off, it will be before dinner."

Of course she was joking. At least I think she was.

She is a wonderfully generous and caring woman, a rare blend of tenderness and steel. But the children and I understand you never can tell her what to do. You can't fool her, either.

I recall, when we were newly married, telling her she must learn to drive and get a license immediately. It was a requirement of modern life, I insisted. Time was of the essence.

Nothing happened. Eventually I stopped talking about it. Then I had a brilliant idea. I told her, "This trial I'm in — it's going to be a long one. I won't be able to drive you to the pediatrician. You'll have to take taxis."

Mary paled at that suggestion. Her constant struggle to balance our family budget — an activity she had assumed after deciding I was inept at it — made her particularly sensitive to the word "taxi."

"We can't afford taxis," she said.

"Well, there isn't any bus, and you can't walk all that way."

"You're an artful one, William Bulger," she said. "I'll get my license. But I know your ways, don't think I don't."

When I was in college, she had urged me to become a teacher. "It would be grand to be an English professor," she would say.

But she didn't protest when I went to law school. And when I ran for office, I told her, by way of comfort, "This may be only for one term — just to get it out of my system, you know. I may decide by then I'm tired of it and stop."

"And I'll stop being Irish as soon as I get tired of it," she said.

Quick as that. No hesitation. I was glad I never had to run against her.

Mary and I have always tried, with only modest success, to insulate our home life from politics. We did not have television in our house until the youngest of our children was in college, because we wanted them to read. That spared us the relentless TV rehash of political news, but we could not cut ourselves off from newspapers and radio as well.

And constituents frequently brought their problems to our front door. Others importuned Mary or the children on the street, and even at church. They would dutifully write down the requests and bring the lists home to give to me.

As I noted before, there are no real vacations in politics, but it is possible — even essential — to escape for brief periods. That is why, one rainy day, we bought a cottage at Popponesset on Cape Cod. There seemed a remoteness to it, and when it was shown to us, all our carefully laid plans for clever bargaining were promptly forgotten and Mary said, "Bill, I love this. We have to have this house."

And so we bought it.

On the drive back to Boston, Mary asked, "What have we done? How can we ever pay for it?"

"Everything will work out. Don't worry about things like that."

"You always say that."

"Well, it's true." But I knew it would be a near thing.

We have never regretted buying the cottage. It was a retreat when things were hectic. When that happened, I would leave Mary and the children on the Cape and commute to the statehouse. Each week I would borrow fifteen books from the Boston Public Library for the children. They were always eager to get them. They had no TV to watch, and you can spend only so much time on a beach. As a result, they are all well read.

We were at our Cape refuge when Governor Sargent sent the state police to find me, because he wanted to appoint me to a judgeship. I appreciated his offer, but I was not interested. However, the event showed how successful our cottage was as a place of escape — even the governor had been unable to reach us without the aid of the constabulary.

In later years, we would vary our visits to the cottage with escapes to the century-old Red Lion Inn, an idyllic hostelry in historic Stockbridge. It is close to Tanglewood, where the Boston Symphony plays each summer, surrounded by leafy splendor.

The inn somehow preserves an air of restful privacy that attracts knowing luminaries — we met Helen Hayes, Paul Newman and many others there. It is owned and operated by a former Republican senator with whom I served, Jack Fitzpatrick, and his wife, Jane, both close friends to Mary and me. They have given millions to the Boston Symphony and support the nearby Norman Rockwell Museum, and many of that artist's paintings hang in their home. Jack is such a man of purpose that he taught me to ski when I was forty-four years old, for which I am not sure I thank him.

Even in Boston, though we were an easy target for everyone, we were able to preserve some sense of privacy. That was possible, I think, because we had so many family traditions. They weren't planned, they just developed, and we clung to them. One example is the way we celebrate birthdays. The entire family gathers, Mary bakes a cake and serves it in Katie Day's dish. That's our Katie Day tradition.

Katie had lived above us when we were at 21 O'Callaghan Way in the Old Harbor project. She was our first close neighbor after we married. She died many years ago.

Every time I saw her cake dish, I remembered her vividly: a tiny sprite of a woman in a severely plain dress, heavy-duty dark stockings and the inevitable spinster's emblem, sturdy black shoes.

We received a blizzard of notes from Katie. Unable to climb down the stairs, she would put her messages in a tin can attached to a string and lower it to our window. She was very big on advice.

I recall one night when our first-born, Bill, was in full voice and it was my turn to walk the floor with him. Mary said, "I had a note from Katie Day this morning. She reminded me to be patient with little Bill because he's just fighting for his life."

"Mary, it's two A.M. — I'm the one fighting for his life."

In retrospect, there was always wisdom in Katie's guidance.

Ravaged by cancer, which had forced her to abandon her vocation as a nun, Katie was an intense little woman, so filled with frustrated energy that she seemed constantly busy though she could barely walk. She was irrepressibly cheerful. Her pain was a private thing — and her eyes sparkled so happily it was easy to forget that all the time she was fighting the enemy within her. I doubt she ever admitted to herself that she was losing the battle.

I drove her to the Lemuel Shattuck Hospital for her radiation treatments, and as time went on and she became weaker, I would have to carry her to the car. Each time she seemed lighter than before. She would sit there beside me, bubbling away with small talk like a fountain of youthful prolixity.

Once she said, "I have a nice cake dish. I'm going to give it to Mary."

"Why would you give your cake dish to Mary?" I asked.

"Why, for little Bill's first birthday cake, of course."

It seemed unlikely that a one-year-old child would eat much birthday cake. But I thought I would leave that explanation to Mary — to whom I left so many difficult things.

Mary accepted Katie Day's cake dish joyously. When we celebrated Bill's first birthday, she filled it with a cake. Bill was fascinated watching Mary blow out the single candle.

Every year since then, Katie Day's cake dish has been used for each birthday in our home. That adds up to some three hundred times we have blown out candles on a cake and thought of Katie Day . . .

Everyone in politics — no matter how much he or she enjoys the stress and the battle — must have a refuge, a sanctuary, a resting place. Mine is with my family. For me, there is no critic's bite, no adversary's sting, no sad defeat that is not healed when I turn to Mary and our children. Their faces, their voices, their laughter — these are the favorite things in my memory. They are always there when I need them.

10

ABOUT THE ONLY members of the media I had not infuriated at one time or another were sportswriters — and I managed to accomplish that on January 6, 1993.

That was the closing night of the previous year's Senate session. The members were weary and shared, as did I, a fervent wish to conclude matters and go home.

Members of the governor's staff seemed desperate to have us act that night on a bill, approved by the House, that had come to the Senate earlier in December. The measure was designed to facilitate construction of a sports arena, a new Boston Garden replacing the ancient, crumbling facility of that name. It was a complex bill, and we had not had sufficient opportunity to study it.

The governor's representatives assured me the measure was simple and straightforward, that it was greatly in the public interest, and that it was essential it be approved before the session ended. In short, I was asked to rush it through, unstudied, in the minutes remaining.

Every alarm bell in my psyche sounded.

The proposal had been vigorously promoted by Michael Goldman, the mortician turned political consultant, whose tactics I had observed in connection with the city's ill-fated incinerator. I did not connect Michael with "simple" or "straightforward."

Leafing through the pages of the bill, I had noted items that translated in my mind into substantial and unparticularized involvement of taxpayer funds. The provisions might be completely in order, but they might also award hidden millions of dollars to the private firm, Delaware North, that owned the Garden.

I concluded we could deal with the matter in a month or so, at the opening of the new session, but that the bill wasn't going to sail through in the dark of this session's final night. Instead, with time for only one bill remaining, I chose a measure filed by a Republican senator, Nancy Achin Sullivan of Lowell, that was designed to aid victims of breast cancer. Frankly, I thought it more urgent and important anyway, and we passed it before the clock struck.

The immediate disapproval of columnists and editorial writers was no more than I expected, but the angry reaction of sportswriters registered eleven on a scale of one to ten. Hockey writers emerged as economists; basketball writers lectured on political science; some fans, aroused by what they were reading, fired off furious letters to the papers, and to me.

It was said I had deprived the city of a new Boston Garden because I hated sports, because I wanted the new building named after me, because I was looking for a payoff, and on and on and on. I suppose I exacerbated the situation by referring to the sportswriters as members of the Toys "R" Us division of journalism.

In fact I enjoy sports, and I have never allowed anything — a bridge, a building or any other structure — to be named after me. The only payoff I sought was for taxpayers, and they got it, $35 million of it, the amount of tax funds buried in provisions we removed from the original bill. In the end, the city was deprived of nothing: the Boston Garden bill — minus the gift of tax dollars — was passed about six weeks later.

Even though members of his staff had tried to railroad the first Boston Garden bill through the Senate, Governor Weld thanked me for having blocked it. "We'd have been embarrassed to discover later that we'd given millions of dollars from the state treasury to a private firm," he said.

Two years later the *Boston Phoenix* acknowledged I had acted
properly. The *Globe* and the *Herald* stopped accusing me of denying the city a modern sports arena — which was pretty close to
praise from those sources.

I was pleased.

Goldman was bitter, as I would discover later.

When Jackie Birmingham got to heaven — and I have no doubt
he did — I am sure that his first thought was of Suitcase Fiddler
and that his first words were "How in hell did I ever get *here?*"

Probably many modest men and women get there with the
same question on their lips. They may be among the first chosen.

Jackie was a Townie, a native and resident of Charlestown. He
worked in Boston's Department of Veterans' Services, which provided a small benefit for jobless veterans who were "ready, willing
and able" to work. It was Jackie's responsibility to investigate
claims and decide on eligibility.

Suitcase Fiddler, also a Townie, applied for the benefit. Jackie
approved. A few months later, Birmingham was caught up in a
broad investigation being conducted by the Suffolk County district attorney.

"Will you represent me, Bill?" he asked.

"What are you supposed to have done?" I asked him.

"I didn't do anything wrong. I okayed unemployment benefits
for Suitcase Fiddler."

From that point, the interview went along these lines:

"This Suitcase Fiddler — was he a jobless veteran?"

"Yeah, but what I'm concerned about is that when I said he was
ready, willing and able to work, he was doing a small bit in the
slammer."

"I can only think of one defense to that, Jackie: you were a
victim of fraud and didn't know — "

"Oh, I knew. I investigated the claim and knew all about it."

"They're not saying you got anything out of this, are they?"

"Good God, of course not. They know better than that."

I think everyone who knew Jackie knew better than that. But I was more wary than Jackie of the climate created by the ongoing investigation.

I suggested he tell me his story.

"Well," he said, "I went to Suitcase's house to tell his wife the sad news — that he wasn't eligible until he got out. She had some cabbage she was boiling up for her kids, a bunch of kids. And that was supper, Bill. That was the whole thing, a head of cabbage." Jackie shook his head. "The place they lived looked tired. She looked tired. Even the kids looked tired. And they all looked at me like they were used to hearing bad news and were just waiting for me to give it to them.

"I did some fast thinking. I made a decision and told her I was approving the claim."

"What was this fast thinking you did?"

"Well, the benefit is very small, you see. It only lasts a few weeks. It isn't like some big hunk of taxpayers' money. I knew Suitcase would be eligible in six months when he got out, so I was just advancing the payment date a little — sort of like a loan. I said to myself, 'Fiddler isn't *able* right now because they won't let him be. But he's sure *ready* and *willing* — and, what the hell, Bill, two out of three ain't bad, things being what they were with his wife and kids."

"I know you didn't mean to do anything wrong, Jackie," I said, "but with this investigation going on, I don't know how much understanding there will be out there."

"Well, that's my story. It's the truth. I'll take the hit."

The district attorney was a rigid, hard-nosed young man whose tolerance of such things I expected to be minimal. But he seemed to sense something special about the circumstances. When I sought to delay any appearance for Jackie before a grand jury, he said, "You're stalling me, aren't you?"

"I'm trying to."

He laughed and said, "I know your client's a decent guy. I'll get back to you."

He never did. The result was that Jackie never appeared, never had to tell his story, never had to take his hit.

Some years later, when Jackie was dying, I visited his home. A hospital bed had been moved into the living room so he could be in the midst of things. His body had suffered the mutilations of disease, and I grieved for an old diminished friend. But he was quite cheerful, grateful for his wife, Agnes, whom he regarded as an impeccable contrast to his imperfections. He spoke with nostalgia, but a happy nostalgia, of things that had happened long ago, things he wished were still before him. He seemed so ill I thought it grand he had the spirit to long for *something* — even yesterday.

After Jackie died, his son, Thomas Birmingham, educated at Harvard and Harvard Law School, a Rhodes scholar, became a state senator. His liberal agenda was not always mine, but he was a decent and brilliant young man. I chose him to be chairman of the most potent and prestigious committee, Ways and Means.

I knew it was the right choice. I also knew it was not the smart choice. As it turned out, the reaction to my selection was far more violent than I had anticipated — but I have never regretted making it.

So often the days that bring struggle and danger arrive like any other day, with no clear warning of what they portend. A politician habitually involved in controversy must be the most vigilant of sentinels at all times — and when the greatest crisis of my career arose, I was asleep at my post.

The first clue came on April 8, 1993, in my fourth decade in public life, when the *Globe* printed a story implying that serious problems were developing for me. I was unimpressed, but for once the paper knew more about what was happening in the Senate than I did. The reporters, Scott Lehigh and Frank Phillips, apparently were aware that some of my colleagues were joining to drive me from office.

In life, the inevitable affirmation of our mortality always takes us by surprise: we never know when we are having our last meal, our last laugh, even our last haircut. It is somewhat the same in

politics: we may realize only by reflection that we
last vote.

Once, long ago, it was the fashion to wear a re:
— a ring or pin, on the stone of which was engra...
crossbones. Perhaps if that fashion had not passed, I might have
seen my political *memento mori* in the story I read that day. But
I did not inquire what lay behind the story. I saw no reason to
do so.

None of that amounts to an excuse, only an explanation.

The story quoted Senators Robert Havern of Arlington and
Michael Barrett of Cambridge as saying the Senate was tense.

I shrugged that off. Havern had four years in office and was
hardly a wizened authority. Barrett was obsessed with a quixotic
fantasy of becoming governor. He hoped to benefit from my perceived unpopularity, and vibrated like a tuning fork in sympathy
with any suggestion critical of me.

The story said I had become "testy." It said my relationship
with some members had "frayed badly." These things, it was
reported, had been caused by my "restive eye on exit." Except for
the quotes of Havern and Barrett, everything was attributed to
"sources" fished from that sea of anonymity which keeps investi-
gative journalism afloat.

There *was* a degree of tension; there is always some of that in
any deliberative body that is getting things done. And there are
always members with complaints:

At the time, there was Lois Pines of Newton, who had come to
the Senate in 1987. She felt ill-used. Her office had grown by
several rooms, yet she constantly bemoaned her lack of space. In
addition, she told me, "I'm not sure you plan to stay. If you do, I
will always vote for you, but I don't like Birmingham or anyone
else in the line of succession."

Another malcontent was William Keating of Sharon, an intensely ambitious and mercurial sort, who had arrived in the Senate in 1985. He was really angry.

A lawyer, Keating represented a new generation of Boston College graduates uninterested in the issues most important to work-

g-class citizens. Despite that and his vertiginous nature, he had many capabilities, and I had appointed him to two chairmanships. But he seemed to have a sense of entitlement to the chairmanship of Ways and Means, and was embittered because I considered him too volatile for a key decisional post. He regaled fellow patrons at the Golden Dome Pub with details of his victimization.

Such things were routine. In the Senate, as in the House, there were always ambitious snipers such as Barrett, groaners such as Pines, people like Keating who lusted for appointments they didn't get to posts for which they were not fit. The players change through the years; the gripes remain the same. To report them as news seemed to me not unlike revealing that there was a gold dome atop the statehouse.

As far as my "restive eye on exit" was concerned, that was, to my certain knowledge, overblown.

One in public office must be ever aware of the impermanence of that status. Even if he or she is so optimistic or cocky or foolish as to dismiss any thought of defeat, as was I, there remains the question of when it is time to do something else with one's life.

I had weighed that option every year for the past decade. It was hardly new.

In the past there had always been something or someone to dispel any notion of immediacy. On the positive side: unsolved problems demanded difficult legislation, or allies needed help and could not be abandoned. On the negative side: the challenge of political foes and the malevolence of some elements of the media had been too invigorating to leave unanswered.

Still, 1993 was admittedly a comfortable time to go. The political sky was clear of thunderheads: we had dug the state from its recession, employment was up, taxes were down. Our bonds, which had declined to near junk levels, were strong again. And that year, when I was reelected president of the Senate, it meant — if I completed the two-year term — that I would have held the office for sixteen years, a satisfyingly round number and twice the longest tenure of any predecessor.

Increasingly, powerful men and women in private industry and in academia were telling me I could make a great deal of money in any number of private fields. And most of them would add, "When you do quit, please talk to me before you take some other offer."

I knew what was available in the private sector. I had known it for many years. Money, for itself, appealed to me now no more than it had in those long-ago days when Tom Finnerty lectured me on the rewards of a full-time law practice. I believe most anyone can become wealthy in the United States; it is one of the risks we face — a risk because money begets boredom, and that is near the summit of life's agonies.

Yet a sensitive nerve end *was* touched when I heard, "Think how much more you could do for your family." After thirty-three years of political office, the time was long overdue to think of greater comfort and security for Mary and our children. But I wanted the change to be the *right* change. I was not "restive" to rush to the nearest golden exit.

I had been urged to run for administrative office, but it held no attraction for me. I had been offered a judgeship, but I wanted to make law, not apply it.

In the state legislature, where I wanted to be, no higher post was available than the one I held. Each day when the sun came up, I read its implicit homily: once you reach your zenith, the only way to go is down. But it was, I believe, Immanuel Kant who noted that the actual proves the possible — if something has happened even once, it can happen again. I knew that same sun often had shown brightly on the careers of men and women until they had *chosen* to seek the shade. I hoped it might happen again — this time, for me.

Thinking of all these things, and evaluating the *Globe* story in its entirety, the conclusions were obvious: either there was nothing of moment behind the story but idle rumor or the reporters knew something I did not know. I carelessly chose the former.

*

For the better part of four decades I have marched in South Boston's St. Patrick's Day parade every year, except in 1994 when it was canceled because the veterans' organization that sponsors it was at odds with a group of homosexuals and lesbians.

Wacko Hurley, the parade marshal, refused to allow the group to march as a unit "to make a statement for their sexual orientation." The lifestyle of the group members was not the issue: the objection was to the "statement." On many occasions in the past, other groups — ranging from political parties to the Ku Klux Klan — had tried to use the parade to make "statements," and all had been excluded.

"Anybody who wants to march can march as individuals," Wacko explained. "We won't care if they're homosexuals or lesbians or even Republicans. The only *statement* the parade makes is a statement honoring a Catholic saint."

In the past, the exclusion of groups promoting special interests never caused controversy. But GLIB, an organization representing the barred homosexual and lesbian unit, appealed to the superior court, where a justice held the ban unlawful. His decision was appealed to the Supreme Judicial Court which, with the sole dissent of Justice Nolan — who had urged me to grant Johnny Powers his pay raise — upheld the superior court's finding.

The GLIB unit marched in the parade in 1992 and 1993, but the veterans' organization canceled its 1994 parade. A parade of sorts, featuring the GLIB group, was arranged by people outside South Boston. As in the busing days, fear of violence was expressed by the media, but of course there was none. The parade met not violence but silence along its route.

The veterans, represented by Chester Darling, a most able lawyer, took the case to federal court, where Judge Mark L. Wolf ruled that GLIB's unit could lawfully be excluded from the 1995 parade, pending a decision by the U.S. Supreme Court. The parade resumed for that year, free of extraneous "statements."

Darling argued that the GLIB group was completely free to march through the streets of South Boston advertising its lifestyle, but not as a part of our St. Patrick's Day parade. "Why," the

Supreme Court was asked, "should a parade honoring a saint of the Catholic Church be required to include a contingent stating its contempt for the saint's teachings?" The Court, in a rare unanimous decision, held that Wacko's ban had been lawful. That was that.

I recall the first time I marched in the parade after Mary and I were married, I invited everybody along the parade route to come to our home for a glass of beer. So many came that our next-door neighbor had to open her home for some. Mary, who had never had a drink, tried to help, but stunned our visitors by putting ice in their beer.

One year I did not march the complete route. It was in the early seventies, and I was asked to assist a woman from New York, a TV personality named Peggy Cass, who had been sent to narrate the parade. She was a witty and delightful person. It was chilly for a mid-March day, and I was grateful when she offered me a cup of coffee, though I would describe it as a cup of Scotch laced with coffee.

"I'd better not drink this, Peggy," I said.

"You're a prohibitionist?"

"No, but I made a trip to Taiwan once . . . Well, it's a long story."

She looked at me strangely, but she was a forgiving sort and we got along famously. Later she took me to New York, where we appeared on *The Tonight Show* with Jack Paar.

Before the parade, I would host my St. Patrick's Day breakfast. Through all the years, except for a single time during the busing struggle, that show went on — in good times and bad, when my party was winning and when it wasn't.

Nothing interfered, not rain or even unseasonable snow. Nothing kept members of both parties, visitors from other states and from abroad, characters and frequently celebrities — actors and actresses, poets and writers, distinguished journalists, athletes — from taking part in our gathering at the old German Club. We sang Irish songs and generally tried for a day to forget being serious about anything, especially anything divisive. I roasted our guests and was the target of their jibes.

At times there were consequences we had not foreseen:

One guest, Elliot Richardson, a most proper Bostonian and a former state attorney general, had achieved much attention when, as a member of the national administration, he defied an order from President Nixon. Now he was seeking the Republican nomination for the U.S. Senate.

The *Globe* was fervently supporting his candidacy, devoting oceans of ink to describing the sheer wonderfulness of him. The Taylors, who published that paper, were themselves charter members of the Yankee old boy club, and I had often expressed my gratitude to them for allowing the rest of us to use their country. I could not now resist having a huge placard prepared, a mock imitation of the *Globe*'s front page. I presented it to Richardson at the breakfast. The headline read, VOTE ELLIOT: HE'S BETTER THAN YOU ARE.

Everyone laughed, including Richardson.

He was a heavy favorite to win the nomination, but it was reported that seventy-five percent of Catholics who voted in the primary cast ballots for his opponent, and Richardson lost. It never occurred to me that the St. Patrick's Day prank was a factor, and I still do not believe it was.

The following winter, on a day when snow was falling in Boston, I heard from Richardson. He was calling from an undisclosed island in the Caribbean. He asked me to join with Art Buchwald in hosting a party to help retire the Richardson campaign debt.

"I was doing well until that unfortunate headline from St. Patrick's Day," he lamented.

"You're giving me too much credit," I told him, "but I'll be there to help you pay off your debt."

South Boston's disproportionate importance in the Boston vote prompted many presidents to call during the breakfast. In recent years, Presidents Reagan and Bush called, as did Vice President Quayle. When President Clinton called, I said, "Mr. President, I knew you had a great sense of humor when you appointed Ray Flynn ambassador to the Vatican. Would you consider our parade marshal, Wacko Hurley, for secretary of defense?"

"He might be a good one for my liberal outreach program," Clinton said.

When the time came and Flynn offered himself to settle the disturbance in Somalia, and then when he proposed that the pope mediate the baseball strike, I wondered whether Clinton might be pondering Wacko Hurley's qualifications . . .

Perhaps the biggest joke was on me:

At one breakfast I introduced the then–state treasurer, Robert Q. Crane. Since the treasurer is by law head of the state Lottery Commission, I described Crane as the biggest bookie in Massachusetts.

I thought that was pretty funny. So did some Boston police officers who were there. Later they were laughing about it in the Victoria Diner.

In a nearby booth sat a woman from Ohio — who happened to be an FBI agent. She heard much of the conversation and filed a report about it. She wrote that I had identified for police the biggest bookie in the state. She said she had been unable to catch the bookie's name, but that the police seemed to be in high spirits over the information.

Her report was leaked, as confidential reports routinely are leaked, and I read of my role as an informant in a gossip column. It was not until I noted the eavesdropping had taken place on March 19 of that year — a day after my annual St. Patrick's Day breakfast — that I understood the basis of the inane rumor.

For six months there were no sequels to the *Globe*'s report of dissension in the Senate, so it appeared my assessment had been accurate. Then, on October 24, the paper revealed that William Keating would challenge me for the Senate presidency.

That caught my attention. Not because Keating was formidable, but because he had retained Michael Goldman to orchestrate his campaign.

While my assessment of Goldman's talents undoubtedly was more modest than his own, he was well connected in the media, and one to be taken seriously. In addition, he was personally motivated. He had major scores to settle with me: I had blocked his effort to have an incinerator sited in South Boston, disappointing an important client. I had cost another of his clients, Boston Garden, a $35 million windfall. Most galling of all, perhaps, I had summarily rejected his offer to work for me in the 75 State Street affair.

Goldman was clever, but he struck me as a nervous man, very tense. He made me think of a conjurer who always feared the ace falling from the sleeve, the rabbit escaping the hat, the trick being found out. Still, he had the attributes for success in his chosen trade: he was able, ambitious, intelligent and the practitioner of an utterly ruthless calculus.

He had, as I mentioned earlier, helped oust Tom McGee as Speaker, a coup some thought gave him great influence in the House. If he could reprise that event at my expense, it would give him the appearance of also being a power in the Senate, which I did not think would distress him. The very thought made my teeth ache.

Thus I knew Keating was not the threat. He was merely a convenient, easily manipulated instrument. It was the consultant who was the danger.

The day following the announcement of his challenge, Keating held a press conference at Boston's Parker House, which a battalion of print, radio and television journalists attended. He was accompanied by Senators Pines, Barrett, Havern, Dianne Wilkerson of Roxbury, Michael Morrissey of Quincy and Daniel Leahy of Lowell. Goldman, aggressively in charge, bustled about arranging everybody: "You stand here . . . you stand there . . . okay, step over here . . . get behind her . . ." That sort of thing.

It was said that a new era was dawning in Massachusetts. To dramatize it, a tape machine in the background blared the Beatles' song "Revolution."

My lieutenants and I watched it all on TV later that day. We thought it a bravura balletic performance. Goldman floated like a butterfly, Keating stung like a bee — as a noted sometime poet might have put it.

"It's time!" Keating thundered. "It's time to end forever the famous lightning power plays and the back-room deals."

His six confederates clustered about him as he spread the good news: an opportunity had finally arrived to get rid of me. He said, "I'd be afraid to go into my election and tell my constituents there was a once-in-a-lifetime chance — a once-in-a-*century* chance — for a change and I sat it out. I'll not tell my constituents that."

I fancied I could hear him asking his fellow senators, "Are *you* going to tell your constituents that?"

Then my mind wandered from the events on the screen to what might lay behind them, for however asleep I had been before, I was awake now.

Believing I was "restive" to depart, Goldman probably thought I would elect to leave graciously rather than suffer an internecine war. It was a not unreasonable expectation. But what was his plan if I did *not* quit? The universe of possible actions at first seemed limited, even blindingly obvious. He could not hope to defeat me in my district, even with the aid of the media. The DeJong contest had proved that. His goal had to be to defeat me in the contest for Senate president.

With Keating?

Surely Goldman was too bright for that. Keating, considered unstable by most senators, could never be elected president, and Goldman had to know it. At some point, after he had served his purpose, Keating would be scuttled for a more viable candidate. I had no doubt that was already in the consultant's playbook.

But where were the votes even for a substitute? Most of the Democrats were pledged to me. Either Goldman was naive or was crafting a scenario too slick to be readily evident.

Forget naive. I chose slick.

Goldman certainly was too shrewd to reveal plans prematurely, but Keating — yes, one might rely on Keating's volatility. So when he and his group returned to the statehouse after their press conference, I called a caucus in my office.

The members were plainly confused. One asked me, "What's going on, Bill?"

I invited Keating to tell us.

He stood up, his back to the huge fireplace, his hands on the tall antique andirons, and addressed the caucus.

"I hope to be the next president of the Senate," he said.

"But why the press conference?" he was asked. "The media can't vote for you."

"The people of Massachusetts don't want Bulger," Keating said.

That was still too vague, too rhetorical. I sat there willing him to be more specific and less prolix. Don't stop now, I was thinking. This is no time for you to start being smart. Tell them the *plan*. Spell it out.

He did. "We're going to stand against the Senate president and make it necessary for every one of you to do the same, or to explain why you're going to be voting for him."

Now he was wound up, infatuated with sudden importance. He could not stop: "We will ride buses into your districts. We will bring support to any Democrat who opposes you if you do not take a pledge to vote against the Senate president. We will campaign vigorously. We have the money, the leadership, the skill and the determination."

Subsequently Barrett, Keating's most vocal ally, warned, "No one can hide in this thing. In the next fourteen months each of us will be asked which side we're on. In 1994 every voter will carry the issue of Bill Bulger's presidency into the voting booth."

So now we knew the plan. I was to be the issue, and a group of Democrats — Keating and his allies — would invade districts to contrive the defeat of other Democrats loyal to me. Nothing like it had ever occurred in our state.

Total silence greeted revelation of the plan. The members stared at Keating in shock, their rising anger almost palpable. I knew the irony of his promise to make the Senate "less dictatorial" — while threatening to defeat any senator who refused to vote for him — was not lost on anyone.

Keating, misreading the reaction, beamed: he appeared to think his colleagues were frightened. I am confident he believed at that moment that senators soon would be saying to me: "Bill, you've been here since the beginning of the world. How much longer? We're all going to be killed if you don't quit." That's what his consultant probably had told him would happen. But his consultant had never served in the Senate.

Instead, once those first frozen moments wore off, Keating's declaration evoked the most spirited reaction I have ever seen in a caucus.

Above the din I heard the voice of Shannon O'Brien, the senator from Holyoke: "You keep your nose out of my district or you'll get it cut off, and that goes for that schmuck you have for a consultant."

Mark Montigny, a senator from southeastern Massachusetts, was so incensed he told Keating, "If I catch you in my district, I'll punch you out of there."

I knew that he had lost any hope of support from incumbents outside his seminal group, and that though he spoke with the tongues of angels, he could not undo his mischief. But he did not try.

"Sorry," Keating said, his face red, his jaw clenched, swelling with menace like a tumescent cloud bank. "We're going to do it."

While the cacophony proceeded, I watched the faces of Keating's partisans. I did not read total approval there. Barrett, of course, looked solid; Wilkerson, a troubled woman, and Morrissey, a personal friend of Keating's, were stone-faced. But Leahy . . . Leahy seemed uncomfortable, and Havern even more so. I made a mental note of that.

Meanwhile, Pines was on her feet. "This isn't necessarily my strategy," she said. "I'm with Bill Keating, but this is *not* my strategy."

"You can't get off the hook like that," said Senator Michael Creedon from Brockton. "If you're part of Keating's thing, you're part of everything he does. That goes for all of you — you're all responsible."

It seemed like a good time to quiet things down. I stood and told the members, "I know the senator's displeasure. I understand it. To those who are joined with him I say, this is the road you have chosen. You are free to see where it leads without any rebuke from me. To all other members I would offer some counsel, just one word: relax."

I stressed the importance of remaining focused on the work for which we had been elected. I noted that the next election was almost a year away, a very long time in politics. "It will be a roller coaster ride," I said, "there will be ups and downs, but we must simply fasten our seat belts." I concluded: "Most people seem pleased with what we have done so far — with the economy, workers' compensation and the like — and we must not be distracted. We must go on and do more. If we do that, everything will turn out well. I promise you, *everything will turn out well.*"

Later, Jim Julian, my administrative assistant, and I went to Locke-Ober, the restaurant where years before I had made a spectacle of myself by ordering lobster Savannah at Ted Kennedy's luncheon.

Kevin Harrington, whom I had succeeded as Senate president, was seated at our left with members of his family. He came to our table, cigar in hand, and sat down. "I hope," he said, "you're giving thought to this Keating thing."

"Why should I do that?"

"Well," he told me through a cloud of cigar smoke, "you're going to have to decide if you want to go through it. This will be difficult, Bill. This is serious."

"You think so, Kevin?"

"Absolutely. The *Globe,* the *Herald,* talk shows and newspapers across the state, they'll all join the effort. They'll all be attacking Senate members. The vote for president is no longer an inside game."

I said it did indeed sound serious.

"Bill, various interest groups will be enlisted by the Keating forces. You won't be able to respond to many of the tactics. They'll have the money, the media — and, face it, the polls show everyone outside your district wants you out."

I said nothing while he studied the burning end of his cigar. Then he asked, "Why do you need it all at this point in your life?"

I agreed, I didn't need it.

"You're at the top of your game," Harrington assured me. "You've restored a comfortable Democratic majority in the chamber. You've just been reelected president. It's a good time for you to find out how comfortable life can be outside that building."

When I said nothing, he added, "You know, I just bought a house in Florida. Life is good. You should think about that. Naturally, I want to help you in whatever course you choose, but you should think about these things."

Clearly Harrington had given much thought to the matter, and I sensed he had discussed it with others. He wanted me to avoid a battle I could not win — to quit. Who, I wondered, did he hope would replace me?

I thanked him for his counsel. After some small talk, he returned to his table.

As Jim and I finished our coffee, I thought about Harrington's suggestion. It was sound advice from a professional. It irritated the canker of self-doubt that already troubled me.

Goldman's plan, whatever it lacked in political protocol, was not without a certain cold-blooded merit:

Festering memories — the detritus of old battlefields such as busing and 75 State Street — would invigorate foes from the past.

Causists and the plethora of dilettantes who resented my disdain for their self-righteousness and quick-fix remedies would rush to enlist in any crusade against me.

I had angered many wealthy men, so any effort against me would be well funded.

Surely the media would smell blood.

The ultimate decision would be in the hands of voters who did not know me, people throughout the state to whom I had been demonized. Media polls reported them as being passionately antagonistic toward me, by a margin of five to one. At last, at long last, they would have an opportunity to express whatever fury they had.

The pressure on senators committed to me could be unbearable.

And the whole thing would be organized by Goldman, a shrewd and practiced manipulator of opinion.

Harrington was right. The easy thing, the smart thing, was to leave while I was ahead.

But there is a vast divide between leaving and being thrown out; and in the Neighborhood that had shaped me, even worse than losing was the sin of quitting. I would not do that. Besides, I could not conceal from myself that, however dumb it might be, I enjoyed battle. I understood the character in the *chanson de geste* who said, "I'd leave paradise to go and fight."

It mattered not if Goldman or Keating or Harrington or anyone else thought I could not win. Even if I felt they might be right — which, in fact, I did — I had to make them prove it. So I gathered my lieutenants, and we went to war.

The last really serious effort to oust me — before this one — had been back in 1973, when I was majority leader of the Senate. On that occasion a bloc of liberal Democrats in the House, led by Barney Frank of Newton — who is now a congressman — wanted to create a district that would guarantee election of a black senator. Frank's group dubbed itself the Democratic Study Group and forged an alliance with the Black Caucus.

"When we sat down together," Frank said, "it was like a brotherhood meeting. Everybody was pledging loyalty to each other all around the table."

All of this allowed Frank and his white allies the luxury of political posturing without any pain or suffering since their seats would be unaffected. It also meant that someone presently in the Senate would be out of a job. As it developed, the someone selected was me.

Frank joined with Republicans in the House to pass the "reform."

I was not opposed to Frank's plan, even though it violated the tacit rule that one branch should not interfere in the affairs of the other, such as redistricting. But then, it was not *my* plan to retire from politics. I told our Democratic caucus, "What this comes down to is a simple question: who'll give up his or her seat? I'm not ready to do that."

The subsequent operation was given a code name, "The Slide," descriptive of the efforts of legislators to accomplish the politically popular objective — at somebody else's expense. One labyrinthine scheme, for example, would have created a district snaking a tortuous path from a black urban area to a rural Republican town.

Finally, the legislature chose a scheme offered by Republican Governor Sargent. The plan collapsed two communities outside Boston into one district and then created a predominantly black district in Boston.

To the chagrin of some, the first beneficiary of the redistricting was a friend of mine, Bill Owens, and the runner-up was an even older friend, Royal Bolling, with whom I had worked in the House.

Frank's original plan would have unseated me. Two decades later, the openly gay congressman was critical of the ban against celebration of the homosexual and lesbian way of life in the St. Patrick's Day parade. But however much I have disagreed with him at times, I have always believed his positions were sincere and not based on personal or ethnic antagonism. We have remained friendly throughout the years, and I have supported him in campaigns.

As I began to assess our strategy in meeting the Keating rebellion, I looked first to its leader, Goldman.

I knew his strengths, and they were many. He was skilled at his craft; he was an accomplished artificer of techniques that swayed public opinion. What were his weaknesses?

Goldman had chosen the song "Revolution," by John Lennon and Paul McCartney, as theme music for the Keating uprising, no doubt thinking it a hymn to insurrection. I had looked up the song and found it to be just the opposite — a crushing rebuff to those who would tear down the existing order.

A minor error, but indicative of imprecision.

Goldman accepted the validity of polls conducted by the *Globe* in the wake of its defamatory attacks on me. For many reasons, I had little faith in polls. In the gubernatorial election of 1982, polls gave Franklin Chase a seventy-five percent favorability rating. Later, it was learned Chase was a fictitious candidate. He did not exist!

A larger error: polls offer a shifty basis for reliance.

Believing the polls, Goldman had premised his entire campaign on the notion that the general electorate would seize its chance to end my influence in the Senate. I felt he might be hasty in assuming voters, whatever their view of me, would want to swap my influence for that of a commercial consultant and his corporate clients.

A still more serious error: ignoring his own vulnerability.

Even if the *Globe* polls were right, I doubted hostility toward me would be definitive. Surely voters would be concerned more with the personality of local candidates, and with local issues, than with me. Men and women are more moved by what they *know* and by what affects them immediately; most voters did not know me personally, and any disapproval they might feel was an abstraction based on hearsay. I posed no threat to specific and instant interests.

This was the worst error of all: to assume I was more important to voters than schools, crime, property taxes and the like.

The longer I performed this mental reconnaissance, the more encouraged I felt, especially as I extrapolated my conclusions. Weaknesses in conception and planning necessarily translate to faulty execution, to mistakes, and I wondered how Goldman would handle setbacks. He knew — he had to know — he had put a substantial stack of chips into this game. Being avid to win, he would desperately fear losing, and fear often begets recklessness. That led me to conclude Goldman was going to make mistakes, and well might try to recover from them with further misjudgments.

What of the man personally? What was he like in his secret self? My experience with him had been on the whole too distant to allow me to form many judgments on that score. I would have to rely on appearances, admittedly a dubious source.

I had read much nonsense on the subject. Some have written that the inner man may be deduced from physiognomy — the shape of ears, the configuration of the nose. There is even a theory that the size of an ego is proportionate to the extent by which the subject's index finger exceeds the length of the ring finger. The usually rational Aristotle insisted that the size and shape of the forehead tell it all. If there is the slightest truth in such theories, which I doubt, it is beyond my comprehension.

I did have one important clue: I had learned Goldman had been vastly amused by a cruel joke describing McGee's abasement. One's eyes and body language may shout lies, but, it has been said, the soul whispers the truth — and it has been my experience that if you would look into another's soul, you would do well to listen to the things at which he laughs.

To defeat a foe brings satisfaction, even joy, but to savor his humiliation, I believe, bespeaks a fragility of character, a want of grit if you will — and that is a flaw rife with danger for those who rely upon such a person.

When I put all of these things together, I counted Goldman's opposition a plus for our side. I have never doubted Heraclitus' words that a man's character is his fate.

Still, the Goldman-Keating apparatus of seven incumbent senators was gaining new adherents. Michael Bissonette of Chicopee, who was running against an open seat, and Warren Tolman, a former representative, declared for Keating, swelling the group to nine. All of them were almost certain to win in the primary. In addition, ten men and women had been encouraged, and in most cases recruited, to run against candidates loyal to me. It was in these contests that the issue would be decided.

Goldman and his slate were omnipresent — on the hustings,

in newspapers, in television interviews, on radio talk shows. The major elements of the media were transported. At long last they had me out of my South Boston enclave, out of the sanctuary that enabled me to wield what they perceived as unfettered power, and into a campaign where the statewide electorate could have at me.

The *Herald* and the *Globe* and a flock of others, both print and electronic communicators, endorsed the entire Keating slate. They proclaimed the central issue, the threshold question, in all forty Senate campaigns was now "Will you pledge to vote against Bulger for Senate president?"

"The 1994 election," the *Globe* explained, "will be a referendum . . . It is welcome, and long overdue." The *Globe* said it was a campaign deserving the support of all voters "who want truly independent senate candidates" — as distinguished, presumably, from those who favored me.

The *Herald* printed a page-one editorial warning the Goldman-Keating team to be alert for dirty tricks. It was written by Shelley Cohen, a bright person with a gift for facile expression. Unfortunately, she was also that paper's practiced revisionist historian — and if a tolerant word about me ever appeared under her byline, it would be a typographical error. Cohen referred to my past "psychological warfare" against Alan Sisitsky. As a result of it, she wrote, "one of the brightest lights in the Massachusetts Senate was strapped to a stretcher and carried out of the State House to McLean Hospital." She didn't deny Sisitsky was unbalanced at the time. She merely said I had unbalanced him.

"The lesson in all this?" Cohen asked. ". . . Bulger plays for keeps. Senator William Keating had better realize that."

Meanwhile, the Citizens' Committee for Political Action, a prim, grim and self-righteous organization to which I was an anathema, was gathering signatures in the ten critical districts. It wanted to place on the ballot a resolution allowing voters to declare whether they wanted the successful candidate in the Democratic primary to vote against me. The instruction would be legally nonbinding, but it purported to reflect the position of the candidate's constituency. It would not help me — how much it might hurt was impossible to know at the time.

But Goldman was making mistakes. When he saw that most Democratic incumbents were standing firmly behind me, he tried to stir religious hatred into the contest: Shannon O'Brien's use of the word "schmuck" in reference to him in the caucus was pointed to as evidence of anti-Semitism.

The word is of Yiddish origin, but has become part of American slang. One hears it applied to and by persons of various races and religions. It is used, I think, for its satisfyingly guttural onomatopoeic disdain, certainly without regard to its ethnicity.

I advised O'Brien to ignore the matter, but Goldman — personally and through Keating — kept at it.

The Committee for a Democratic Senate, a group with ties to me, raised questions concerning financial relationships between Goldman and candidates pledged to oppose me.

Keating said we were making Goldman a major issue solely because he was Jewish. He said my supporters and I were engaging in "the kind of ethnic, tribal politics that I had hoped we would have left behind a long time ago."

Among the humbling truths we must live with is the fact that of all species only human beings are able to lie, and they often do. I advised my supporters: "Be patient. Wait. The most dangerous thing to do in politics is to lie. Let them go on doing it until they learn that the hard way."

They went on. On Yom Kippur eve, Goldman told the press, "This is when we go to forgive anyone who has wronged us . . . I intend to do that tonight."

The Jewish community was annoyed, as I expected it would be — not at us, but at the reckless allegations. Stephen Grossman, president of the American Israel Public Affairs Committee, said the various charges "trivialize the notion of anti-Semitism." Leonard Zakim, executive director of the Anti-Defamation League of B'nai B'rith, said, "There's an inappropriateness to the charge of anti-Semitism."

The most scathing criticism came from Cheryl Cronin, the lawyer who had raised the issues about Goldman's financing. Because of her name, and because of Goldman's carelessness with detail, it had not occurred to him that she might be Jewish. She was.

In a letter to Keating she said, "Michael Goldman is no 'victim of anti-Semitism,' and asserting that he is in this matter is a grave dishonor to the all too many true victims of anti-Semitism . . . Most tragically these victims include people like my 87-year-old aunt, who has spent the last fifty-one years of her life alone since her husband was killed by the Nazis at Auschwitz. Such exploitation to advance your own political agenda is nothing less than shameful."

The drumbeat continued, however. During a debate on redistricting that Keating opposed, he attacked Birmingham, Bertonazzi and me by likening the Senate leadership to that of the German Reich! He recounted Elie Wiesel's poignant tale of the Lutheran minister who ignored cries for help from Jews, Catholics, Gypsies and trade unionists, only to find no one left to speak in his defense when the Nazis came for him.

One of Keating's targets, Thomas Birmingham, whose wife is Jewish, responded to Keating with a cold fury more stinging than anger. "I hope," he said, "that the gross comparison which has just been made, which atrociously violates the memories of those who died under Nazism, is never replicated in this body."

The most devastating response came from Wiesel himself. The Nobelist wrote in the *Globe:* "I deeply resent my name being used by Sen. William R. Keating in his polemic with Senate President William Bulger's supporters . . . The story of Pastor Martin Niemoeller is well known to teachers and students of the Holocaust. To compare Massachusetts senators to Nazis in Hitler's Germany is a distortion of history and a dishonor to political discourse."

That was the end of *that.* More than ever, I believed we had an asset in Goldman.

But his plan, aside from the red herring of anti-Semitism, was novel: the iconoclasm of running Democrats against Democrats as a means of seizing the Senate presidency provoked the interest that attaches to newness. Our plan, on the other hand, was designed along familiar lines. Seeing it unfold was, by comparison, like watching an old grainy filmstrip of the Coolidge inauguration.

I hoped it would prove to be our tortoise to his hare.

At the caucus where Keating had outlined his rebellion, I had been impressed by expressions of discomfort on the faces of two of his adherents, Leahy and Havern. Subsequently, I talked with each many times, quite frankly encouraging their disenchantment. I don't know whether I had any effect on either, but in time both defected. Leahy said he had never bound himself to vote for Keating, and would not. Havern said he was alienated by Keating's campaign strategy and declared himself an independent.

Then Goldman made a remark — jocular but derogatory — about a city in Michael Bissonette's district. Bissonette, pledged to Keating and sure to be nominated, since he was running unopposed, was so angered that he announced *he* would no longer support Keating.

The Keating nine suddenly had shrunk to the Keating six.

The defectors were uncommitted, however. They would not vote for Keating, but they might not vote for me. So our strategy remained unchanged: my future still would be decided in the ten districts where Goldman and Keating had recruited what we called their mercenaries.

We campaigned everywhere, but especially there.

In those key districts, seven candidates were pledged to me. Two were technically independent, but I was confident I could count on both. That left one race, in which Brian McDonald of Weymouth was running. I did not know whether McDonald would vote for me, but I knew his opponent would not. I was for McDonald.

When asked for advice, which happened often, I gave it. "Where I'm concerned," I would say, "take a position for me or remain uncommitted. Neither one is carved in stone. But once you select one, refuse to debate it. Concentrate on local issues that concern your constituents. That's what will decide your election."

I hoped I was right.

Advertising money was needed. Our foes were well financed, so the candidates I backed needed substantial funds — more than they could raise alone — to be heard above the din Goldman was making.

A great number of people throughout the state, many of them close friends, contacted me with offers of help. I told them: "I'm unopposed. But there are people in other senatorial contests who need all the help they can get — people I hope will win. Perhaps you and your friends will do what you can for them."

They did. They performed magnificently.

Still, we were underdogs. I conducted no polls but others did, and they indicated we would lose in most if not all of the ten key districts. We had a lot of work to do.

We were strong in the basics. My organization reflected thirty-three years of professional experience, and we knew where to find hordes of enthusiastic and resourceful amateurs. Men and women expert in defining issues, organizing rallies, contacting voters and arranging rides to the polls went to every district where guidance was needed. They advised how to design ads and when to run them to be most effective. They helped candidates avoid pitfalls — there were very few political tricks they had not dealt with in the past. They brought big-city expertise even to the smallest towns.

The people of South Boston, who as I have noted earlier love politics with a special passion, were aroused. They felt the attack on me was an attack on the Neighborhood. They would not condone that. If Tennessee is the Volunteer State, ours is the Volunteer District.

They would leave home at four or five in the morning to carry signs for friendly candidates in places many of them had never visited before. The early start enabled them to control the major intersections and occupy other desirable spots to stand with their placards.

Such assemblies are called stand-outs — and there would be thirty or forty chanting enthusiasts clustered together at each of them, trying to look like locals. They were all volunteers. They used their own cars, paid for their own gas, bought their own lunches or carried sandwiches in paper bags. They simply wanted to be part of the action, so they went where it was and paid to get there.

We'd see them leaving South Boston, a huge caravan of vehicles overflowing with people. Yet they were quite artful at infiltrating their target destinations so they would not look like carloads of Boston activists descending on suburban communities.

Occasionally there were problems. When a group went to the city of Lynn to demonstrate, they had no difficulty parking cars unobtrusively at scattered spots before establishing their stand-outs. Parking a willing but unsophisticated colleague proved infinitely more challenging.

His name was Jimmy Buffalo.

Conrad Bailey, who led that group, had a modest view of Jimmy's judgment, and thought it would be best if Buffalo were not part of the demonstration. So he said, "Jimmy, you've got a special job. You sit in that doughnut shop over there and keep your ears open and your mouth shut. Whatever you do, don't tip anybody that you're from South Boston."

"I want to carry a sign," Buffalo protested.

"We have to know what the locals are talking about," Conrad explained. "That's *very* important. There's lots of guys to carry signs — I figure you got the smarts to listen and not attract attention."

Buffalo, suddenly important, went to his post, where he sat with a cup of coffee and a plate of doughnuts in front of him, listening. In one of those incredible coincidences that cannot happen but frequently do, someone came into the shop and asked, "Hey, anyone here know how to get to South Boston?"

Buffalo leaped from his chair, shouldering patrons aside, and charged through the door. He ran across the street and told Bailey, "They're wise to us, Conrad. I spotted it right away and got out in a hurry."

"What are you talking about?"

"Some guy come in yellin' does anybody know the way to South Boston."

"So?"

"They may be hicks around here, Conrad, but *everybody* knows the way to Southie. That was just the wise-ass way of saying they know where we was from."

Bailey looked across the street. He saw a gathering there, men and women who had followed Buffalo out of the doughnut shop and pedestrians who had stopped and joined them, undoubtedly to learn what was happening. Obviously, they had been told about the wild man who had run amok in the shop, because now all of them were clustered near the doorway, staring in apparent bewilderment at Buffalo and our group.

So Buffalo was given a sign to carry after all, and that made him very happy. Our opponent's name had been hastily written on the sign, but that mattered not at all to Buffalo, since he didn't know who was running for office anyway. That meant the locals saw a group of normal-appearing men with signs supporting our candidate, and one person — the weird one who had disturbed the peace of the doughnut shop — urging support for our foe.

The stand-out in Lynn was considered a grand success . . .

Some of the individual campaigns were noteworthy:

There was Marian Walsh: she was pitted against the Goldman mercenary James Hennigan III. Besides painting her as mindlessly obedient to my dictates, Hennigan pounded on her pro-life position. There was a huge Irish population in her district, many of them people who had moved there from South Boston. We contacted all of them we could find, and we found most of them.

There was John Flood of Canton, a former representative: he had been invited to Goldman's office, where he agreed to run against Paul White of Boston, a stalwart ally of mine. Flood was cursed with a personality that antagonized many, and I was among them. But in the past, when he was experiencing difficult times, he had asked me to help. It was widely known I had tried to help Flood in out of the rain, so he was asked why he had turned against me.

"Well," he explained, "as a matter of fact I resented having to ask him for help."

After that, I suggested Paul White should ask Flood about his service as a lobbyist for the tobacco industry, a group devoted to spreading a poisonous habit among young people. Flood spent the rest of his campaign trying to answer that. Meanwhile, I attended house parties for White and addressed neighborhood groups in his behalf.

There was Michael Creedon: helping him against his Brockton opponent, Anne McCormack, was difficult. Mike was a solid ally, but he rarely would take seriously counsel suggesting any inadequacy in his performance. And so he was sometimes given to unhappy modes of expression. Once, referring to Anne, he said, "If she gets to the Senate, the boys will just send her out for coffee."

I groaned when I heard of that. Goldman must have been thrilled. Creedon's quip grossly distorted the attitude toward women in the Senate. Prior to Thomas Birmingham, I had appointed Patricia McGovern chairman of Ways and Means, the first woman to hold that post; she had held it with the approval of her colleagues until her retirement. Still, Creedon's words would arouse every feminist in the district and rally them to McCormack's support. Mike had no regrets; he felt he had won a victory by stressing Anne's inexperience. It seemed clear to me that another such victory might destroy him. That one was going to hurt; and it did.

There was Freddie Berry: he was running against John Keenan, a young Harvard graduate given to febrile vituperation and wholly manipulated by Goldman. Keenan appeared on TV with Goldman to assail me, and wrote a passionate polemic for the *Globe* condemning my tyrannical influence in the Senate.

We gave a copy of Goldman's client list to Berry to distribute publicly. Henceforth, when Keenan would say Berry was beholden to me, Fred would list the firms to whom the consultant was beholden. That put Keenan on the defensive. He began trying to distance himself from Goldman. It was too late for that.

There was Jim Jajuga, a former state policeman: he had been a declared foe when he first came to the Senate, but had gradually changed his mind and become supportive of me. In the election he was uncommitted, but he would not pledge to vote against me. I felt so sure of his support that I went to his district to speak in his behalf. Jim's local paper, the *Lawrence Eagle-Tribune,* was furious.

"Jim," I advised, "remember the words of Edmund Burke, who said, 'Your representative owes you not his industry only, but his judgment, and he betrays instead of serving you when he sacrifices it to your opinion.'"

"That's true," Jim said.

I suggested he write it down, and he did.

And so it went, on and on, working without rest, never stopping; winning some battles, losing some; encouraging some candidates, comforting others; even helping some who were too intimidated by the media ever to vote for me, but who promised to vote "present" . . . My larder was not so full that I could scorn even half a loaf.

As the primary drew near, it was clear we had made some gains. But the prevailing view was that the Goldman-Keating candidates — or at least most of them — would prevail. Some reporters who had baited me for years actually spoke to me in gentle, almost funereal, tones, as one might at a wake. I didn't care for that at all: I preferred the days when they growled at me.

On primary eve, Don Aucoin's analysis on page one of the *Globe* said the primary would in part be a referendum on my sixteen-year Senate presidency — "whether Bulger likes it or not." Those words indicated what the *Globe* thought the result would be. But on primary day, when John Henning, a TV commentator, asked me what I thought now that the polls were closed, I said, "We'll win. Count on it."

That night our campaign office looked like a modest version of a military communications center. Every phone was in use. Every fax machine was busy. We were compiling returns, actual and estimated, from every area and analyzing them as they came in.

In the beginning, results were spotty. Then we were doing well.

Then, as the night wore on, we were doing better . . . and better. By ten-thirty, two and a half hours after the polls closed, I told my aides, "All of the candidates Goldman recruited are gone. All of them. Our allies have won. We've pitched a shutout."

That was verified when the ballots were finally counted two days later. Out of the nineteen candidates Keating had said would vote for him, ten lost to my supporters, two defected to vote for me, one voted "present," another withdrew his support for Keating but lost in the general election to a Republican. In all, there were only five votes for Keating, less support than he had in his news conference.

CCPAX had failed in nine of the ten key districts to get enough signatures to place its "Vote Against Bulger" directive on the ballot. And in the one district where it did get on the ballot, the voters said no!

Michael Barrett's decision to give up his Senate seat and run for governor had not proved a glittering career move. He had made his opposition to me the centerpiece of his campaign — and he had been demolished. It seemed as though misfortune clung to Barrett with singular fidelity.

Goldman made $83,000 from Keating's abortive coup, $39,395 from Keating alone. Not only had all his challengers in the Senate districts been trounced, his lieutenant governor candidate was beaten by a political rookie, one of his congressional candidates lost the primary, and the other won the primary only to lose in the general election.

"Once a mortician," Jim Julian said, "always a mortician."

Goldman's final score — except for his bank account — zero.

Jack Meyers of the *Boston Herald* called the results "an awesome display of political muscle."

A kinder, gentler Michael Goldman appeared on a TV panel show, where he gave me much credit for helping to solve the state's economic problems. He expressed hope there would be less divisiveness.

The *Globe*, of course, conducted another poll, which it said showed the majority of voters wanted me out of office.

11

W HEN IT ALL BEGAN for me — I realize now — I was almost totally innocent of any understanding of the life I had chosen. I expected to create great legislation without knowledge of the process; to be effective with no awareness of the anatomy of political power; to continue in office with only a rudimentary grasp of politics.

Experience is indeed a hard school, but it was the only one I had. From it I have learned a bit about legislating and about the structure of political power — and, perhaps most important of all, the art of politics.

First, legislation:

To make law, to make what you believe is *good* law, to see laws you have sponsored or effectively supported improve the happiness of people, is the ultimate satisfaction.

As of this writing, our commonwealth is, as all states are and probably always will be, far short of where we want to go. There is so much still undone — so much. Yet our people are vigorous, our economy is strong, and much has been accomplished. Taking it all in all, there is reason for optimism.

The legislative terrain abounds in difficult crags and arid dunes that test the purpose and endurance of lawmakers and that too often slow progress to a crawl. Thus complaints against legislators are endemic in a democracy, and with good cause. The process *is* slow and obfuscated by bicker and parliamentary maneuver.

It takes time to write a law. In our nation the legislature is not dominant as once it was in England, until George III proved that he could manipulate lawmakers by awarding them honors and estates. That caused our forefathers to forsake Locke's theory that the legislature must be supreme, and to embrace instead Montesquieu's doctrine of separation of powers. This concept of separate but equal branches of government means we must draft each law with care lest its purpose be frustrated by judicial interpretation or administrative application.

This is aggravated in any situs, such as mine, where it is traditional for legislators to file many bills — even bills they personally oppose — at the request of private citizens. The result in Massachusetts is that we must consider about 8,000 bills in a year, 2,000 filed in the Senate and 6,000 filed in the House. Each bill must be given a public hearing before committees of the House and Senate, where proponents and those in opposition may testify. That, too, takes time.

Like legislators everywhere, we must listen to the antinomic counsel of expert witnesses. The sheer volume of such people is brain-numbing because of the popular notion that a person competent in one area is equally qualified in every area. Noted mathematicians may advise us on sociology, artists counsel us on road construction, pediatricians hold forth on care for the elderly. Then there are the self-proclaimed prophets — economists are very active in this line. They consume much time, often reappearing in succeeding years to explain why their earlier predictions did not materialize. That takes more time. It all makes for lengthy proceedings, often terminating in final sessions that run into the dawn of the following day.

Yet we must not only hear such people, we must *listen* to them: often the most unlikely advisers offer useful guidance. And fatuous as some forecasters may seem, we must listen to them also, for it is reckless to be too swift to condemn prophets.

I recall from long ago that my childhood friend Eddie Curran would tell us such things as, "My father says it's going to be a cold winter" or "My father says the Red Sox won't win the pennant."

Since it inevitably got cold in our winters, and since the Red Sox had elevated disappointment to an art form, such previsions proved remarkably accurate. We were very impressed.

When television came along, Eddie Curran told us, "My father says TV won't last — it will be dead in a few years."

As time went on and antennas began to appear on every roof, we all lost faith in Eddie Curran's father. Henceforth, when Eddie would begin a sentence with the words "My father says . . ." someone would interrupt and say, "Tell us what he thinks about television."

But, I don't know . . . There *is* life in the medium — programs that do not insult the intellect — but as a whole TV is vegetative. It is supported by income from mindless sitcoms, cacophony served up as music, voyeuristic trash so often offered as drama and comedy. Perhaps, after all, Eddie Curran's father wasn't so wrong.

All that aside, the fact remains that we legislators require an unmercifully long time to get our job done. It is quite reasonable that we should be asked why we haven't found a way to hasten it.

The answer is that the legislation a democratic system produces is particulate. It may begin with linear simplicity, but along the way it becomes a mosaic of many parts. Its tessellated structure consists of purpose, craft and art, frequently of courage, almost always of compromise — an admixture of interests necessary to achieve its passage.

Just as the laws of aerodynamics indicate that a bee cannot fly, the fact that the legislative procedure is cumbersome, dilatory, often parochial and at times indecorous indicates it, too, is unworkable.

Somehow the bee flies, somehow our system works. On rare occasions the net result is exquisitely good; generally it tends, at least, to be more beneficial than harmful.

What alternative do we have? There have been kings and any number of uncrowned despots who have governed swiftly, wisely and in the best interests of their people. Then the good sovereign dies; the unlimited power survives and in time inevitably falls into the hands of an idiot prince or some other successor, inept and often cruel. That, of course, is why men and women devoted their lives, often quite literally, to invent and establish our process, a process that is not and cannot be tidy and neat, because when democracy — real democracy — is at work, it sweats.

Perhaps our system is a work in progress, but it is all we have.

After legislation, an understanding of both power and politics completes the politician's trinity:

After the Democratic revival in Massachusetts in 1992, I received a note from a dedicated media critic. It said, in part: "Your accomplishments in this remarkable event served your party well, but all they really revealed about *you* is that you are a politician . . . effective at what you do, but still merely a politician."

Because I respected the writer's ethics, though not her views, my first reaction was to respond. I wrote, in part: "Oscar Wilde observed that what is true in a man's life is not what he does, but the legend which grows up around him. I think you have bought into the legend about me: I would remind you that this 'mere politician' has had a not insignificant role in funding for public education and the beginning of a meaningful right of school choice; hundreds of millions of dollars for the health care and shelter of the state's homeless; and a litany of other worthwhile things ranging from protection for abused children and battered women to building public swimming pools and skating rinks — even down to such relative minutiae as providing lighting for Boston Common.

"You are aware, I hope, that this 'mere politician' sponsored initiatives helpful to business; but that he also was the one who spoke on the floor of the Senate against the lobbyists of powerful industries when they sought to block legislation designed to protect the poor."

I hesitated, because I prefer to write one-page letters, and this one, besides the self-serving ring such letters have, threatened to go on interminably. The most difficult problem with a résumé is when to stop, without omissions for which you later reproach yourself.

Perhaps, I thought, it would be useful to conclude the letter with a reference to the Charles Street jail and the rare media approbation I had received in regard to that matter. The challenge was how to explain this in ten lines, which was all I could get on the single page, even by cramming. That wasn't easy.

Boston's Charles Street jail was an ancient and ill-preserved architectural corpse, and for thirteen years the city had tried to find a site for a new structure. Conditions for inmates had so deteriorated that the Supreme Judicial Court said a high-rise would have to be built in the prison yard if a new site could not be found. That plan was described as the "worst possible idea and the worst possible place, but the only one without serious opposition."

There was, in my opinion, an ideal piece of land, but only part of it was owned by the state. The rest was the property of the world-renowned Massachusetts General Hospital, which abutted the jail, and which itself desperately needed to expand. We could, by our power of eminent domain, take the hospital land, but that clearly was not in the public interest.

As the deadline for construction drew near, I visited Drs. Robert Buchanan and Thomas Durant and the hospital's general counsel, Ernest Haddad. I proposed a swap: their parcel of land for the old jail site. The hospital was delighted. I hurried about touching all the legislative bases until the plan was approved.

To my astonishment, even the media applauded. The *Herald* said, "Senate President William Bulger, who originally proposed the land swap idea, deserves a good deal of the credit for helping bring this together . . . He has done his city an incalculable good deed." The *Globe* said "all parties are to be congratulated," which, coming from that quarter, I considered absolutely dazzling praise . . .

At that point in my thoughts, I abandoned the letter and put what I had written into my files. It had suddenly occurred to me that I had no objection to being called a "mere politician."

Contrary to the pejorative implication intended by my angry correspondent, I deem "politician" descriptive of a member of a noble profession, a practitioner of the art and craft of politics.

And to be to any degree "effective" at what I do had required a lifetime of learning — perhaps as much preparation as it takes to be an "effective" journalist.

I recalled a few of those lessons I had learned along the way:

I thought of a day when Dennis Donovan had called. As soon as I recognized his voice on the phone, I winced.

"It's the planes, Bill," he was saying. "You have to do something about the planes."

Dennis was a stout supporter, and I was fond of him. His problems ranged from the exotic to the impossible, and he seemed unable to believe I could not solve them. This, I suspected, was no exception.

"Right, Dennis. What are the planes doing?"

"They're drowning out the TV when I'm trying to watch *Gunsmoke*."

"You want the planes to stop flying during *Gunsmoke*?"

"I know they have to come over *sometimes*," said Dennis, ever the voice of reason, "but they shouldn't be always drowning out the most popular show on TV."

I groped for an answer. Finally I said, "The next time it happens, get the number of the plane."

That seemed to satisfy him. As far as I know, he's still trying to read the numbers, because I have heard no more of it.

Donovan's dilemma taught me this: when a constituent insists you halt the sun, and when you know he will not accept the answer that you are not Joshua, you can avoid losing a friend by making him part of the effort. It is useful to remember that.

There are other ways to cope with unreasonable demands, of course, a galaxy of them, dependent upon the circumstances and the personalities. I have been discovering them ever since 1964, when Bridie Connolly told me to close down a busy South Boston artery. In that year Mary and I lived at 1596 Columbia Road and I was being challenged by a tough opponent, Jerry O'Leary, who was running once again for representative.

Bridie, a native of County Cork, was our landlady. She lived on the third floor. She said the noise and poisonous exhaust from vehicles on Columbia Road were hastening her demise, which was "coming soon enough as it is," and insisted I put a stop to it.

Like the rest of us, Bridie had been dying all her life. But in her case she worked at it, constantly issuing bulletins of her physical decline while giving every evidence of enormous health and vigor.

Though ever complaining, she was also ever active, ever alert — and ever mindful of the date the rent was due. One day she told me, "Sick as I am, what with the traffic and all — which you ain't done a thing about — I'll still give you some good advice, sonny."

"What would that be, Bridie?"

"You'd best start setting a bit aside for rent money in case Mr. O'Leary beats you, which there are many who say he will."

"Don't pay any attention to her," Mary's mother told me. "She's just worried about her rent. Cork people are like that. They'd squeeze the buffalo off a nickel."

But I did pay attention. I detected a disposition on Bridie's part to defect to O'Leary, and I needed every vote I could get.

The next time I saw Bridie I became even more concerned, because she walked past me as though we were strangers. So I said: "About the rent — "

Bridie stopped. I had her complete attention immediately.

"Don't worry about the rent, Bridie — even if I lose."

The sharp black eyes bored into me, waiting for the rest.

"Oh, there may be a few months when I can't pay, but I know you'll be good about it. Even the law won't let me be evicted for that in an emergency."

She looked as though I had struck her. I went on: "That will only be for a little while, anyway. Then I'll be back on my feet and able to start paying again. So don't you worry."

She stared at me in stunned silence. I sensed that it wasn't the traffic that brought that waxen pallor and frozen cast to her face.

When I arrived with the next month's rent just before the election, she was beaming — or as close to a beam as she was capable. "You'll be fine," she said. "My cousins, the Hanrahans, are voting for you. The Sullivans are voting for you. So are the O'Reillys and the Finleys and my in-laws, the Joyces. I've talked to everybody and I've got them all talking to everybody else."

"Bridie, that's very generous of you. I really thank you."

"Oh, you'll win for sure," she said as she stood there counting the rent money.

Constituents expect one in public office to use political power in their behalf, but many do not understand its anatomy.

There are three kinds of power in politics: one that you own and two that you borrow for a while. The power one owns consists of acquired political knowledge gained mostly from experience — though in part intuitively. It is an enduring resource. No one can take it away. Borrowed powers are those inherent in office and those that are perceived to exist there. Such powers, both real and imagined, are achieved through election to office. The perception usually exceeds the reality, and often outlasts it to some degree, but both are generally conterminous with tenure.

Constituents such as Donovan or Bridie seek the exercise of perceived power — the power to stop traffic or control planes. But there is an interesting variation on that theme: some people pursue the appearance of power not in the politician, but in themselves. A good illustration is one Snuffy Dillon, a gnarled and balding constituent with a voice that could halt traffic on a Los Angeles freeway during rush hour.

His name is a familiar trivia question to many basketball fans who recall the night the Boston Celtics held a ceremony to retire the jersey of its former basketball star Bob Cousy. There came a moment during the proceedings when a reverential hush settled on Boston Garden, a silence shattered by a stentorian voice shouting, "We luvya, Cooze!"

That was Snuffy, holding forth from the balcony. The shattering voice carried not only to the rafters of the Garden but to all parts of the nation electronically tuned in for the game. Media representatives descended on him with cameras and microphones, bringing his grin and V-for-victory sign to radio, television screens and front pages. It was Snuffy's fifteen minutes of fame.

I knew him in a less flamboyant context. He was a dogged

pursuer of comely South Boston widows — he called them "grass widows" — who had been assigned to apartments in the Columbia Point housing project. All Snuffy's widows had a single wish: to be transferred to the Old Harbor project in the heart of their old Neighborhood.

I would receive telephone calls, usually after midnight: "Bill, this is Snuffy Dillon. Howareya?"

I knew he was sitting beside one of his widows and talking for her benefit.

"Look, Bill, I'm here with Agnes, Aggy Dooley, at Columbia Point. She needs a transfer to Old Harbor. Okay? Here, Aggy, say hello to my pal Bill, the senator."

I would chat with Dillon's friend and explain to her that there was a long waiting line and that it was unlikely I could help. "But I'll try," I'd assure her. "Snuffy's a very important constituent. You give him the information, and I'll send a letter to the housing authorities."

I would in fact send a letter memorializing her request, but I had no power of any sort to do more except in cases of great hardship. Snuffy was well aware of that — all he wanted to do was impress his friend with his importance.

He was happy; and Dillon's "grass widow" at least knew that, however fruitless it might be, an official letter would be sent on her behalf. It is the kind of accommodation that requires only patience on the part of the politician, while creating the appearance of power in the constituent.

Individual votes like Donovan's and Bridie's and Dillon's are precious, but votes are needed en masse. Those are hard to come by.

Helping young people get summer jobs or into schools or colleges, helping their parents find work or resist the antics of an overreaching bureaucracy, helping the elderly to get housing or the sick to get care — these are the joys of public office. But only the fittest survive to realize them. And such things alone will not keep you in office.

I knew, as all politicians must come to know, that people forget or, once satisfied, lose interest; and that no amount of service will routinely transmute itself into votes.

For that alchemy I have looked to Franna Burke.

Franna had worked for Bill Foley, the city councilor, and for three Senate presidents: John Powers, Maurice Donahue and Kevin Harrington. When I became Senate president, he came to work for me.

In Massachusetts, he was the best at what he did, and what he did was get votes. Because of him, South Boston had the highest percentage of registered voters of any section of the city. It also had the highest turnout of voters. And it was all due to Franna.

When someone would come seeking help — and they came in great numbers — Franna would check the voting list, and if he didn't find the name he'd say, "You're not registered. You go down to city hall and register. They'll give you a slip, and you bring it back and show it to me. Then I'll know you can vote for us."

Franna sent them by the thousands to get registered. When they brought back their slips, Franna would say, "Great — now you can vote for us. We'll work for you."

"Franna," I asked, "why do these people you deal with always seem to turn out and vote for us? People come to me and I help them, but many of them don't vote at all."

"You don't trade with them," he said. "You can't. I can."

And he did — and they faithfully voted for me.

They turned out for me throughout the eighties when I had to run for reelection to the Senate five times. They turned out so solidly that I was unopposed in the Democratic primaries until 1988, when my opponent was Stephen C. Holt of Boston. I defeated Holt approximately two to one and won the general election five to one. Franna Burke was responsible for much of that.

It would be idyllic if we didn't need to organize such support, if all people voted as a civic duty. But they do not, as the percentage of nonvoters attests. In the real world, the rock of political power is quarried *quid* by *quo* — as Franna does it.

The moil of politics is a great Aurelian web of many strands, and no one can get to a position to serve the public for any length of time unless he or she learns how to spin that web. It is a complex whole of so many parts, so many threads: magic tricks to appease unreasonable constituents; a genuine sense of empathy to buoy the hopes of the hopeless whose sad exigencies one cannot remedy; tactics and tenacity to build and maintain a solid base of support; boundless physical endurance to survive the debates, even the fundraisers and the banquets and the wakes — and so much more . . . so many threads.

That is what being a politician is all about. It is the fun of having a box in a theater that never closes; but it is also the work of being an actor in the theater, and having many roles in the same play. And it is, at the same time, being part of a very real world where one must campaign for one's life. In that world there is no time for fantasy; the time is always *now,* always today, and in each day, if you would win, you must achieve something of value, however small, *something,* before a westering sun signals the end of that day's opportunities.

One must learn such things to be elected — and to stay elected. But if politics demands hard work and inflicts pain, it also offers an occasional touch of poetry. It is at various times, and in varying degrees, the fount of realized hopes and the grief business, a sanguinary sport and the conjurer's art . . .

Politicians didn't invent any of that; democracy did.

I disdain none of it. I love it all.

But just as the merry-go-round is wearing on the public and the media, it is tiring to the legislator. And so I am asked with increasing frequency, "How long? When will you decide you have had enough?"

In all candor, I do not know. It may be years from now. It may be tomorrow. From the beginning, my thought has always been this: I would stay in politics as long as the party was fun. When it became dull or tedious, it would be good to go quickly and with a decent grace. I should hate to linger in the doorway like an awkward guest, one who could not bring himself to say his thanks, bid a cheerful farewell and be about his way.

That view has not changed, nor will it — while the music lasts.

Afterword

Accomplished and experienced authors, from whom I am at a far remove, are probably never satisfied with their efforts. I share with them — undoubtedly with greater cause — that discomfort. Most of this memoir was dictated to a hand-held tape recorder in airport waiting rooms or written during flights or scribbled in a notebook while I was a passenger in automobiles. I doubt that I would have done better under optimal conditions because I lack the professional's experience, craft of composition and acquired felicity of expression. My only satisfaction — besides the happy astonishment of actually finishing the thing — is the knowledge that, warts and all, I wrote it; it is not my memoir as told to someone else.

Soon after its completion, I was offered and accepted the presidency of the University of Massachusetts. With its five campuses and more than fifty thousand students, it is a huge complex.

My old friend and trusted adviser Dan Holland, one-time secretary to James Michael Curley and now a most capable and successful lawyer, said, "So you finally have had enough of public service." For the only time I can remember, Dan was wrong.

I see my decision as a change in venue, not in career. The music to which I refer in this book is the harmony that public service has brought to my life for the thirty-four years I have spent in the legislature. The music goes on, strange and clear and sweet as ever, in the challenge of leading the University of Massachusetts to the realization of its potential as one of the very best, as well as one of the biggest, universities in the nation. I can think of no greater public service I might perform.